DATE DUE

GAYLORD			PRINTED IN U.S.A.

The Church and the City

THE AMERICAN HERITAGE SERIES

THE

American Heritage

Series

UNDER THE GENERAL EDITORSHIP OF

LEONARD W. LEVY AND ALFRED YOUNG

The Church and the City

1865-1910

EDITED BY

ROBERT D. CROSS

Columbia University

THE BOBBS-MERRILL COMPANY, INC.

Indianapolis *and* New York

The center of the community of an old New England village is the meetinghouse. It recalls a time when the church not only provided guidance on the life hereafter; it also afforded guidance on the details of daily life and a forum for public issues. Time brought many changes both to the old communities and to the newer westerly settlements, resulting in more than one church in a given place. The venerated identification of church with community and of congregation with "the people" was strained almost to the point of disruption.

New immigrants bearing new religions intensified the strains; but it was the rapid growth of the cities that most seriously challenged the old church order in America. Far more people congregated in a neighborhood than any "congregation" could contain, and the same neighborhood juxtaposed people of alien origins, languages, creeds, and affiliations. Between the Civil War and World War One there was a crucial confrontation of the old church order and the cities that grew so spectacularly during this period.

Robert D. Cross focuses on this critical time in our history when the quality of American life was dramatically affected in part by the impact of the cities on the churches. He contends persuasively that the result was not a "de-Christianization," such as had been predicted by great sociologists like Simmel and Weber, and allegedly found in European and Latin American cities in the nineteenth century. Whether Americans were too deeply committed to religion, theologically or socially; or the protection of religious freedom was so effective that every form of spontaneous variation was given a chance in the new environment; or Americans were especially talented in developing new church organizations or formulating new religious heresies; the churches in the cities in America at the turn of the century were anything but moribund. Beecher, Moody, Eddy, Rainsford, Russell, and others whom Professor Cross describes and whose words he presents were creative, forceful leaders. Each in his own way met the new challenges of secularism, urbanism, and industrialism. What they called their "churches" bore only a limited resemblence to the old meetinghouse on the village green. Yet the range of their experiments and the intensity of their diverse beliefs testify to the magnitude of the new challenges and the resiliency of an American religious tradition.

This book is part of a series whose aim is to provide the essential primary sources of the American experience, especially of American thought, from the colonial period to the present. The series when completed will constitute a documentary library of our history. These volumes will fill a need of libraries, scholars, students, and even general readers for authoritative collections of original material. These materials will illuminate the thought of significant individuals, such as James Madison and Louis Brandeis; groups, such as Puritan political theorists and American Catholic leaders on social policy; and movements, such as those of the Anti-Federalists or the Populists. There are a surprising number of subjects traditionally studied in American history for which there are no documentary anthologies. This series will be by far the most comprehensive and authoritative of its kind. It will also have the distinction of presenting representative pieces of substantial length that have not been butchered into snippets.

Leonard W. Levy
Alfred Young

CONTENTS

Introduction   xi

Selected Bibliography   xliii

PART ONE

The Predicament of the City Churches

1. The Contrast Between Country and City   3
   John Lancaster Spalding, "The Country" and
       "The City," 1880

2. Church Life in New York City   29
   James M. King, "The Present Condition of New York
       City Above Fourteenth Street," 1888

3. Church Life in New York City   33
   Adolphus F. Schauffler, "The Present Condition of New
       York City Below Fourteenth Street," 1888

4. The Fratricide of the Churches   40
   Washington Gladden, "The Church," 1897

PART TWO

The Downtown Churches

5. The Chosen Role of the Downtown Church   55
   Morgan Dix, Address at Trinity Church, New York,
       Ascension Day, 1871

6. The Downtown Church Arraigned   69
   Ray Stannard Baker, "A Study of Trinity—The Richest
       Church in America," 1910

PART THREE

Transplanted Rural Churches

7. The Old Faith Reasserted 99
Lewis R. Dunn, "Cleansed by the Blood," 1882

8. The Ghetto Congregations of the Immigrants 114
Anton H. Walburg, "The Question of Nationality," 1889

PART FOUR

Adaptations

9. The Neighborhood Church Eulogized 127
James Parton, "Henry Ward Beecher and His Church,"
1867

10. The New Opportunities of the Minister 154
Henry Ward Beecher, "Sphere of the
Christian Minister," 1869

11. The Gospel of Sweet Manhood 182
Henry Ward Beecher, "What Is Salvation?" 1872

12. Conversion 202
Dwight L. Moody, "Faith," 1876

13. The Responsibilities of the Converted 213
Dwight L. Moody, "Address to Young Converts," 1876

14. God's Plan of the Ages 227
Charles Taze Russell, "The Day of Jehovah," 1906

15. Testimonies of the Gifts of Pentecost 262
Frederick G. Henke, "The Gift of Tongues and Related
Phenomena at the Present Day," 1909

16. Religion as Healing 267
Mary Baker Eddy, "Precept and Practice," 1902

17. Christian Science Defended 290
Mary Baker Eddy, "Questions and Answers," 1896

PART FIVE

Attempts at Reintegration

18. A New Type of Pastorate   305
    W. S. Rainsford, "Three Episodes in the
        Reconstruction of a Downtown Church," 1922

19. The Institutional Church   331
    Charles Stelzle, "The Institutional Church," 1907

Index   353

INTRODUCTION

I

In the fifty years between the close of the Civil War and the onset of World War I, American cities grew rapidly. Although early in the nineteenth century religious spokesmen like Lyman Beecher had been aware of the need to "evangelize" the growing city populations, most had been preoccupied with the challenges and opportunities presented by the "frontier." The emphasis shifted after the Civil War. A flood of books with titles like *The Challenge of the City, The Redemption of the City, If Christ Came to Chicago,* and *Christianity's Storm Centre: A Study of the Modern City* demonstrated how acute the problem had come to seem.[1] It was not, of course, in the bookstore that religion's response was most authoritatively rendered, but in the behavior of the churches—not only the churches which found the community in which they were established swelling into a metropolis, but also the new churches of one kind or another appearing in the cities. No more in this era than in any other in American history was all religious life lived within the churches; then as always there were sturdy individualists to whom religion was gravely important but to whom church membership seemed an irrelevance if not a spiritual handicap. But for the vast majority of religiously concerned Americans, the churches were the normal vehicle of religious life, making the conduct and welfare of

---

[1] Josiah Strong, *The Challenge of the City* (New York: Missionary Education Movement, 1907); Charles H. Sears, *The Redemption of the City* (Philadelphia: Griffith and Rowland Press, 1911); William T. Stead, *If Christ Came to Chicago* (Chicago: Laird and Lee, 1894); Charles Stelzle, *Christianity's Storm Centre: A Study of the Modern City* (New York: Fleming Revell, 1907).

these churches the best barometer of American religion's response to the city.

It was clear from the start that the response would be remarkably multiform. There were already in the 1840's many mansions in American religion; each variant form reflected a unique set of notions not only about church membership and organization and worship, but also about the church's proper role in "the world."[2] Furthermore, in practice if not always in ecclesiastical theory, initiative in responding to new situations rested mostly in the hands of the local church. When such a varied and decentralized institution was confronted with the fact of city growth, dynamic both in its pace and in its apparent unpredictability, it is hardly surprising that church life in the cities was soon almost incredibly diverse in character. (So diverse, in fact, that for many years it was regarded as simple chaos, a judgment of God upon American religiosity.) About the turn of the century, churchmen like H. Paul Douglass began to survey the urban scene more matter-of-factly, and to discern patterns in the kind of religious responses they found.[3] In recent years, such churchmen have been joined by professional sociologists, and together they have evolved quite sophisticated typologies—never in the belief, however, that any typology could do full justice either to the whole range of response or to the uniqueness of the individual churches.[4] Still,

---

[2] Two useful nineteenth-century surveys of the range of religious organization are Robert Baird, *Religion in the U. S. of A.* (Glasgow: Blackie, 1844) and Daniel Dorchester, *Christianity in the United States* (New York: Hunt and Eaton, 1888). The classic analysis of the correlation in America between sectarian difference and social attitude is H. Richard Niebuhr, *The Social Sources of Denominationalism* (Hamden, Conn.: Shoe String Press, 1954).

[3] Typical of Douglass' many works on urban religion is his *One Thousand City Churches* (New York: George H. Doran, 1926).

[4] A good summary and critique of seven of the most widely accepted typologies is Frederick A. Shippey, "The Variety of City Churches," *Review of Religious Research*, II (Summer, 1960), 8–19.

these efforts at classification make it possible now to distinguish four general modes of churchly response.

Transformations include the changes that took place in long-established churches when the towns in which they stood rapidly expanded into cities. Suddenly they found themselves "downtown" churches with a conspicuous location, an equally conspicuous loss of neighborhood membership, and consequently a pressing need to redefine their mode of preaching to the community.

Transplantations characterize the attempts—always unsuccessful in the long run—to create, in the midst of a city, churches identical to warmly remembered ones in town or country. Immigrant groups usually created "ethnic churches," and migrants from the American countryside often founded "village churches" in a fond attempt to create at least one bulwark against urban demoralization.

Adaptations, by far the largest category of urban churches, resulted from single-minded attempts to cope with some specific challenge of the city. Viewed from the perspective of the traditional church in America or Europe, these adaptations seemed heretical for their emphasis or overemphasis on some belief or practice. (1) Neighborhood churches, on the way to becoming the "suburban church" of the mid-twentieth century, defined their ambit in terms of a neighborhood that was not the whole of a community, nor even a cross section of it, but a highly stratified segment. (2) Some churches came to specialize as centers of revivalist exhortation. (3) Adventism, always stimulated by untoward developments in the surrounding culture, was given renewed expression by Charles Taze Russell and the group that came to be known as Jehovah's Witnesses. (4) A congeries of short-lived but intense Pentecostal churches matched the Witnesses' hostility to the culture in which they found themselves, but drew upon the opportunities the city offered for an autonomous religious life. (5) Christian Science exemplified the special anxiety of city-dwellers about health and well-being, and their receptivity to "new thought" which offered a gnostic solution to uncertainties about both this world and the next.

Reintegrations were typified by the "institutional church," which self-consciously sought to restore the old identification of the church with the whole community. Since the population of most cities was far too large for a single congregation to encompass, the institutional church resolved at least to draw its membership from a real cross section of the city, not simply some congenial social class or ethnic group. "Transplanted" or "adapted" churches might in time follow the path of "reintegration"; in the late nineteenth and early twentieth centuries, however, it was the churches "transformed" by urbanization into downtown churches which were most likely to make this transition. But there was nothing inevitable about it, even for the "transformed."

II

The churches located near the center of a growing city faced a difficult choice. Almost inevitably, the bulk of the congregation of "Old First Church"—of "Center Church"—of "Trinity Church"—moved to less crowded, more fashionable neighborhoods; their former homes were made over into places of business, or were subdivided into boarding houses, or were replaced by barracks and tenements to accommodate a flood of new inhabitants. Many of the newcomers were immigrants from Europe, deterred by language and faith from joining the old church on the green. Others, fresh from the American countryside, were nearly as uprooted psychologically, and at least as unlikely to find the old church a purveyor of the kind of religious life they had been accustomed to. Some were the "derelicts" that find shelter in the heart of large cities. In the middle of the nineteenth century, the old churches in the southern reaches of Manhattan found themselves surrounded by Irish and German Catholics, by people from the provinces, by a large fraction of the Negro population, and by the city's professional criminals. In the area known as the Five Points, all of these lived in close proximity, physically near the old churches, but in spirit hopelessly remote.[5] Some of the congregations, in despair, sold their buildings to commercial enterprises (or, occasionally, to immigrant religious groups) and built new churches "uptown" or in the suburbs. Those that resolved to stay where they had always been encountered the vicissitudes of the "downtown" church.

There were, of course, a few compensations. Trinity Church in New York, for example, benefited from the steady increase in the value of its extensive property holdings. But for the bulk of the people in the neighborhood the church as landlord did not arouse the same affection as had the church as house of worship. By the turn of the twentieth century, in fact, Trinity had become a byword for its profit-minded operation of some of the worst tenement-houses in the city.[6] Trinity's role changed in other ways as well. Increasingly, it became a kind of cathedral, in effect if not in ecclesiastical law. Testifying by its presence to the existence in city culture of religion as an institution, it ceased being the meetinghouse around which the life of the city, or even a fair cross section of the city, revolved.[7]

In most "downtown" churches the number of religious services declined; even so, attendance became increasingly sparse. By the end of the century, it had become conventional for city

---

[5] The situation did not become any simpler later in the century; a clergyman in a downtown New York church in the 1890's declared that "on one side of me is a block in which, the police say, thirty-nine languages and dialects are spoken. Within four blocks is a city more foreign than any city in Europe this side of Constantinople." Quoted in Amory H. Bradford (ed.), *Christ and the Church* (New York; Fleming Revell, 1895), pp. 196–197.

[6] See Document 6.

[7] For two different but not contradictory views, see Document 5, and the first pages of Document 8.

newspapers to note the meager congregations at Sunday morning services in the famous old churches. Budgets were met by income from property, from pew rents, and from the large donations of the few wealthy families that maintained a traditional loyalty; some contributions also came from parvenus seeking the prestige which conspicuous support of the older churches—Trinity, Brick Presbyterian, Temple Emanu-El—still brought. Great emphasis was placed on church architecture, on carefully elaborated ritual and liturgy; organized religion would thus demand respect from the passer-by, even if it did not bring in flocks of members. It became increasingly important to have a minister of high social standing; Episcopalians, Reformed Jews and others frequently imported them from Europe. Dignity, social grace, learning, and eloquence were required of him. It would be an especial accolade for the church if ceremony and sermon were so distinguished that prominent visitors to the city regarded a visit to the church as one of "the things to be done." Such visitors fit easily into Sunday congregations made up not of the families of the neighborhood but of a handful of individuals from various parts of the city.

Under such circumstances, it would have been miraculous if the minister proved a pastor to his neighborhood. Phillips Brooks, of Trinity Church, Boston, was admirably suited by the remarkable sweetness of his character to be such a pastor. But his influence extended little beyond the narrow circle of his upper-class Episcopalian congregation. Much the same might be said about Morgan Dix of Trinity Church, New York, and about Gustav Gottheil of Emanu-El. Priests to their "own" people, they felt little incentive to explore the way religion affected, or failed to affect, the rest of the city.

Though the downtown church of the late nineteenth century touched the lives of a far smaller percentage of the population than had its ancestor on the village green, it preserved, simply by staying in the center of the city, a potential for future importance which the churches which moved uptown or to the suburbs decisively abdicated. Its location gave it the moral right, and its financial resources gave it the means, to experiment with new techniques of "churching" the urban population. An easy but in the long run unsuccessful mode was to support a flock of mission churches or chapels. Premised, tacitly, on the belief that different social classes "do not like to worship together," such colonialist enterprises sometimes developed into viable churches—especially if they were planted in the midst of a population group so bound together by a common foreign language, national consciousness, or color as to be able to resist the disintegrating forces in urban life. More often, the life of a mission church was short, and marred by feelings of dependence and hostility. Charles Stelzle remembered about his youth in lower New York City that "none of the chapel people was ever invited to a business meeting of the home church, even though legally they were members of the church. They had nothing whatever to say, not even with reference to the chapel which they attended and helped support. . . . No wonder it was hard to get workingmen to take an interest in that kind of enterprise."[8] The decision of Trinity Church in 1908 to close St. John's Chapel in the belief that the money could be expended better elsewhere led the conservative Episcopal newspaper *The Churchman* to complain that "no account was taken of the people in St. John's parish, of their rights, of their hopes or of their souls."[9]

The major alternative to creating separate chapels was to make unusual efforts to attract to the downtown churches themselves the large unchurched population. As early as 1856, the New York Sunday School Union had tried to allocate to each downtown church responsibility for a certain territory of

---

[8] Charles Stelzle, *A Son of the Bowery* (New York: George H. Doran, 1926), p. 63.

[9] Quoted in Ray Stannard Baker, *The Spiritual Unrest* (New York: Frederick Stokes, 1910), p. 42.

the city; members of that church were to visit each person in the area at least weekly in order to bring him into active church life. Essentially similar plans were experimented with in other cities before the Civil War; and the Home Evangelization program, the Evangelical Alliance, and the Federation of Churches and Christian Workers in New York made brave efforts in the late nineteenth century. On the whole, they were no more successful than had been the chapels and mission churches.[10] Only very slowly some of the downtown churches came to realize that the transformation worked on society by the city was so intense that the character of the church had to be transformed if a genuine reintegration of church and culture was to be accomplished. The institutional church, about which more will be said later, emerged between 1890 and 1910 as the most ambitious attempt at this larger task.

III

Just as some of the older residents tried to preserve what they remembered as the major characteristics of their churches, so many of the newcomers tried to transplant the rural or small-town church into their new environment. Especially in the first years of industrial cities like Holyoke, Massachusetts, in the mid-nineteenth century, or Gastonia, North Carolina, in the 1920's, a high percentage of the Protestant population was right off the farm, and right out of the rural churches.[11] For them, the old-time religion was the strongest surrogate of the continuity they wished to preserve with their former lives. In

---

[10] The failure of most earlier efforts is discussed in Walter Laidlaw, "A Cooperative Church Parish System," *American Journal of Sociology*, III (May, 1898), 795–808.

[11] The situation in Holyoke is referred to briefly in Constance M. Green, *Holyoke* (New Haven: Yale University Press, 1939). For Gastonia, see Liston Pope's excellent study, *Millhands and Preachers* (New Haven: Yale University Press, 1942).

the churches they built and supported, they tried to keep much
the same patterns of service. They wanted no doctrinal or
theological concessions to the spirit of the times, or the ethos
of city culture; "you have to carry a bucket of blood into the
pulpit to satisfy these people," a Gastonia minister remarked.[12]

Baptists and Methodists predominated in the countryside,
and so it was natural that the bulk of the transplanted churches
were of these denominations. But a sizable number of the
emigrants to the cities brought with them such a compelling
concern for "perfection" that many "holiness" churches were
also founded. The origins of such churches lay in the revivalism
of the early and middle nineteenth century. As Timothy Smith
has shown, the ardent search for God's grace not only led many
leaders of the old Calvinist faiths—like Charles G. Finney—to
stress the possibility of perfectionism; it also gave renewed
intensity to Methodist belief in sanctification through the benefits of the "second blessing."[13] The National Holiness Association represented a massive attempt to foster personal holiness.
Most of its leaders were Methodists, and most hoped to in-
tensify religious life within Methodist churches, rather than to
create a new denomination. But like earlier awakening or
reform movements in American Protestantism, the holiness
group encountered opposition within the settled churches. Not
all bishops, conferences, or ministers could approve of the emo-
tionalism the holiness meetings engendered and found praise-
worthy. Churches, whether in the country or the city, sometimes boggled at the willingness of the holiness advocates to
experiment with new measures of preaching revival, of seeking out converts, and of caring for the needy. As a result, the
late nineteenth century saw the gradual, often reluctant,
coalescence of new denominations, such as the Church of the

---

[12] Pope, *Millhands and Preachers*, p. 88.
[13] Timothy Smith, *Revivalism and Social Reform* (New York: Abingdon Press, 1957).

Nazarene and the Church of God.[14] Some migrants to the city had made the transition before leaving the country; for them, membership in a holiness congregation was completely natural, an act that reaffirmed a previous commitment. Others left the countryside before breaking with an older denomination, but, faced in the city with the need to affiliate with a different congregation in any event, chose a holiness group as best fulfilling long-cherished preferences. For both, the holiness congregation was a kind of transplantation—a re-creation of the rural past.

A similar spirit characterized the attempts of immigrant groups to preserve unmodified in American cities the religious life they had known in European villages. Such people were doubly alienated from the "downtown" churches they encountered. So, within a few months of the arrival of the first sizable numbers of Jews from Eastern Europe, New York was dotted with synagogues, each seeking to re-create the special religious life of a *shtetl*, or small village. Those Lutherans from Germany or Scandinavia who settled in the cities tried to find, in churches effectively limited to members speaking the mother tongue, something of the church life they remembered. Catholic immigrants, belonging to a Church which in theory organized local churches by territorial rather than ethnic boundaries, were not always so successful in finding churches limited to their own "kind."[15] But by the end of the nineteenth century, many American dioceses had provided "national"

---

14 Timothy Smith, *Called Unto Holiness. The Story of the Nazarenes: The Formative Years* (Kansas City: Nazarene Publishing House, 1962) is the best study of a holiness group's development. Professor Smith regards the Nazarenes as more of a creative adaptation to city needs, and less of a transplantation from the countryside, than I.

15 The much controverted "Cahenslyite" episode in American Catholic history turned around the reluctance, or the inability, of Irish-American bishops to provide immigrant Catholics with parishes and priests of their own nationality. See Document 7, and Colman J. Barry, *The Catholic Church and German Americans* (Washington: Catholic University Press, 1953).

parishes which encompassed all those speaking a similar foreign language. In those national parishes where the Church could also provide a priest of the same nationality, parishioners were able to enjoy the round of services and festivals cherished in the old country.

Such churches were inevitably transient. Sometimes, a peculiarly rigid social-economic structure such as prevailed in a small Southern industrial city would keep a group together for a generation or more; sometimes the centripetal forces of a foreign-language ethnic group enabled its members for a period of time not only to renounce the opportunity to scatter through the whole city but also to resist temptations to adapt their "country" church to city life. (Of course, the country churches willy-nilly made some adaptations immediately; the very determination to transplant and maintain an institution exotic to the city created a beleaguered spirit which they had not previously had.) But usually within a decade or so, the transplanted churches from the country, like those older churches which had experienced the transformation of their community into a city, were forced to make much more radical adaptations. Though at any given moment a considerable proportion of a city's churches might be striving to remain country churches, a growing number had adapted in dramatic fashion.

IV

The much more complex, heterogeneous life of the cities produces institutions that are far more specialized than those which flourish in rural culture. Furthermore, just as city-dwellers expect of such institutions rather precise intellectual and moral services, so the leaders of such institutions come to approximate functionaries with highly specialized skills. So it was with most of the churches which adapted to the ways of city life in late nineteenth-century America. Compared with the traditional churches, many of these adaptations—even some of those the age most admired—seem almost grotesque, heretically preoccupied with responding to some limited aspect of urban life, and stressing some limited theme in the churches' armory of beliefs and modes of worship.

The "neighborhood" church neatly illustrates both the plausibility and the peril of adaptation. As Springfield, Massachusetts, grew from a frontier town to a considerable city and its population spread out away from the original cluster on the Connecticut River, those who thought of themselves as Congregationalists but did not wish to journey into the center of town to "Old First Church" founded successively a North and a South Congregational Church, a Faith Church, a Hope Church, until more than a dozen neighborhood churches had been created. Such cellular division was sometimes justified as creating new, reasonably sized and reasonably located churches, each as concerned as the original church with the total gospel of the Church to the World. But Springfield was not, any more than were other cities, a cluster of generally similar neighborhoods, but an area that was highly stratified according to income, class, and ethnic group. As a result, each new congregation tended to be markedly segregated, and thereby highly susceptible to a very specialized notion of the nature of the Church and of its proper relations with the World. An extreme but illuminating example of the neighborhood church was Plymouth Congregational, founded in the 1840's in the City of Brooklyn, for many decades a suburb for up-and-coming New Yorkers. For forty years its minister and central figure was Henry Ward Beecher.

Perhaps because of his expansive, ebullient personality, perhaps because he was the son of Lyman Beecher, one of the great churchmen of the prewar years, but mostly because of the demands of his congregation, Beecher enjoyed a singularly close relationship with his flock.[16] Instead of speaking from a pulpit far back from or high above the congregation, Beecher

---

[16] See Document 9.

had one constructed as much in the center of the church as possible. His sermons frequently elicited emotional outbursts. At the weekly prayer meeting, he delighted to emphasize his communion with his people by sitting on a chair where he could share rather than direct the flow of testimony. Everything about his role militated against prophetic preaching against the sins of his people. It was not that Beecher felt inhibitions about the subjects to which the minister ought to address himself. Shrugging off the tradition that enjoined the minister to concentrate on simple evangelical truths, Beecher claimed the right and duty to speak on politics, economic life, the most recent innovations in the world of culture—all the themes of interest to his congregation.[17] But the evils which excited his alarm were those that came from without the circle of his congregation's lives, and threatened their social and psychological well-being. The old doctrines of hell and eternal damnation, for example, seemed increasingly incongruous to both Beecher and his thriving, prospering people, and Beecher soon avowed that the God they all worshiped was a God of love, who would not conceivably deal harshly with creatures made in His own image."[18] "You are Gods," he once told his congregation; "you are crystalline, your faces are radiant."[19] Aware that the newly bruited doctrines of Darwinism threw into doubt the power of God as well as His amiability, Beecher was not long in assuring his people that evolution, rightly construed, implied only that God chose to create by retail, rather than wholesale. (The metaphor, no less than the sentiment, was harmonious to the sensibilities of his bourgeois audience.) Equally important, he vindicated the righteousness of middle-class economic behavior against the polite innuendoes of the wealthy, and the protests and occasionally obstreperous revolts of the poor. Justifying the *douceurs* of prosperity, he slashed at the immorali-

---

[17] See Document 10.

[18] See Document 11.

[19] Constance Rourke, *Trumpets of Jubilee* (New York: Harcourt Brace, Harbinger edition, 1963), p. 129.

ties that luxury induced in the wealthy; preaching a Protestant ethic of hard work, he denounced working-class demands for better wages and living conditions, as evidence of unfitness to live. If few neighborhood or suburban churches were so imaginatively and fulsomely served as was Plymouth Congregational, most of them encountered a version of the Gospel so edited and distorted as to be almost a parody. Many developments in American culture helped promote this kind of Christianity, but it could hardly have been sustained in the churches if the sociology of metropolitan life had not produced parishes so stratified and so unrepresentative of the full spectrum of potential churchgoers.

No doubt the social homogeneity of the suburban or neighborhood church sometimes allowed a congregation to transcend other kinds of stratification. In a new area, representatives of different denominations often found it possible to unite in a community church which ignored theological or liturgical distinctions which had long lost their meaning. A similar development was possible for the children and grandchildren of European immigrants who wished to belong to a church which preserved the central faiths of their fathers without the admixtures of language and custom which now seemed alien and un-American. The unification movements among the bewildering variety of Scandinavian Lutheran churches were markedly aided by the proliferation of community churches. Some of the ethnic tensions in American Catholicism were allayed by the same development. Probably the most dramatic example was the emergence in suburban areas of Conservative Judaism which proffered a more plausible, more American version of Judaism than the Orthodoxy that had been transplanted from *shtetl* to urban ghetto; Conservatism also provided a viable common ground for Jews of "German" and of "Eastern European" origin.[20]

---

[20] Marshall Sklare, *Conservative Judaism* (Glencoe, Illinois: Free Press, 1955).

For former country folk deprived of a genuinely country church and not yet settled into a neighborhood church, revivalism often afforded a consoling sense of continuity. (It had been one of the strong appeals of the transplanted holiness churches, but it also proved powerful even when sharply separated from regular congregational life.) To church leaders it seemed wholly natural that revivals, which had played a crucial part in bringing religion to the unchurched West, should be used to Christianize the "city wilderness." As early as 1857, the Baptist minister Henry Clay Fish had exclaimed, "What can save our large cities, but a powerful revival of religion?"[21] Superficially, at least, the city seemed an even easier place to conduct a revival than the open country, where the people had to be collected, housed, and supervised, or the small town, where the numbers available were strictly limited. But early nineteenth-century revivalists had noticed that their success was greater in small towns than in cities. To Finney, city people were too engrossed in worldly ambitions; "see how crazy these are who are scrambling to get up . . . ," he said, "enlarging their houses, changing their styles of living. . . . It is like climbing up [the] masthead to be thrown off into the ocean. To enjoy God you must come down, not go up there," as the city continually tempted.[22] By the 1840's, however, it appeared that the right kind of revival could "succeed" in the great city. Emphasis upon the theological niceties of a single denomination was inappropriate for a heterogeneous city audience; furthermore, the newspapers and other impersonal modes of communication on which a city revival depended for its notoriety were not inclined to herald purely sectarian efforts. As a consequence, revivalism developed in considerable autonomy from the congregations existent in the city. Churches developed, like Tremont Temple in Boston, which offered a

---

[21] Smith, *Revivalism and Social Reform*, p. 49.
[22] William G. McLaughlin, *Modern Revivalism: Charles Grandison Finney to Billy Graham* (New York: Ronald Press, 1955), p. 119.

steady fare of revival services. Inevitably they came to place emphasis not on the continuing religious life of their audiences, but on the success of the revivals in producing numerous convictions of sin.

The dramatic but curiously limited effect of urban revivalism was perfectly illustrated by the career of its greatest exponent, Dwight L. Moody. After a pious upbringing in East Northfield, Massachusetts, he sought a business career in Boston. When converted, he felt that the cities in England and America were his destined field; "if we can stir them, we shall stir the whole nation," he said.[23] Never ordained as a minister, he felt no obligation to any denomination, and preferred to conduct his revivals in a special tabernacle rather than a church. He recognized that careful planning was necessary to provide the advance publicity; to secure the necessary funds; to coordinate the ushers, choirs, and auxiliary ministers; to keep the meeting to a brisk schedule of sermon, gospel hymn, and exhortation; to obviate—and if necessary to suppress—hysterical outbreaks. He would no doubt have been gratified by the contemporary's observation that Moody made the business of revivals businesslike.[24] His goal was so simple that it was easy to pursue it matter-of-factly. He once defined his duty as to ask at least one stranger a day, "Are you a Christian?" By the end of his life, he had asked several million, with an energy and persuasiveness unsurpassed in his era. Speaking as he felt he was to people no more than a generation away from active church life, he did not imagine that complicated arguments were necessary; the main task would be to confront as many hearers as possible with the challenge: were they for or against Christ?

Concentrating on this one task, he made no effort to respond to the peculiar difficulties of urban culture. "The old-time

---

[23] *Ibid.*, p. 166.
[24] Gamaliel Bradford, *Dwight L. Moody, A Worker in Souls* (New York: George H. Doran, 1927), pp. 227–263.

religion" was "good enough" for him; knowing the Bible, he saw no need to read or consider Darwin. A natural kindliness made him worry about difficulties of the poor in keeping warm in the winter, but he refused to be distracted from his revivalist efforts into any prolonged consideration of the social-economic order.[25] Critics of a later era could without much difficulty construct from Moody's occasional remarks a ready acquiescence in *laissez faire*, but his attitude was less affirmation than simple indifference. No doubt his aloofness to worldly concerns was strengthened in Moody by a belief in an imminent Second Coming. (But even those revivalists without millennial expectations showed far more interest in the moment of grace than in the subsequent life of the faithful in the world.)

This same set of priorities conditioned Moody's attitude toward the urban churches. Though he supported their work, it did not seem to worry him greatly that revivalists like himself were not notably successful in persuading non-church members who "decided" for Christ to join a congregation. Sometimes he seemed to be reconciled to the prospect that his converts would maintain a vicarious relationship to the churches; once, seeking money for a Sunday School, he sold "stock certificates" which would entitle investors to *watch* Sunday School members studying. Earlier, in the smaller cities and towns, "seasons of revival" had meant revival for the congregations as well as for the individuals. But big-city revivalism in Moody's day developed into a functional substitute for church life. Like the "adaptations" of the neighborhood church, revivalism forfeited much that it purportedly sought to preserve.

Like the neighborhood church, too, revivalism appealed only to special segments of the city population. Moody believed that the poorer classes were those most cut off from

---

[25] See Document 13.

religion; he made them the target of his revivals, and when he founded the Moody Bible Institute in 1886 he charged its students to devote their lives to evangelizing the poor. Yet, like most other urban revivalists, he drew most of his audiences from the middle and lower-middle classes, especially those who in their own lives or family traditions had had some contact with organized Protestantism. When he tried to conduct a revival on Fourteenth Street and Second Avenue in New York, the attendance was so sparse that he sent out men to try to round up listeners from the nearby cafes. " 'Don't you want to come up to the church . . . and hear Dwight L. Moody preach?' the chairman said to four men who sat at a cardtable near the door. 'Who the hell is Moody?' one of them replied. And that was all there was to it."[26] Moody's complete defeat on the Lower East Side neatly symbolized the limits of revivalism's ability even to begin the process of reestablishing the old church order among the city's poorer people.

The striking growth of what came to be known as Jehovah's Witnesses demonstrated that many of those whom revivalism could not reach sought a more radical rejection of contemporary culture than men like Moody demanded. In the 1840's pre-millennialism had attracted a large following; when William Miller's predictions of a day of judgment had not been fulfilled, some had been disillusioned, but a variety of adventist churches remained in existence. Then in 1872, Charles Taze Russell, dissatisfied not only with his early Congregationalism but also with the "infidelity" to which "science" and "modern thought" had led him, found in the eschatological promises of the Bible a guarantee that Christ would soon return to rule on earth. In that overwhelming perspective, the creeds and practices of the churches seemed worse than temporizing; not preaching the truth, they were necessarily

---

[26] The incident is recounted in Stelzle, *A Son of the Bowery*, p. 119.

diabolic agencies. Zion's Watch Tower Society, which Russell organized in 1884, tolerated no compromise with the world, no participation in rituals or worship which tried to sanctify modes of accommodation. Society members were to devote all their efforts to "witnessing" and "publishing" Christ's imminent coming. Free of the need to follow conventional modes of action, Russell was able to develop modes of "evangelism" peculiarly suited to the masses of unchurched city dwellers. He developed an illustrated lecture, or sermon, "The Photo Drama of Creation," and transcribed his words on to phonograph records that could be played to many more people than Moody could ever have reached, and in situations and places where neither Moody nor any other regular revivalist would ever have been accepted.[27] Unencumbered by a theological tradition (Russellites declared for example that the Trinity was a vulgar error), he could depict "the divine plan of the ages" with the clarity of an architectural drawing; even the barely literate could see in the chart which prefaced most collections of Russell's writings the point in history where mankind stood. Though the movement avoided stipulating an exact day in which Christ would sit in judgment, 1914 was generally thought to mark the beginning of Christ's reconquest of the world. As important as the danger was the promise, epitomized in the slogan made popular by the Witnesses in the twentieth century, that "millions now living will never die." Simple in the demands they made upon the believer, unqualified in the denunciations they uttered against the government, the other churches, indeed modern culture generally, Jehovah's Witnesses exerted a growing appeal to the lower social and economic classes in American cities.[28] By the twentieth century, observers recognized that the Witnesses were proselyting

---

[27] Charles S. Braden, *These Also Believe. A Study of Modern American Cults and Minority Religious Movements* (New York: Macmillan, 1949), p. 361.
[28] See Document 14.

successfully among the habitués of city missions, which apparently could reach down-and-outers, but could not mold them into any kind of church.[29] Symbolically, when Jehovah's Witnesses established themselves in Brooklyn, they turned a former mission of Plymouth Church into their headquarters. Though they did not themselves develop congregational life of the once familiar type, they made out of one strain of traditional religion an adaptation to felt needs that was more viable than either the mission ventures of transformed churches or the adaptations of revivalism.

The Witnesses were held to their single religious purpose first by the charismatic leadership of Russell and later by a highly centralized organization dominated by "Judge" Rutherford. In marked contrast were the flock of largely autonomous local groups which began to appear, as it seemed, spontaneously in many of the large cities about the turn of the century. Sharing with the Holiness churches an almost unlimited trust in the leadings of religious emotion, and with the Witnesses a strong conviction of a not too distant Second Coming, these churches were often lumped with Holiness groups and the Witnesses as manifestations of Pentecostalism. But while all did indeed believe that the special gifts of the Pentecost would be bestowed on men again, both Witnesses and Holiness groups remained extremely wary toward contemporaries claiming the gift of "tongues" and of healing.

The gift of tongues, or *glossolalia,* was not only an easy development of the hyper-excitement of the protracted religious meetings these groups treasured; it met the needs of simple, untutored people anxious to take a leading part in meetings.[30] Honorific distinctions in favor of a professional minister disappeared; formal training, logic, even Biblical

---

[29] Theodore Abel, *Protestant Missions to Catholic Immigrants* (New York: Institute of Social and Religious Research, 1933), pp. 54–55.

[30] See F. G. Henke, "The Gift of Tongues and Related Phenomena at the Present Day," *American Journal of Theology,* XIII (1909), 196–201.

scholarship lost most importance. Above all, command of the language, which more than anything else inhibited European immigrants and slow-speaking country folk from masterful participation in urban culture, now was irrelevant, for might not God choose to speak through His people in any language, any accent?

The gift of tongues first came to public attention in 1905 in Los Angeles, but it is likely that there had been manifestations earlier.[31] From the first, Pentecostalists were an affront to most other churches. H. Paul Douglass, one of the most devoted workers for the Christianization of the city in the twentieth century, declared after a survey of St. Louis in the early 1920's: "It is a challenging and indeed shocking discovery that there are so many examples of these wild religious tendencies in St. Louis, and that so many of the humbler and newer people of the city are actually receiving from them a poor and unnourishing imitation of the Bread of Life." It appalled Douglass to realize that this "spiritual underworld" serving so crudely "that seething, unregulated and untamed stream of emotional religion" should provide so many "humble believers" the "only congenial religious home in St. Louis." Moreover, these sects were often impossibly "dogmatic, perhaps conceited, critical, and impatient with others."[32] But if the Pentecostals sneered at the churches of the "world," they did not discriminate among social classes and ethnic groups; nothing better illustrated their sectarian preoccupation with the leadings of the Holy Spirit than their obliviousness to the "color line" which cut across almost every aspect of American life. Shortlived, tumultuous, and strife-torn as some of these Pentecostal churches were, they brought congregations of

---

[31] Nils Bloch-Hoell, *The Pentecostal Movement* (Oslo: Universitetsforlaget, 1964), especially pp. 45–51.

[32] *The St. Louis Church Survey* (New York: George H. Doran, 1924), pp. 119–120.

striking catholicity together in worship services that were uniquely absorbing.

One of the prized Pentecostal gifts was that of healing. Like the gift of tongues, it proved to have extraordinary appeal to the lower-class folk who flocked into "storefront" churches. But the conviction that organized religion should assume responsibility for bodily ailments was not confined to any one sect or any one social class. In the Episcopal Church, a group of ministers led by Drs. Elwood Worcester and Samuel McComb of Emmanuel Church, Boston, began to treat parishioners suffering from "functional nervous disorders." But the shining example of the attempt of religion to guide the faithful to victory over illness was Christian Science. It was the achievement of Mary Baker Eddy that the Church of Christ (Scientist) which she founded in 1879 was premised on the guidance given by the Scriptures to "Science and Health."

The central strategy of Christian Science was a denial of the reality of matter; for this there were abundant precedents in American transcendentalism, and Mrs. Eddy not surprisingly always had to cope with numerous competing brands of gnosticism. But Mrs. Eddy had unusual powers both of inspiration and organization. Students spoke "of a certain spiritual and emotional exaltation which she was able to impart . . . , a feeling so strong that it was like the birth of a new understanding and seemed to open to them a new heaven and a new earth." Those who "were imaginative and emotional, and especially those who had something of the mystic in their nature, came out . . . to find that for them the world had changed. They lived by a new set of values; the color seemed to fade out of the physical world about them; men and women became shadow-like. . . . The reality of pain and pleasure, sin and grief, love and death, once denied, the only positive thing in their lives was their belief. . . ."[33] Once

---

[33] Quoted in Georgine Milmine, "Mary Baker Eddy," *McClure's Magazine*, XXIX (July, 1907), 108–109.

Mrs. Eddy became convinced that the only way to preserve the purity of this gospel against the distortions of her "enemies" (whom she believed informed with "malicious animal magnetism") was to establish a church, she created an institution which placed all power in her hands, and which made the study of her words the primary religious duty. She built and ruled so well that at her death in 1910 her church was able to survive her.

It was, however, a church with a very special appeal as well as a very special doctrine and government.[34] Most of the members had not long before been members of the older Protestant churches; most were middle or upper-middle class; almost all were living in cities; the preponderance of woman members was exceptional, even for the American churches.[35] All of this seemed reasonable and natural to Mrs. Eddy. Though she would have denied that Christian Science was simply an adaptation of Protestantism, she always believed that a sound Protestant background was virtually a prerequisite for seeing the light. Christian Science, like Beecher's Plymouth Church, purveyed a singularly straitened version of Christianity to a peculiarly middle-class segment of the urban population.

V

By the last decades of the nineteenth century there was an enormous variety of urban churches—downtown, country, immigrant, neighborhood, revivalist, Witnesses, Pentecostal, Christian Science; but those which were churches were not urban in anything but location, and those which were urban were not churches, at least in the traditional sense of being

---

[34] See Documents 16 and 17.

[35] See David O. Moberg, *The Church as a Social Institution* (Englewood Cliffs, N. J.: Prentice-Hall, 1962), p. 396; see also the perceptive English study, Bryan R. Wilson, *Sects and Society. A Sociological Study of the Elim Tabernacle, Christian Science, and Christadelphians* (Berkeley: University of California Press, 1961), p. 350.

the religious expression of the community. Many prominent churchmen made no secret of their sense that the many expedients did not constitute a triumph of religion in its new tasks.

Among Catholic leaders, much of the discontent focused on the difficulties posed for the Church by the ethnic heterogeneity of the city. Once these were overcome it was plausible to imagine that urban Catholic churches would suffer none of the distortions obvious in Protestant adaptions. Parish boundaries seldom coincided with lines dividing social classes, so that most parishes would come closer to approximating "the whole Church in microcosm" than the average Protestant downtown or neighborhood church. The Church's hierarchical structure seemed also to guarantee that no parish, whatever its social composition, would become too parochial in outlook. Furthermore, by the late nineteenth century, urban Catholic parishes had begun to develop that bewildering array of parochial schools, sodalities, confraternities, and societies—something for every condition of man—for which the modern American Catholic parish is famous. Yet, as a few of the more "Americanist" clergy recognized, the typical urban parishes fell short in two ways of being the authentic voice of their communities—as by ancient rural custom, and theological claim, they ought to be. Recoiling from the city because it was not the country, and because it seemed, to a Catholic population still of immigrant stock, formidably "American," they tended to remain aloof from attempts to civilize the city. Also, obsessed by the dangers to the faith engendered in a religiously heterogeneous city, most Catholics contented themselves with resisting error; they were almost sectlike in their disposition to preserve Catholicism from contact with the non-Catholic world.[36] Though Protestants regularly hailed the

_____

[36] Robert D. Cross, *The Emergence of Liberal Catholicism in America* (Cambridge, Mass.: Harvard University Press, 1958), especially chapter 2.

success of Catholics in transcending the social divisions rending urban Protestantism, the more perceptive Catholics were anything but satisfied with the Church's response to the city.[37]

A growing number of Protestant leaders concluded that churches could not simply react to urban life; if they hoped to re-establish the harmonious relationship between religion and culture, they would have to take an active responsibility for reshaping that culture, even if that required marked departures from the usual modes of church action. In reaching this perception, churchmen were aided not only by their recognition of the partial failures of the city churches, but also by the partial successes of such enterprises as the YMCA and the Salvation Army. Though making no claims to being churches, such responses to what Aaron Abell has felicitously called "the urban impact" demonstrated that religion could be presented to some elements in the city, only if the men of God would seek to meet certain creaturely needs.[38] Equally influential was the gradual formulation of a "social gospel"—what Henry May and Charles Hopkins have ably discussed in terms of the Protestant churches, but which had parallels in Catholicism and Judaism as well.[39] Finding its great appeal among those least trammeled with congregational responsibilities— among seminary teachers, bishops, and denominational officials the social gospel gave sanction to those ministers and laymen anxious to redefine the gospel to meet specifically urban needs.

---

[37] Robert D. Cross, "The Changing Image of the City among American Catholics," *Catholic Historical Review*, XLVIII (April, 1962), 33–52.

[38] Aaron I. Abell, *The Urban Impact on American Protestantism* (Cambridge, Mass.: Harvard University Press, 1943).

[39] Charles H. Hopkins, *The Rise of the Social Gospel in American Protestantism* (New Haven: Yale University Press, 1940); Henry F. May, *Protestant Churches and Industrial America* (New York: Octagon Books, 1963). For some reverberations in the Catholic Church, see Abell, *American Catholicism and Social Action* (Garden City, N. Y.: Doubleday, 1960).

This attitude was especially attractive to Episcopalians, who maintained a disproportionate number of "downtown" churches; who had, as a church, never acquiesced completely in the "denominational" assumption that the responsibility for the welfare of society could be shared with other religious organizations; and whose parishes frequently included enough of the city's wealthiest citizens to permit very costly innovations in the ministry to the city. St. George's, for example, on the East Side of New York, had been surrounded by new immigrants, few of them Episcopalian. The handful of wealthy members, including J. P. Morgan, invited to the pulpit the Reverend William S. Rainsford, an English cleric of considerable experience with the problems of London and Toronto as well as New York.[40] Determined to preside over a community church, even if that required using much of the church's resources to create the community, Rainsford soon had developed a parish program to meet the social and economic needs of every sort and condition of urban man. He attained notoriety by his proposal to establish, as an alternative to the saloon, a church club where the workingman could enjoy his glass in edifying circumstances; more important were his programs of industrial education. That such enterprises were not simply alternatives to church life—like the earlier ventures of city missions, or the Salvation Army and YMCA—seemed demonstrated when the membership of St. George's grew from 200 to 4,000, with much of the increase coming from people of humble circumstances, both foreign-born and American. This mode of reintegrating church and community became celebrated as the institutional church.

Although the majority of institutional churches grew out of "downtown" Episcopal and Congregational churches of high social standing and low membership, Grace Church in Philadelphia illustrated that a city Baptist church might also become

---

[40] See Document 18.

"institutional." In 1882, Russell Conwell brought to the pastorate of Grace no majestic ecclesiastical tradition, but the conviction that churches to succeed must prove more relevant to social problems than they had been to him as a country boy seeking his fortune in the city.[41] As an adjunct to Grace Church, he built Samaritan Hospital, and also Baptist Temple, eventually the center for Temple College and for a whole complex of recreational and social clubs. Grace Church soon claimed to have the largest congregation in the United States.

The conspicuous success of congregations like St. George's and Grace made it plausible for the Open and Institutional Church League, founded in 1894, to boast that "the burning question, 'how to reach the masses,' is practically solved,"[42] for the institutional church seemed to possess the "comprehensiveness" essential to a true congregation. But the League failed to recognize just how precarious was the life of most institutional churches. Both St. George's and Grace at the end of the century depended too much on charismatic ministerial leadership to prove that many churches could reach, let alone hold, the "masses." Rainsford had to struggle continuously to preserve the peaceful coexistence of rich and poor in one church. J. P. Morgan found it almost intolerable to imagine that the vestry, whom he was accustomed to entertain at his home, should contain men he did not "know socially"; and Alfred Mahan quit St. George's in revulsion against Rainsford's democratizing policies. Conwell, spared such problems by the relative absence of wealthy men in his congregation, was continually obliged to seek outside funds to continue his institutional church. Whether he secured money from friendly businessmen like the Wanamakers, or raised it by touring the country delivering his paean to self-help, entitled "Acres of

---

[41] Agnes R. Burr, *Russell H. Conwell and His Work* (Philadelphia: John Winston, 1917).

[42] Quoted in Abell, *The Urban Impact on American Protestantism,* p. 161.

Diamonds," he symbolized the adventitious existence of his church—a missionary venture if not in its character at least in its dependence upon other churches and churchmen. Even the League, acknowledging that more cooperation between denominations would be necessary to sustain institutional churches in some parts of some cities, implicitly retreated from the old faith in the autonomous congregation.

Furthermore, commitment to the social gospel involved the institutional churches in some of the ambiguities of that movement. Faith that a program of action satisfactory to all social classes could be agreed on was soon shaken by the intransigence of the congregations. Early in the twentieth century, Charles Stelzle became convinced that the institutional church would never even consider the socialistic ideas which, he thought, were talismanic to many city workers;[43] his own inability to get support from the Presbyterian Church for radical congregational experiments was paralleled in subsequent decades by the rebuffs many social gospelers received from their denominations.[44] Most congregations would endorse the social gospel only if it did not involve pronounced departures from middle-class values.

Conversely, to the extent that institutional churches committed themselves to programs of more or less radical social action, they did so on the assumption—explicit in Rainsford's case—that either a healthy community would be swiftly restored, or that the state would see its duty and relieve the churches of their social responsibilities. Either eventuality was conducive of disillusion. As the municipalities, or private agencies like the settlement houses, increased the range of

---

[43] Compare Document 19 with Stelzle, *American Social and Religious Conditions* (New York: Fleming Revell, 1912).

[44] For the history of the later years of the Social Gospel, see Paul A. Carter, *The Decline and Revival of the Social Gospel* (Ithaca, N. Y.: Cornell University Press, 1956) and Donald Meyer, *The Protestant Search for Political Realism* (Berkeley: University of California Press, 1960).

community service, the institutional churches lost much of their sense of mission. Perhaps more ominous was the discovery that social amelioration did not by itself automatically produce a population naturally inclined toward congregational life. The dawning realization that alienation from the churches was not simply a by-product of problems of society was central to the neo-orthodox revolt of the 1930's from the social gospel on which the institutional churches were premised.

VI

For all its limitations, the institutional church constituted the most coherent effort to re-establish the congregation as the normal vehicle of religious life in the city. Its obvious successes encouraged churches threatened by a changing city environment not to desert to the suburbs. Its very willingness to experiment with new modes of evangelism made it an important precedent for contemporary enterprises like the East Harlem Protestant Parish, with its determination to construct a congregational life in a demoralized neighborhood.[45] On the other hand, the institutional church has never been so generally accepted as to preclude the continued existence— and in some cases the steady growth—of more specialized adaptations to the urban scene.

The number of neighborhood churches has increased during the twentieth century. As suburbia has grown more rapidly than center-city, new congregations have been established at an astonishing rate, each usually drawing on a highly stratified segment of the population. The consequence has been

---

[45] For the implications of the experience in this parish, as seen by one of its leaders, see George R. Webber, *The Congregation in Mission* (New York: Abingdon Press, 1964). For contemporary Catholic concern about the urban parish, see Dennis Clark, *Cities in Crisis* (New York: Sheed and Ward, 1960), and the references in Cross, "The Changing Image."

much like that exhibited in Beecher's Plymouth Church; within the last decade some Protestant, Catholic, and Jewish spokesmen have gloried in the obvious vitality of these churches, while others have deplored the "suburban captivity."[46]

The relatively steady abandonment in many suburban churches of traditional theology in favor of a gospel of social adjustment and mental health has further narrowed the gap separating them from the gnostic cults once represented almost exclusively by Christian Science, but now including New Thought, Unity, Psychiana, and I Am. Of these, only Christian Science maintains any semblance of congregational life, but the strong group identification of their members renders these cults almost as close to the old church order as many of the suburban churches.

The rural churches established in the cities in the late nineteenth century have been markedly affected by urban life. The Church of God (Anderson, Indiana), for example, one of the larger holiness bodies, has steadily accommodated to the religious diversity of the city by shedding its hostility to other denominations. As members slowly abandon their peculiarities of dress and expression, the church concentrates on maintaining the allegiance of the younger generation; it

relaxes its program of grab-him-by-the-lapel evangelism, puts robes on the choir and candles on the altar, divides the chancel, replaces folding chairs with oaken pews, and calls a college-trained minister. . . . It moves out of its plain rectangular white frame building into a stone gothic or redwood contemporary structure. It is now respectable.[47]

---

[46] Representative views are those of Andrew Greeley, *The Church and the Suburbs* (New York: Sheed and Ward, 1959); Albert J. Gordon, *Jews in Suburbia* (Boston: Beacon Press, 1959); and Gibson Winter, *The Suburban Captivity of the Churches* (Garden City, N. Y.: Doubleday, 1961).

[47] Val B. Clear, "The Urbanization of a Holiness Body," *The City Church*, IX (July-August, 1958), 2–3, 7–11.

Such transformed churches, of course, do not appeal so strongly any more to the migrants from the countryside. But with the restriction in the 1920's of immigration from abroad, and with the reduction of the American rural population, the number of country folk in the city has decreased; the likelihood has therefore decreased of creating a church which continues the special version of religious life cherished in one's own country or region. However, the ability of revivalists like Billy Graham to mount revival crusades demonstrates that there are still many people in the cities who are not completely satisfied with the ethos of the city churches.

Meanwhile, the probability has steadily grown that newcomers will be attracted to one of the cultic or Pentecostal groups authentic to the cities. Some of these groups owe their existence to a charismatic leader like Daddy Grace or Father Divine; others are sustained by a special myth like that which connects the "Black Jews" with the Lost Tribes; still others have stressed a single doctrine like the rapidly growing Jehovah's Witnesses, or a single gift, like some of the healing cults.[48] In 1958, Henry Van Dusen, President of Union Theological Seminary, estimated that a third of all believers now adhere to radical sects or cults, and that, taken together, they comprise the most rapidly growing component of American religion.[49] About the same time, two sociologists noted how Puerto Rican migrants to New York, not strongly drawn to the Roman Catholic parishes, have flocked into Pentecostal churches. Not only do these churches offer a stringent moral code in reassuring contrast to the apparent normlessness of the city; they also provide frequent meetings, in which newcomers

---

[48] See G. Norman Eddy, "Store-Front Religion," in Robert Lee (ed.), *Cities and Churches. Readings on the Urban Church* (Philadelphia: Westminster Press, 1962). See also Elmer T. Clark, *The Small Sects in America* (Nashville: Cokesbury Press, 1937).

[49] "The Third Force in Christendom," *Life,* XLIV (June 9, 1958), p. 23.

are welcomed, in which the modes of worship are simple, and in which participation in songs and "tongues" is warmly cherished. "The first time I went there, I was impressed by the way everyone shook hands with me," reported one member. Another said that "I was sick, they came to my home to say a prayer for me." "I used to go to the Catholic Church," a third explained; "there nobody knew me. . . . Now in my church they call me sister."[50] Such testimonies reaffirm that a need for congregational communion continues to be a strong theme in American religious life. Under the social confusions, the economic difficulties, and the psychological tensions engendered by urban life, congregationalism has developed in ways often unfamiliar and almost always profoundly unsatisfactory to leaders whose ideal has remained the village church on the green.

---

[50] Renato Poblete and Thomas F. O'Dea, "Anomie and the 'Quest for Community': The Formation of Sects among the Puerto Ricans of New York," *American Catholic Sociological Review,* XXI (Spring, 1960), 18–36.

Nelson Burr's remarkable two-volume *Critical Bibliography of Religion in America* (Princeton: Princeton University Press, 1957) affords the interested student a wide variety of sources, both primary and secondary, on almost every conceivable topic of American religious history. The most useful general summary volume is Clifton E. Olmstead, *History of Religion in the United States* (Englewood Cliffs, N. J.: Prentice-Hall, 1960). Henry F. May's article, "The Recovery of American Religious History," *American Historical Review,* LXX (October, 1964), 79–92, nicely organizes the most recent scholarship.

Three works present challenging interpretations of the main contours of American religious history: Sidney Mead, *The Lively Experiment* (New York: Harper & Row, 1963); Winthrop S. Hudson, *The Great Tradition of the American Churches* (New York: Harper, 1953); and H. Shelton Smith, *et al., American Christianity: An Historical Interpretation with Representative Documents* (2 vols.; New York: Scribner, 1960). In the Chicago History of American Civilization are to be found John Tracy Ellis, *American Catholicism* (Chicago: University of Chicago Press, 1956), Nathan Glazer, *American Judaism* (Chicago: University of Chicago Press, 1957), and Winthrop S. Hudson, *American Protestantism* (Chicago: University of Chicago Press, 1961); all of these are available in paperback. Also available in paperback is Franklin H. Littell, *From State Church to Pluralism* (Garden City, N. Y.: Anchor, 1962).

The best general study of American society in the era when the churches first unavoidably confronted "the city" is Arthur M. Schlesinger, *The Rise of the City, 1878–1898* (New

York: Macmillan, 1933). Though there have been historical studies of almost every city in America, only men of sociological imagination have made any attempt to generalize. Lewis Mumford, in *Technics and Civilization* (New York: Harcourt, Brace, 1934) and his more recent *The City in History* (New York: Harcourt, Brace, 1961), is grandly gloomy about the survival of religion (or anything else traditional) in modern cities. Robert Park, *et al.*, in *The City* (Chicago: University of Chicago Press, 1925) were almost equally apocalyptic. The classic statement of the destructive effect of city life on religion is Louis Wirth's "Urbanism as a Way of Life," a 1938 essay reprinted in Paul Hatt and A. J. Reiss, eds., *Reader in Urban Sociology* (Glencoe, Illinois: Free Press, 1951). For a recent cogent criticism of this dogmatism, see Maurice Stein, *The Eclipse of Community* (Princeton: Princeton University Press, 1960). See also the suggestive summary of European scholarship by Joseph Folliet, "The Effect of City Life upon Spiritual Life," in R. M. Fisher, ed., *The Metropolis in Modern Life* (New York: Columbia University Press, 1955).

Several special studies of religion in American cities in the late nineteenth century will help the reader find his way through the enormous volume of sermons, parish histories, biographies, and denominational self-praise. Francis P. Weisenburger, *Ordeal of Faith: The Crisis of Church-Going America 1865–1900* (New York: Philosophical Library, 1959), though a bit mechanical, asks some important questions. Aaron I. Abell's two books, *The Urban Impact on American Protestantism* (Cambridge: Harvard University Press, 1943), and *American Catholicism and Social Action* (Garden City, N Y.: Doubleday, 1960) are very judicious; unfortunately, there are no comparable volumes on the Jewish experience or on that of the sects and cults; the extensive twentieth-century interest in these themes has produced books, noted in Burr's biography, that throw light on their origins in the late nineteenth century. Though Henry May was primarily concerned with the shock of industrialism, his *Protestant Churches in Industrial America* (New York: Octagon Books, 1963) makes highly useful discriminations about the modes and the chronology of Protestant response to a rapidly changing environment.

Other bibliographical suggestions may be found in the footnotes to the Introduction to this volume, and in the Headnotes to the Documents which follow.

PART ONE

THE PREDICAMENT OF
THE CITY CHURCHES

1. THE CONTRAST BETWEEN
COUNTRY AND CITY

The Country and The City, 1880

BY JOHN LANCASTER SPALDING

Almost every American churchman, in considering the problems of the city, contrasted them with the pastoral harmonies of rural culture. John Lancaster Spalding (1840–1916) was brought up on a Kentucky plantation, studied in Europe, and then returned to serve four years as a parish priest in New York City in the 1870's. His remarkable intelligence and polished literary style enabled him to give normative expression to the anguish of a religious people moving toward a new environment. The logical remedy, Spalding declared, was to "colonize" oppressed city dwellers in the country. Spokesmen of other denominations made similar recommendations, and were similarly ignored.

Of course, as a member of a church committed to the parochial organization of the whole nation—cities as well as countryside—Spalding never despaired of the possibilities of congregational life anywhere. Indeed, later in life, he wrote volume after volume on the power of education to help men

From John Lancaster Spalding, *The Religious Mission of the Irish People and Catholic Colonization* (New York: Catholic Colonization Society, 1880), pp. 64–100.

transcend mere environmental obstacles. For an excellent recent essay on Spalding, see John Tracy Ellis, John Lancaster Spalding *(Milwaukee: Bruce, 1962).*

Most Catholics, Protestants, and Jews lacked Spalding's later optimism about the city; and when they roused themselves to action, Charles Stelzle complained in 1907, they seemed disposed "to meet town conditions by an elaborate country church programme" (pp. 339-340).

THE COUNTRY

Human character is shaped by its surroundings. This is the meaning of the proverb that we are creatures of circumstance. God's grace even works through the natural medium in which the soul lives, and its action is hindered by untoward conditions, so that it is held to be a miracle of grace if one remain pure amid evil associations. Every special mode of life creates a separate type of character, and the virtues and vices of races and nations are traceable in a great degree to the surroundings in which they have lived and labored.

When we compare Christian with pagan civilization the most obvious fact which meets our view is a change in the distribution of population. In Greece and Rome the owners of the soil were collected together in cities. Their history is the history of cities and towns. There was no country population, except the slaves whom the proprietors kept upon the land. "Rome," says Guizot, "has left us nothing but monuments impressed with the municipal stamp and intended for populations amassed upon a single spot. From whatever point of view you consider the Roman world, you find this almost exclusive preponderance of cities and the social non-existence of the country." But when the new society was constituted by the help of the Catholic Church upon the ruins of the great pagan empire, the social preponderance passed from the city to the country; and little by little the soil of Europe was covered with castle and cloister and the thatch-roofed cottage of the peasant.

The family became the social unit, and its purity and typical character were preserved and developed by isolation from the corrupt mass of mankind, and by the healthful atmosphere of its natural surroundings. This was an immense advance, and its influence upon the course of Christian history has been incalculable. To make the cultivation of the soil honorable was a return to the ways of God, who had destined man, even before his fall, to till the earth, and who, after the original sin, had made this destiny a part of the redeeming punishment. And this was the life of the chosen people. Abraham and Isaac and Jacob were shepherds and husbandmen, and when their descendants had been made the slaves of industry, hewers of wood and drawers of water, they were led out of bondage, by the divine command, into the land of promise, where all, from the chief of the tribe of Juda to the least of the house of Benjamin, returned to the agricultural and pastoral life of their fathers. The land was divided among the tribes and families, with the provision that no perpetual alienation should ever take place, and at the end of every fifty years all lands reverted to the original owners or their descendants. Every man sat beneath his own fig-tree and ate the fruit of his own vine. God did not promise silver and gold and precious stones, but he promised seasonable rains, abundant harvests, ripe fruits, numerous flocks, quiet sleep, safety and peace.

These were the temporal blessings which the children of Israel were taught to expect from his providence. They were the farmers of God, the most purely agricultural people that has ever existed. Even their religion bore the impress of husbandry. The sacrificial offerings were the first-fruits of the flocks and the fields. The Passover was celebrated when the ears of corn began to show. The feast of Pentecost pointed to the ripened grain, and the feast of Tabernacles announced the garnered harvest. Whenever the Bible speaks of labor, of business, of possessions, it speaks of the land and its tillage. How full it is of imagery drawn from the golden grain, from vineyard and meadow, from rain and sunshine, from the melting snow and the flowing stream! On every side we hear the lowing of oxen and the bleating of sheep. The King is a shepherd, and the people are his flock. King Saul was driving his team afield when news was brought him that the city of Jabes was in danger; David was watching sheep when Samuel sent for him to anoint him king; Eliseus was following one of his father's twelve ploughs when he was called to prophesy. A shepherd might become a king or a prophet, and the king and the prophet were shepherds. All were "sons of Abraham, and never in bondage to any man." They were, as Moses had said, a people of kings and priests, ennobled and sanctified by the possession of the soil. "You shall love labor," said the holy writings, "and husbandry created by the Most High God"—*Non oderis laboriosa opera et rusticationem creatam ab Altissimo.*

This was the divine political economy; these were the teachings of God; and they are the teachings also of the best human reason. To dwell upon the land and to eat the bread of toil is man's natural condition. "This country life," says Cicero, "teaches economy, industry, and justice"; and a modern thinker has added that agriculture is the mother of good sense. "The strongest men and the bravest soldiers," said Cato, "are farmers' sons; and those who are occupied with the cares of husbandry are freest from evil designs." It is good to dwell in the presence of nature; to see the sun rise and set; to be over-canopied by the blue heaven with its fleecy clouds; to see the flowers bloom and the green fruit swell to melting pulp; to be awakened by songs of birds and lowing of cattle; to breathe fresh air blown from meadows and waving fields of corn; to hear the rain that makes the earth green and glad; to watch the snowflakes that, falling swift and noiseless as the foot of time, enfold it in its winding-sheet. For the young, above all, the earth, with its dower of river, wood, and vale, is God's

university. It never grows old, but is re-created for each new-
born generation, to fill the heart of the human child with
reverence, wonder, awe, delight, ecstasy. The love of nature is a
sacred element of human feeling, and if this sentiment is not
awakened in the child I see not how the man shall be full-
grown and complete. "The dweller in the country," says St.
Chrysostom, "has a higher enjoyment than the rich inhabitant
of the city. To him belong the beauty of the heavens, the
splendors of the light, the purity of the air, the sweetness of
quiet sleep. You shall find in this life true contentment and
security, good name and health, and the fewest dangers to the
soul. This people dwells in peace, leading a modest and
venerable life." And if we go to the highest authority, in heaven
and on earth, we shall learn the same lesson. The birth of
Christ was announced first not to kings, or philosophers, or
men of wealth, but to shepherds watching beside their flocks
on the hills around Bethlehem. Herod's palace was not far off;
but there song, and dance, and revelry went on, and no messenger from heaven heralded the glad tidings to the dwellers in
houses of kings, who are clothed in soft garments. And Christ
himself, setting the supreme example to the conduct and
thoughts of men, spent nearly his whole life in the fields, looking with a tenderness almost akin to human love upon the
grazing flocks, the whitening harvest, the budding trees, the
lilies, and the birds, and the grass, which to-day is green and
to-morrow is cast into the oven. He walks by the seashore, he
goes up into the mountain, he withdraws into the desert, but
he will not so much as sleep within the walls of Jerusalem. The
noise and stir of the crowded city jar upon the sweetness and
serenity which mark all his thoughts and ways. An air of Godlike simplicity breathes round him, and this is not the atmosphere of great cities. The beatitudes were spoken while he
sat upon the hillside, overlooking the landscape that served as
a background to the listening multitudes; and to understand
the peace and delight of the life which they trace out one

should dwell in the open country and breathe the pure air of heaven. In the city neither the rich nor the poor can realize the infinite charm of the Christian ideal. The heart is troubled there, and God is not in the whirlwind of human passion. "To watch the corn grow and the blossoms set," says Ruskin; "to draw hard breath over ploughshare or spade; to read, to think, to love, to hope, to pray—these are the things that make men happy; they have always had the power of doing this; they never will have power to do more. The world's prosperity or adversity depends upon our knowing and teaching these few things; but upon iron, or glass, or electricity, or steam in no wise."

What deep Christian instinct was there not in the love of the ancient monks for nature and solitude—*sedebit solitarius et tacebit!* "I approve," said St. Ivo, in the twelfth century, "the life of those men for whom a city is but a prison, who find their paradise in solitude, who live there by the labor of their hands, or who seek to renew their souls by the sweetness of a life of contemplation—men who drink with the lips of their heart at the fountain of life." Montalembert has called attention to the beautiful names which symbolize the natural scenery that surrounded the mediæval monasteries, and has quoted in this connection Alcuin's touching adieu to his cloister when called to the court of Charlemagne. "O my cell," cried he, "sweet and well-beloved home, adieu for ever! I shall see no more the woods which enfold thee with their interlacing branches and flowery verdure, nor thy fields full of wholesome and aromatic herbs, nor thy streams of fish, nor thy orchards, nor thy gardens where the lily mingles with the rose. I shall hear no more the birds who, like ourselves, sing matins and, in their way, praise the Lord of all; nor those words of sweet and holy wisdom which sound in the same breath as the praises of the Most High from lips and hearts always peaceful."

The monks who converted the barbarians and preserved the writings of the Greeks and Romans were the pioneer farmers of Christendom. "They carried," says Montalembert, "labor,

fertility, human strength and intelligence into those solitudes
which till then had been abandoned to wild beasts and to the
disorder of spontaneous vegetation." They felled the forest,
they drained the marsh, they planted fruit-trees and the vine,
they domesticated the animals which in the chaos of barbarian
invasions had gone back to the savage state. There was Telio,
a British monk, who introduced the apple-tree into Armorica.
There was St. Fiacre, an Irish monk, who cleared the forest
around Meaux, and who is still the patron saint of the French
gardener; and there was Theodulph, born of an illustrious
family in Aquitaine, who, having become a monk, drove his
yoke of oxen in the plough for twenty-two years. After these
twenty-two years of ploughing he was elected abbot. "Then,"
says Montalembert, "the inhabitants of the nearest village took
his plough and hung it up in their church as a relic. It was so,
in fact—a noble and holy relic of one of those lives of perpetual labor and superhuman virtue whose example has exercised a more fruitful and lasting influence than that of the
proudest conquerors. It seems to me that we should all contemplate with emotion, if it still existed, that monk's plough,
doubly sacred by religion and by labor, by history and by
virtue. For myself, I feel that I should kiss it as willingly as the
sword of Charlemagne or the pen of Bossuet." The plough and
the cross, he adds, formed the ensign and emblazonry of the
entire history of the monks during these early ages—*cruce et
aratro!* And there was Ermenfried, a nobleman of the court of
King Clotaire II., who, having become a monk, was accustomed
to kiss with tender respect the hard hands of the ploughmen.
"I have surveyed the annals of all nations, ancient and
modern," says the writer whom I have just quoted, "but I have
found nothing which has moved me more, or better explained
the true causes of the victory of Christianity over the ancient
world, than the image of this German, this son of the victors of
Rome and conquerors of Gaul, become a monk and kissing before the altar of Christ the hard hand of the Gaulish husbandmen in that forgotten corner of Jura, without even suspecting

that an obscure witness took note of it for forgetful posterity." And there was Columba, who had a poet's love of nature, and who, when death was near, was unwilling to die until he had taken leave of his monks, who were at work in the fields on the western side of holy Iona. Drawn in an ox-cart, his white head bowed by age and long prayer, he went among them, greater than a Roman conqueror returning over the Sacred Way with captive kings bound to his triumphal car. And as he homeward went by slow degrees, lingering as loath to bid farewell to the fields he loved, the old farm-horse, white, too, with age and set free from work, came up to him and put his head upon his shoulder. "The horse loves me," says Columba to Diarmid. "Leave him with me; let him weep for my departure."

The farmer's life, I know as well as any man, is not ideal; no human life is so. It has its cares, its disappointments, its hardships, its narrowness, its unloveliness. Less than any other, probably, does it suit a sentimentalist. The farmer must learn to be content with hard work and small gains. He must dress coarsely and wait long. His hands will grow hard and his knees stiff. He must love plain living, but not high thinking. He is married to the earth, and, like all the wedded, must needs learn patience. He is bound to a single spot and moves within a narrow circle. But in return he is nature's freeman, dependent upon God's providence and his own strong arm. He is no man's hired servant. He has health, and appetite, and soothest sleep. He sits beside his own hearthstone; and his children around him look up to him as a father and a king, for he is a sovereign owner of the soil:

> A man he seems of cheerful yesterdays
> And confident to-morrows, with a face
> Not worldly-minded, for it bears too much
> Of nature's impress—gayety and health,
> Freedom and hope—but keen withal and shrewd.
> His gestures note; and hark! his tones of voice
> Are all vivacious as his mien and looks.

"The first farmer," says Emerson, "was the first man, and all historic nobility rests on possession and use of land. Men do not like hard work, but every man has an exceptional respect for tillage, and a feeling that this is the original calling of his race, that he himself is only excused from it by some circumstance that made him delegate it for a time to other hands. If he have not some skill which recommends him to the farmer, some product for which the farmer will give him corn, he must himself return into his due place among the planters. And the profession has in all eyes its ancient charm as standing nearest to God, the First Cause. Then the beauty of nature, the tranquillity and innocence of the countryman, his independence and his pleasing arts; the care of bees, of poultry, of sheep, of cows, the dairy, the care of hay, of fruits, of orchards and forests, and the reaction of these on the workman in giving him a strength and plain dignity, like the face and manners of nature, all men acknowledge. . . . The farmer is a hoarded capital of health, as the farm is the capital of wealth; and it is from him that the health and power, moral and intellectual, of the cities come. The city is always recruited from the country. The men in cities who are the centres of energy, the driving-wheels of trade, politics, or political arts, and the women of beauty and genius, are the children or grandchildren of farmers, and are spending the energies which their fathers' hardy, silent life accumulated in frosty furrows, in poverty, necessity, and darkness."[1]

The farmer is the strongest and the healthiest member of the social body; he is also the most religious and the most moral. The children of farmers who carry into the cities fresh blood and new energy carry thither also a deeper religious faith and greater moral earnestness. The forces with which the husbandman deals are boundless and immeasurable; they are above and beyond him, a part of an infinitely mysterious Providence. The

---

[1] *Society and Solitude*, p. 125. [(Boston: Fields, Osgood, 1872), pp. 123–125. Ed.]

sunshine, and the rain, and the changing seasons of the revolving year are under the control of no man. They are manifestations of a higher power, and proclaim the wisdom and goodness
of God. Explain them never so much, and express them in all
possible formulas of matter and motion, and the mystery still
remains to fill the heart with reverence and awe. In the city, on
the other hand, where the eye meets nothing that the hand of
man has not shaped and polished, the tendency is to flippancy
and rationalism. These populations have seen so many sleight-
of-hand tricks that they cannot admire the rising sun or the
waving wheat-fields, or think God's universe wonderful, and
so they lose reverence and faith. Let us listen to the words of
an unbeliever, since it is lawful to be taught by an enemy.
"Thus it was," says Buckle, "that the want of great cities, and of
that form of industry which belongs to them, made the
spiritual classes more numerous than they would otherwise
have been; and what is very observable is that it not only increased their number, but also increased the disposition of the
people to obey them. Agriculturists are naturally, and by the
very circumstances of their daily life, more superstitious than
manufacturers, because the events with which they deal are
more mysterious—that is to say, more difficult to generalize and
predict. Hence it is that, as a body, the inhabitants of agricultural districts pay greater respect to the teachings of their
clergy than the inhabitants of manufacturing districts. The
growth of cities has, therefore, been a main cause of the decline of ecclesiastical power."[2]

The farmer is conservative. He clings to ancient ways and
traditions as he clings to the soil. He is not a theorist and cannot give arguments for his faith, but the excellent good sense
of which agriculture is the mother teaches him that it is good to
believe in God and the soul; that infidelity is a miscreed, be-
gotten of unwisdom. He is as heedless of the newest opinions

---

[2] *A History of Civilization*, 2:151. [H. T. Buckle, *History of Civilization in England* (2nd edn., London: J. W. Parker, 1861). Ed.]

as of the latest fashions, and is content to walk in the way in which his fathers trod. He is unprogressive; and this is doubtless a defect, but a saving one, for the upward march of the race is not secure unless the mass of mankind remain steadfast by their ancient moorings. He stands, like a portion of nature, permanent and changeless, the firm foundation to the whole social fabric. The lawyer, the doctor, and the preacher are the ministers of disease. They are nourished by the sins and infirmities of man. They were not in Paradise—could never have been there. Man, the farmer, was there, and the minister of nature was the minister of health and the minister of God.

The higher moral purity of the farmer is beyond question. "The city population of France," says Michelet, "which is but one fifth of the nation, furnishes two-fifth of the criminals."[3] The following table of statistics, showing the relative percentage of illegitimate births in city and country compared with the total number of births, has been drawn up by Wappäus:

	CITY	COUNTRY
France	15.13	4.24
Netherlands	7.71	2.84
Belgium	14.49	5.88
Sweden	27.44	7.50
Denmark	16.05	10.06
Prussia	9.80	6.60
Hanover	17.42	9.06

The average for the city is double that of the country. Statistics show, in like manner, that the number of divorces is nearly twice as great in the city as in the country; and the city is, the world over, the hot-bed and focus of the social evil and of drunkenness. It is also the favorite home of the suicide. The researches of Legoyt have established that in France the number of suicides among the industrial classes is nearly twice that

---

[3] *Le peuple,* p. 20. [Paris: comptoir des imprimeurs-unis, 1846. Ed.]

of the agricultural classes, while the liberal professions show a still higher proportion. The greater frequency and fruitfulness of marriage among country populations is another evidence of the superior morality of the farmer as compared with the inhabitant of the city.

The higher death-rate among city populations, though partly due to physical causes, is also, in no small degree, attributable to their lowered moral life; and this is equally true of insanity, which is far more common in the city than in the country. The physical deterioration and diminished vitality of city populations throw additional light upon their moral condition. Were it not for the uninterrupted influx of healthy country blood the cities would become depopulated; and, due allowance being made for this revitalizing of city populations, the average duration of life is from eight to ten years longer in the country than in the city.

"It is undeniably proven," says Oettinger, "that industrial populations are inferior to the agricultural classes in ability to bear arms. Industrialism, it would seem, unnerves a people and renders them unfit for service. Engel has shown that in Saxony twenty-six per cent. of the country population and only nineteen per cent. of city people were fit for military service. In Prussia the researches of Helwing have led to similar results, which are, moreover, in perfect accord with the earlier investigations of Süssmilch, who calls attention to the ethical phase of the problem when he says that the peasant is braver and truer 'because he fights for his property and family, whereas the factory-hand has seldom a hearth and home.' "[4] Dr. Bartholomäi has shown that there is a gradual and progressive diminution in the power of endurance among the laboring classes of Berlin; and this is no doubt true of all city populations.

Mr. Lecky, all of whose sympathies lead him to prefer the

---

[4] *Moralstatistik*, p. 384. [Alexander von Oettingen, *Die Moralstatistik in ihrer Bedeutung für eine Christliche Socialethik* (2nd edn., Erlangen: Deichert, 1874). Ed.]

civilization of the city to that of the country, writes the following sentence: "The promotion of industrial veracity is probably the single form in which the growth of manufactures exercises a favorable influence upon morals";[5] and we may fairly question whether he is able to establish even this single exception to what he admits to be a general rule. The dishonesties of trade, the adulterations of articles of commerce, the fraudulent failures, the short weights and measures, and the merchant's lie, which is so much a matter of course that only simpletons fall into the snare, would certainly demand some little explanation. The city, however, must and will exist. Its influence upon civilization is not only great but in many ways beneficial. It is the centre of the manufacturing and commercial interests; it is also the focus of intellectual light. The immediate contact of great multitudes does, indeed, tend to develop the lower and more animal side of man's nature, but it acts also as a stimulant upon his spiritual faculties, and the presence of the wretchedness and degradation which vice is sure to beget will not fail to rouse the better sort of men to higher efforts of unselfish devotion. All that I wish to say is that the agricultural life more than that of the city conduces to happiness and morality, and that it harmonizes better with the Christian ideal.

THE CITY

A noticeable feature in our modern social life is the accelerated growth of cities and towns. The stream of population is from the country towards commercial and industrial centres. In Great Britain, from 1811 to 1821, the number of agricultural families sank from thirty-five per cent. to twenty-eight per cent. of the entire population; and in 1851 it had fallen to twenty-three per cent. From 1831 to 1841 there was an increase of forty-six per cent. in the manufacturing and commercial popu-

---

[5] *European Morals*, 1:139. [*History of European Morals from Augustus to Charlemagne* (2nd edn., London: Longmans, Green, 1869). Ed.]

lation, while there was during the same period a falling-off of twenty-two per cent. in the agricultural classes. In France, from 1851 to 1856, the country population fell from fifty-six per cent. to fifty-two per cent. of the whole people, and in the same time the industrial and commercial classes increased from twenty-seven to thirty-three per cent. The same movement of population is found to exist throughout the civilized world; and it is of course strongest where the manufacturing interests are most powerful. There is not merely a tendency to abandon the country for the town, but there seems to exist a morbid yearning for the life of great cities. The population of Berlin was doubled from 1852 to 1872, and the increase during the last seven years has been still more rapid. The growth of London and Paris during the last quarter of a century has been prodigious; and, in America, New York, Philadelphia, and Chicago are striking examples of the suddenness with which, in the present phase of civilization, great centres of population are created.

The causes to which this tendency is to be ascribed are many. The city is a mystery and the source of boundless wonder to the young who have always lived in the country; and, as the real life is never altogether satisfactory, it is natural that in their dreams of happiness they should look to the city as their future home. They see but the surfaces of things, and have never learned that all that glitters is not gold. And when they are told that in the great city they will readily find employment at good wages, they are filled with feverish desire to plunge into the great ocean of humanity to see what pearl they may bring up. How many a country boy have they not read of who, having entered the metropolis without friends or money, worked his way up until he became the owner of millions and dwelt in a palace—and for the mass of mankind, whether young or old, to have millions and to dwell in a palace is more than to be a saint or a hero, or Plato or Shakspere. It is a part of the blessedness of youth that the young believe whatever good fortune has happened to any man will somehow or other come to them.

Then the air of the city, with the stir of the multitude and the whirl of business and pleasure, intoxicates, and men are drawn into the vortex by the craving for excitement, which is often so great that honor and all that is most precious are sacrificed to the indulgence of a fatal appetite. Those who desire to lead a life of dissipation are drawn to the city by the feeling that it will offer them better opportunity and greater security from the consequences of evil-doing; and those who have lost their good name are anxious to bury themselves in the promiscuous crowd from the sight of those who know them. There are also multitudes of people for whom to think or act for themselves is a weary burden of which they are glad to be relieved. They ask only that some one hire them, and are content to eat the bread of servitude. They have no thought of the morrow, and never suspect that their condition is wretched until no one will pay for their labor longer and they are left without food or shelter. Of these people the city or the factory town is the natural home. And then there are numbers who, having met with some success in smaller places, are persuaded that their talent is exceptional and demands a wider field. The city, too, is the paradise of adventurers and speculators, and there is the great matrimonial exchange which calls into play all the fine and subtle powers of woman. But it is needless to trace causes and motives, since commerce and manufacture create centres of population by virtue of the law of demand and supply.

The gates of the city have in our day been thrown wide open to the multitude. Formerly it was necessary to serve an apprenticeship before one was permitted to labor at a trade, but machinery has done away with trades. The workman now is only part of the machine. He requires little training and less skill. And because anybody can do this work it is easy to find people who will do it cheaply, and so wages sink until the operative receives barely enough to keep him from starvation. If, from whatever cause, he ceases to work, he is at once a pauper; and yet there are numbers waiting to take his place.

The way to the city is open to all—*Facilis descensus, sed revocare gressus.*

The country once abandoned is like a divorced wife. She will hardly be taken back, and if she is received again she will not be the mistress of the heart she once was. Those who have lived as servants in the houses of the rich will scorn the farmer's simple fare, and those who have labored in the factory will lack the energy to buffet the storm and breathe the crisp air of the open country.

The benefits which accrue to the great body of people from the cheap and suicidal labor of the operatives are undeniable and real. It is mere declamation to affirm that machinery is the slave of capitalists and works in their interest alone. Cheap labor means cheap clothing, cheap houses, and cheap food. Never in the history of the human race have the multitude been clothed and lodged as in our day; and this progress we owe to machinery and the factory slave. To make the great body of the people more comfortable the social evolution has brought forth a new species, a race of human machines whose destiny is to be a part of the iron mechanism which transforms the world. This race forms a people apart; nothing like it has ever been seen until now either in pagan or Christian civilization. They have the name of freemen, but are indeed slaves; they make the most costly fabrics and are clothed in rags; they work in palaces and live in tenements and hovels. Their labor is the most painful and the most fatal to human life; and their wages are so low that mothers and children are forced to throw themselves into the jaws of Moloch to escape starvation. When they are old or infirm they are thrown into the street or the poorhouse, and the rich man who has hired them is guiltless, it is held, before God and men. When the wheels of machinery stop the whole race is driven to the public trough, to be fed like cattle, until the shambles are again in readiness. They reproduce themselves, but their children are doomed from their very birth, and the race is saved from annihilation only by constantly absorbing fresh multitudes of other populations. They know that they are wretched, and yet have not the courage even to hope that they shall ever be less miserable. Where the type is perfect, as in England, they are "without God and without hope." . . . Enter one of these palaces of industrialism. The noise is deafening, the air stifles you, and the pale, weary forms stand impassive, as conscious that they are bound to the wheel of destiny. The work is never done and it never varies. The human hand must keep time to a ceaseless and measured movement, which imposes silence and causes the vast pile to tremble. Even the power of thought is made captive and bound in irons; the great machine alone seems to live and to be the cause of the automatic motion of the human body. In other ages those who worked sang at their labor; and even in the South, in the days of slavery, the plaintive melodies of the Negro humanized his toil and helped to relieve the sadness of his heart; but here man grows dumb, and works, like the horse and the ox, in silence. Reverie itself, that sweet solace of the weary, is not possible within this temple of Mammon, where God's image is made

> The senseless member of a vast machine,
> Serving as doth a spindle or a wheel.

Moral degradation accompanies great physical wretchedness; and the low moral state of manufacturing populations affords inexhaustible matter for discussion and consideration. The conditions of life are not favorable to purity, and the grossest sensuality prevails. Where people have no settled home and no local traditions the loss of good name is often looked upon as a mere trifle; and the sense of shame is stifled in the young who from their earliest years have lived in an atmosphere polluted by foul language. In the city old age and childhood are thrust out of sight, and the domestic morals and simple manners, which are above all price, cease to be handed down as sacred heirlooms.

One of the greatest evils which afflicts a manufacturing population is the breaking down of the family life. What family life is possible where there is no continuity, where there are no traditions that descend from father to son? The soul of the family is respect for ancestors, and where there are no traditions this respect dies out and the family becomes an accidental collection of individual existences. A home is essential to the family, and the traditional spirit is transmitted with the home from father to son. With the possession of a fireside the family receives a life of its own, and its permanency and complete identity can be assured only by the hereditary transmission of the home. To take from it the perpetuity of its fireside is to deprive it of a great part of its strength. A house that is occupied but not owned is not a home. A true family ought to be abiding; it ought to endure while the nation exists. It reposes upon love and religion; it is nurtured by traditions of honor and virtue; and the symbol of its continuity and permanence is the home owned and transmitted from generation to generation.

Now, the poor in our great cities and manufacturing towns have no homes. They live in tenements and hired rooms; or if the more fortunate own their cottages they can have little hope of leaving them to their children, who will go to swell the great floating population that is up for universal hire, and which, work failing, sinks lower to join the army of paupers and outcasts who form, to use the modern phrase, the dangerous classes of our great commercial and manufacturing centres. What hope can we have of men or women whose childhood has never been *consecrated* by home-life to pure thoughts and generous deeds, and who too often carry through the world the heavy burden of physical and moral disease planted in the infant heart, in which the whole human being was yet enfolded like the rose within the tender bud? Lodging-houses where people sleep and eat are not homes. Hired rooms which are changed from year to year, and often from month to month, are not homes. The operative's cottage, without yard or garden, without flowers or privacy, is not a home. The house which is empty day after day, because the mother and her little ones are chained to the great machine in the factory mill, is the grave of the family, not its home. . . .

In vain, or almost in vain, are schools and asylums built for the children of the poor in our great cities. The mechanical spirit of the age must, of course, find expression everywhere, and be applied, with superstitious confidence, to processes which are vital and not mechanical. It is not, therefore, surprising that there should be a wide-spread belief that men can be educated by machinery in very much the same way as it works up raw material into finished products; so that a youth who has been run through the school drill is thought to be prepared for his life-work, as wheat which has been under the millstone is ready for the baker's hand. This is a false belief, whether it be held by the advocates of secular or religious systems of education. Catholics, in their logical and well-founded rejection of the Common School System of this country, are led often to exaggerate the advantages which may be hoped for from a different system, and they sometimes speak and write as though all would be well if only prayers were said and the catechism taught in the schoolroom. No man living, I imagine, is more persuaded of the necessity of religious education than myself, and yet I am convinced that even well-organized parochial schools will accomplish comparatively little with children who have no home training, which is the foundation of all education and of all true manhood.

The teaching of religious doctrines and practices in the school-room necessarily partakes of the defects of all school exercises. It is mechanical and becomes an affair of routine. The personal influence, indeed, of the teacher which is able to awaken the mind is able also to kindle in the heart sentiments of piety; but those who possess or exercise this power are a few out of a multitude, and the proportion is smallest in the large and crowded schools of the great cities; while there, also, the pupil finds the greatest difficulty in bringing himself into intimate and vital relations with his teacher. The child's daily companions, his recreations, the scenes that surround him; the physical aspect even of his home, the presence of his father and mother day by day, and the unconscious drinking in of their thoughts and sentiments, their hopes and fears; the family devotions, in which the father becomes a priest and the home God's sanctuary—these are the living forces that mould and fashion the human heart: and when later on he is taught how to use the instruments and aids of thought—such as books and the pen—the sense of increased power will but stimulate him to bring out more clearly the fair image which has been already impressed upon his stainless imagination. The child is born into the family, which takes hold of him before the church or the state; and as its influence is the first to which he is made subject, it is for this reason the most important.

The family is not a piece of mechanism. It is the natural condition in which human life everywhere exists. It is at the beginning and at the end of all other forms of association; and it, together with religion and property, forms the social trilogy, which emanates from the creative power. In the beginning it is society itself, and all larger associations of men rest upon it as their only secure foundation. Wherever its power is weakened, or its sanctity profaned, or its beauty tarnished, there the strength and loveliness of human life grow less. The teachings of the father and mother have, from nature, almost a sacramental character; and it would seem to be a postulate of reason itself that, given a revelation, marriage should be lifted into the supernatural order and receive a special consecration.

Now, whether we consider the rich or the poor, it is evident that the life of the city interferes with the power and sanctity of the family. The simple pleasures of domestic life lose their charm for those who have once plunged into the dissipations of the fashionable world; and to be rich in the modern city is to be drawn with almost resistless force into what is called society, which, while it imposes the heaviest burdens upon its votaries, unfits them for the right fulfilment of the more serious duties, because its necessary tendency is to produce a frivolous and artificial type of character. A fashionable woman can hardly create a happy home or be the mother of true men. The woman of wealth may, indeed, resist this temptation and find her happiness in the fulfilment of duty, but she cannot change the conditions of city life which make the club-house, the theatre, and the ball-room the enemies of home. Amid these surroundings the family is secularized and parental authority loses its religious sanction. The children assert their individual liberty, and an egotistic spirit breaks up the sacred reunion of the fireside, which is possible only when love and reverence have made unselfish devotion a second nature.

Ancestral traditions are not so much forgotten as buried, since they recall, along with memories of virtue and honor, the story of poverty and humble beginnings. To appear now is more than to be, and simple truth is less than a fine house. The relations of life grow superficial and external, and companions are sought, not for their inward worth, but for some showy or adventitious quality, such as wealth, or manner, or birth; and as these may readily co-exist with the worst forms of vice, the depraved gain admittance into the sanctuary of the family and its sacred character is profaned.

But it is in the squalid quarters of the poor that we should study the results of the influences of the city upon home-life. There the home is not owned; it cannot be transmitted; it has no privacy; it has no mystery; it has no charm. It is a rented room in some promiscuous tenement; it is a shanty in some filthy street or alley. The good and the bad are huddled together; and the poisoned air does not sooner take the bloom from the cheek of childhood than the presence of sin and misery withers the freshness of the heart. The children rush from the narrow quarters and stifling air into the street, and the gutters are their playgrounds. The sounds that greet their ears are the yells of the hawkers of wares and the blasphemous and obscene oaths of the rabble. Through all the changing year they see only the dirty street and the dingy houses. Spring and summer, and autumn and winter, enacting, as they pass over the great world's stage, the divine drama of God to soften and purify the human heart, come and go, and come again; but for these poor waifs no flowers bloom, no birds sing, no brook murmurs in the glade with the sunfish playing in its rippling waters. Not for them does the ripe fruit hang from the bending bough; not for them waves the golden corn. The love of liberty which Nature gives never springs within their breast. They are born in prison and will wear the chain of servitude. No possible school system can make good the lack of sunshine and pure air, and the large freedom with which the growing soul is clothed when it is permitted to fly, like the birds of heaven, through boundless space, where no barrier rises to hem it in except where earth and heaven meet, and this recedes before the advancing step.

Happy is the country child. With bare head and bare feet he wanders through wood and field, or watches the grazing flocks, or drives the cattle home at milking-time; and all his dreams of peace and love gather round his mother and the home fireside. He is a conqueror, who leads in the halter, submissive to his will, the wild colt and lowing heifer. His ruddy cheek and eager eye tell of health and strength. The sinews that throw the world are building up in him. In a little while you may push him out into the open sea of life and he will not be afraid. Let his after-lot be what it will, he has had at the outset twelve years of sweet liberty, and the dews of this fair dawn will keep still some freshness in his heart. But the factory child is weak in body, weak in soul. His whole nature "is subdued to what it works in." He treads a narrow path until all thought of larger life dies out of him. He lives in the mill and in the street. His home is in the promiscuous crowd. His mother is a drudge and his father is not happy at his own fireside. The dreary room and the close air drive him forth with his children into the street, where the whiskey-shop glares in his face to lure him to shame and death. How is it possible to be severe in judging the poor laborers of commercial cities and manufacturing towns? The marvel is that there is not more vice, that any noble life can thrive amid these surroundings. No labor is healthful which does not bear with it the promise of leading to better things. The curse of the slave is that he must work, and yet remain without hope of ever being other than he is. The looking forward to the fruits of one's toil is the food of hope. Without this the soul languishes.

> We perish also, for we live by hope
> And by desire; we see by the glad light
> And breathe the sweet air of futurity;
> And so we live, or else we have no life.

But what future in this world can these our poor brothers who are bound to the wheel of fate look for? Poverty is at the cradle and poverty is at the grave. Between life's entrance and exit there is hard work and scant food. We must have set phrases to brace our consciences, and so we say these people are wretched because they are improvident and thriftless. Let us hear the remark of M. Villermé, who has devoted much thought to the study of the condition of the working-classes in France. Four things, he says, are required that these laborers may have a sufficiency—that they be always in good health; that they always find employment; that no household have more than two children; and, finally, that they have not a single vice. Illness, or lack of work, or a numerous offspring, or some habit of indulgence will leave them without enough to eat and wear. Are the factory hands of Fall River and Providence, or the laborers of New York and Boston, much better off? And now that we are fairly in the great world-market, to compete with the nations of Europe wages must be cut down to the point at which existence is barely possible. The laborer who marries and takes his wife into a hired room will, if he remain in the great city, have her carried to her grave from a hired room. Much, no doubt, may be accomplished by wise economy; but when one man's wages must fill half a dozen hungry mouths, clothe as many bodies, and pay the rent, there can be no thought of saving. Then there is sickness, and stoppage of work, and a hundred incidental expenses, so that the poor are nearly always in debt. This habitual indebtedness unnerves a man and too often sears his conscience.

These poor people are kind-hearted, and misery loves company. They will meet together; they will seek to dull the sense of pain; they will believe that sorrow can be drowned. But, for them, to drink at all means excess and the death of their better selves. Drunkenness is not merely a passion; it is a disease. In the ill-fed and wretchedly-lodged populations of the great cities and factory towns the whiskey pest is endemic. Like the yellow fever, it is produced by local and atmospheric conditions. The weak body which is compelled to perform its allotted task finds at first an apparent increase of strength from alcoholic liquors, and the laborer readily persuades himself that a stimulant of this kind is a necessity. He has now given himself over to the enemy of all that he ought to love. The drink prepared for him is a poisonous adulteration. Quicker than alcohol it will deprive the soul of its control over the higher nervous centres, and the unhappy man is delivered up to his animal instincts. Statisticians have observed that the consumption of alcohol increases in times of scarcity; and here again we have evidence of the existence of a general law which impels the wretched to this fatal indulgence.

In Prussia there is a constant ratio between the number of illegitimate children and the quantity of brandy which is consumed. The consumption of brandy is greatest in Brandenburg and Pomerania, and there the proportion of illegitimate children is highest. In Westphalia and the Rhine Province there are fewest illegitimate children and the least consumption of brandy. In England Neison reckons that there are twenty-nine women for every hundred men who drink; and we find accordingly that the number of criminals in that country is nearly four times greater among men than among women.

"It is statistically proven," says Von Oettinger, "that the average length of life, even in such highly-developed states as Prussia, has diminished during the last twenty years; and the researches of Engel, Frantz, and others show that there is a causal relation between this phenomenon and the increased use of intoxicating liquors."[6]

Neison has established in a very striking manner the tendency of the use of alcoholic beverages to lower the vital powers and shorten the average duration of life. He found, taking persons of the same age, that fifty-eight in the thousand of those addicted to drink die annually, while the death-rate of others was but nineteen in the thousand. The mortality among drinkers was three times greater than among the remaining population. If the habitual use of intoxicating drink is, at best, but a slow way of committing suicide, the destruction of the poor who are able to get only adulterated liquors is inevitable, and in their case this method of suicide can hardly be called slow. It is an admitted fact, moreover, that a large proportion of those who take their lives, as of those who lose their reason, are the victims of intemperance. The individual does not suffer alone from this appalling evil; it works decay and degeneracy in whole populations. The disease is transmitted to the offspring and tells upon the community. The seeds of some kind of degeneracy will rarely be found wanting in the children of the intemperate; and if they seem to escape the curse the bitter fruit will be gathered by their descendants. There is yet another disease, which I may not name, but which festers in the city, and which rises from its slums like a miasm to taint the blood and rot the bones of whole generations.

---

[6] [Oettingen,] *Moralstatistik*, p. 647.

It is far from my thought to say that the city is wholly evil. It has a great and high social mission. It is the most complex and difficult work of civilized man, and its fascination is felt by all. It is full, and will be full, though all the world should speak ill of it. But if those I love were rich I should not wish them to live in the city; and if they were poor, and made it their dwelling-place, I should despair of them.

2. CHURCH LIFE IN

NEW YORK CITY

The Present Condition of New York City
Above Fourteenth Street, 1888

BY JAMES M. KING

By the 1880's, it was obvious to Protestants of New York City
that their churches were not drawing a very high percentage
of the city's population into congregational life. In 1840, one
group estimated, there was one Protestant church to every
2,000 inhabitants; in 1880, the ratio was one to 3,000; and by
1887, it was closer to one to 4,000. In alarm a group of promi-
nent clergy and laity called a "Christian Conference" to meet
at Chickering Hall in December, 1888. A series of addresses
confirmed in detail the extent of Protestant failure.

King was a Methodist minister, already famous for his at-
tacks on such cancers as Rum, Romanism, and Tammany Hall;
in 1899, he would publish FACING THE TWENTIETH CENTURY
(New York: American Union League Society, 1899). That book
like the portion of his 1888 speech reprinted here, was more
eloquent in lamenting present evils than imaginative in point-
ing toward constructive reforms.

From *The Religious Condition of New York City* (New York: Baker
and Taylor, n.d.), pp. 11–13.

. . . The population of this city, Protestant in sympathy, is perhaps 500,000. The churches have a seating capacity of about 300,000, and the average attendance on church services is perhaps 150,000. And 100,000 would be a liberal estimate for the membership of Protestant churches.

The private and public beneficence of the city is undoubtedly largely in the hands of Protestantism. The disparity in numbers need not cause despair.

But we must always bear in mind that the law in religion is as rigid as in nature, that no effect is produced without an adequate cause. It is within our power to make such alliance with God as to remove from the domain of debate the question of final victory. But we must not underestimate the strength of the opposition.

The forces opposed to the extension of Protestantism are many and powerful, and all are enrolled within these mute figures:

(1) Romanism, with its magnificent ecclesiastical machinery and its blind loyalty to a foreign politico-ecclesiastical power.

(2) Indifferentism, with all its phases of pronounced or practical infidelity.

(3) Judaism, with its century-walled exclusiveness.

(4) The inactivity and selfishness of professing Christians.

(5) That portion of the foreign element which is difficult to assimilate, and it is this element that multiplies by births more rapidly than the native, and makes legislative, social, and religious problems difficult of solution. According to the census of 1880, two-fifths of the population of the city were foreign born, and three-fourths of these were of two nationalities, Irish and German. The boundaries of the abodes of the most undesirable and dangerous of our foreign population, the Italians and Bohemians, are as sharply defined as though impassable walls were built about them.

(6) Ten thousand saloons, or *one* to every 150 of the inhabitants of the entire city, stand over against the 355 Protestant

churches, or *one* to 4464 of the inhabitants of the entire city, as a constant menace. They breed poverty and crime. They increase in ratio faster than the churches and schools. They are open day and night. They make Legislators, Aldermen, District Attorneys, and Judges. They modestly claim to control 40,000 votes in this city; and twenty men, mostly brewers, hold 4710 chattel mortgages on saloon fixtures to the value of $4,959,578. Where is there another instance of such absolute power in the hands of twenty men?

The present Excise Board claim a reduction of ten per cent. in the number of licenses under their administration, and this has been taken off of our estimates. But we have not put into our estimates the unlicensed places where liquor is sold (Mr. Graham puts the number at 1000), and the groceries and drug-stores where immense quantities of liquors are sold, and where what are called the better classes are demoralized.

The stars on the maps tell the location of the churches; but if the saloons were represented by small clouds, the light of the stars would be obscured.

(7) The floating population temporarily resident must be added as a large demoralizing element. Multitudes come to this city and contribute to its dissipation and to the support of its demoralizing diversions, who at home at least abstain from these things.

(8) Thirty-two thousand three hundred and ninety tenement-houses contain an average of thirty-three persons each, with 1,079,728 tenants and with 237,972 families. Home is virtually banished by these abodes, and physical and moral misery necessitated. How can Christianity reach these people? Eight hundred and fifty-six of these tenements have been built in the last six months, and 63,393 souls moved into them.

(9) The hiving of respectable people in the common order of flats is a foe to the Christian Church and the Christian life, in that it destroys the individuality of the tenant, and with it also largely the sense of responsibility. They are often worse

than the tenement-houses, because more inaccessible, and because the people in them are capable of broader usefulness and beneficence when their individuality and responsibility assert themselves. This is not designed as a reflection upon the character of the people who are compelled to stay in these flats if they live in the city at all, but is simply the statement of a painful fact known to many thoughtful Christian workers. . . .

The suggestion often made that the well-to-do should continue to reside in the midst of the tenement-house sections is not in accordance with sanctified common-sense.

We can find no fault with the desire of the people in the lower districts to better their condition by moving uptown. The purpose and tendency of Christianity is to move everybody up-town, if not in locality, at least in condition. . . .

3. CHURCH LIFE IN
NEW YORK CITY

The Present Condition of New York City
Below Fourteenth Street, 1888

BY ADOLPHUS F. SCHAUFFLER

---

*Schauffler (1845–1919), who followed King to the platform of
the Christian Conference described in the Headnote to Document 2, was a Presbyterian minister, a pastor at the City Mission, and an active member of the International Sunday School
Union. Eventually he published several works on Sunday School
administration. Like Spalding, he viewed the situation in New
York City from the perspective of a rural youth; see his* MEM-
ORIES OF A HAPPY BOYHOOD 'LONG AGO AND FAR AWAY' *(New
York: Fleming Revell, 1919).*

There are those who have the impression in summer that, because they have gone out of town, therefore everybody has
left town. The everybody that has left town in summer is perhaps one hundred or one hundred and fifty thousand of the
population, leaving about fourteen hundred and fifty thousand

---

From *The Religious Condition of New York City* (New York: Baker
and Taylor, n.d.), pp. 15–25.

of the people in town. It is never true that everybody has left town; nor is it true that anything like half of our population has gone to the hillsides and valleys of New England, or to the beautiful lands across the sea. Some people also labor under the hallucination that because they have moved up-town, therefore there is nobody left down-town. And there are some who think that down-town—that is to say, south of Fourteenth Street, as a convenient dividing line—that down-town will sometime be like the City of London, a place of storehouses and wholesale business places, with none but janitors resident there. If that ever is to be the case, neither you nor I will live to see it; because down-town is more densely populated to-day than it ever was before, in spite of the fact that up-town is growing at a prodigious rate.

We have here [referring to map upon platform] the north line of Fourteenth Street. The southern portion of the city is divided into wards, this line being the Bowery, this Broadway, this Canal Street running across here, and Rivington and Division Streets down here; here the Bowery runs into Chatham Street, the Elysium of the followers and descendants of Jacob [laughter]; and the line then running into Broadway, and down to the Battery and Bowling Green.

In the First Ward, which is the oldest ward on the Island of Manhattan, the population in 1880 was 17,000 in round numbers. There are there to-day four churches and chapels, in reality only two churches and two chapels, the chapels being very small and adapted to seamen or emigrants, and perhaps holding 100 to 150 when they are crowded. How many times they are crowded I cannot say. Of course, the great church of this ward is Trinity Church, of ancient renown and grand good work. . . . The total population, that is to say that south of Fourteenth Street, as at present approximated, is 621,000. I say approximated, because we have no definite facts later than the census of 1880; and the total number of churches in this population being 127. When I say the total number of

churches, that includes the Catholic churches and Jewish synagogues . . . as well as Protestant places of worship. In 1868
there were 141 places of worship, Protestant, Catholic, and
Jewish, south of that line. There are now, with nearly 200,000
people more, only 127 Protestant, Jewish, and Roman Catholic
places of worship. That is to say, a city twice as large as New
Haven has moved in south of Fourteenth Street, and fourteen
Protestant churches have moved out. They stand as follows:
Since 1888, Baptist churches, four less; Methodist churches,
two less; Presbyterian, six less; Episcopal, four less; Reformed
Presbyterian, one less; Jewish synagogues, one more (with an
enormous addition to the population); and Roman Catholic,
two more. One Jewish synagogue and two Roman Catholic
churches more; and all the balance of Protestant places of worship less.

Now we stand still worse than even these figures would
show, because while the churches north of Fourteenth Street
are very many and large, seating from 1000 to 2000, many of
the places of worship south of Fourteenth Street are very small.
There are the mission stations like No. 36 Bowery, and like
the Y. M. C. A. on the Bowery, where they have religious
services, and like the Seaman's Chapel in the First Ward. There
are a number of Protestant places of worship that do not seat
in their utmost capacity more than 150. I know there is Trinity, and Grace, and the Broome Street Tabernacle, and St.
Matthew's, and other large churches, but there are too many
small churches, as compared with the density of the population—that is, taking the population as native and foreign born.

I find that in the census of 1880 there were 278,000 native
foreigners, very many being children of foreign born parents,
and 231 foreign born; nearly one out of two, south of that line,
born in a foreign country and imported here to be amalga-
mated and digested by our American principles of Christian
civilization.

Now, this is an enormous population. Five of our largest

territories combined do not show the population of Manhattan Island itself. Five of our largest territories combined; and while we hear cries for help from out west, we want to remember that many a western state and many a western territory is better supplied with churches and accommodations for church privileges than Manhattan Island itself in the north, leave alone this southern section of the town.

Now, as matter of fact, the Protestant population—Presbyterian, Episcopal, Baptist, and Methodist—has very largely moved north. The churches that were down-town have moved up-town; the value of the property has increased, and they have moved out and gone north. A piece of land that was bought for $20,000 could be sold for $120,000, because business has made the situation valuable; and the churches have sold out down-town, some of them, and moved north, and have established themselves there.

We do not find fault with the churches for moving up-town, but we call your attention to the fact that the southern part of the island is proportionately being abandoned. They have moved away, and left valuable churches, and left us with a lack of Sunday-school facilities; and the result is that the power is in the north, while the evil is down in the south, for the most part.

. . . We have more tenement-houses relatively than all the rest of the city put together. It is par excellence a place of tenement-houses, where from twenty to twenty-five families live in one house. I divide tenements into three classes. The first is the good tenement-house, which is a kind of modified French flat,—it is not so flat as it is tall, but they call it a flat—where there is some one to answer the door, and to tell you where to go in that great beehive of humanity, and find the one you are looking for. Then there is the next one, which is a grade lower. You pull the door-bell, either the first, second, third, fourth, or fifth, and an invisible power opens the door, and leaves you to stumble your way up as best you can, and find those you have called to see. Then the next lower grade in tenement-houses is what I call the slam-bang kind, where the door keeps slam-banging all the time, where peddlers and Jews and the city missionaries all go in and out, and find their way through the place as best they can through the pitch darkness that pervades the place—so dark, that to illustrate it perhaps I would better tell a little experience that I went through, that happened some time ago. I remember going into one of these great, large tenement-houses on a very warm, bright noonday. The place was in pitch darkness, and as I made my way upstairs my knee struck something soft, and I heard the cry of a child. She had been sitting there all alone in the darkness, and I never knew of her presence until I had knocked against her. I always listened at the bottom of the stairs to see if anybody was going up or coming down, and to give the signal that I was coming up; but there was perfect silence, and I nearly killed the little one by pushing her against the brass-headed stairs where she was.

In that tenement population there are thousands of church members who have come to New York and moved into the tenement-houses, and know not where to go. And if we are to reach them in that southern part of the island, they have got to be reached by the Christian going into the tenement-houses and reaching them there and drawing them out of that house into some place of worship, where they shall hear of God, and of the great truth, and of eternal things.

But the situation is still worse, if anything, than I have indicated, for while we have some churches that are full, like the University Place Church, Grace Church, St. Matthew's, and others that I could name, there are others that are pitifully empty. I made the rounds some time ago on a beautiful Sunday morning in some of those churches, and some of them fairly large—and this was the count on a bright Sunday morning: In four churches there was one with 126 people, another 38, another 28, and another 110. Those are the numbers in the four churches that I visited that morning, and that I counted myself. If anybody tells you that he estimates that in his church there are 500 in the congregation, you can cut him down 50 per cent., and you will be about right.

There was a gentleman once who called upon me to speak in a hall. I asked him how many it would hold, and he said it would hold about 1200, and that it would be jammed right up. When I got there I saw that the house wouldn't hold more than 600, and when the audience assembled I counted them, and there were just 137 people there; and just then the enthusiastic brother nudged me in the ribs, and said, "Magnificent congregation, isn't it?"

If anybody estimates the congregation, cut him down half, and you will still be beyond the number a little.

The next Sunday was a beautiful Sunday, and I went forth once more to count the people, and I found them: In four churches there were 58 in one, 48, 28, and in another 26—and a bright Sunday morning it was, too.

That was, of course, in the southern part of the island; and I could go on the next Sunday morning, on a beautiful day, to four more, and on the next Sunday to four more, and I shouldn't find 100 in any one of them.

This will set forth a little of the state of things in the southern part of the city.

There are good churches, doing good work, but they are like angels' visits, few and far between; whereas there are other churches that are struggling to maintain themselves, and overcoming obstacles almost insurmountable, and are more than measurably successful.

I have been requested to close by telling what is needed. Do I need to do that? I have told you what there is, and having stated that, doesn't that show what there is needed? But I will tell you what is needed. We don't want any more brick and mortar around; but we do want, and desperately too, more flesh and blood. Brick and mortar are very good in their place, and in their time, but I would rather have poor brick and mortar and good flesh and blood than good brick and mortar and poor flesh and blood. We want to increase our good flesh and blood; and we want consecrated flesh and blood; and if we cannot get it in the line of voluntary laborers, we must have paid workers down there. . . .

. . . The Anarchist has established his Sunday-school, of which he has three in Chicago, and I believe will have some in New York, unless we are careful, to teach men to hate God and hate their fellow-men. And if you and I are going to do away with this danger in this city, we have got to forestall that start of Anarchist teachings, in order that we may meet this condition and preoccupy the mind with divine teachings and the word of God. But if we do not do that, Anarchy is going to do her work, and whoever does it most earnestly will win the day. Shall it be Christianity, or shall it be Anarchy? . . .

4. THE FRATRICIDE

OF THE CHURCHES

The Church, 1897

BY WASHINGTON GLADDEN

Gladden (1836–1918), born in a small town in Pennsylvania, discovered during an early pastorate in the industrial city of North Adams, Massachusetts, how signally most churches failed to speak persuasively to both capitalists and laborers. As a minister in Springfield, Massachusetts, and then for thirty-five years in Columbus, Ohio, he learned how much more willing Protestant denominations were to compete with each other than they were to join in helping the "Church" serve the "Community"—as he felt it had in the countryside. He was saddened by the realization that many Protestants who did propose modes of cooperation were openly anti-Catholic; like James King, they regarded Catholic immigrants in the city as evidence of the failure of Christianity, and as necessary targets for missionary efforts. By contrast, Gladden spoke out against the efforts in the 1890's of the American Protective Association to proscribe Catholics, and he responded warmly to those

---

From Washington Gladden, *Social Facts and Forces* (New York: Putnam's, 1897), pp. 192–218.

Catholics—like Archbishop John Ireland of St. Paul and the Paulist Fathers—who hoped for closer relations with American Protestants.

Gladden was neither by temperament nor by conviction a radical. His lecture on "The Church," given first in Chicago in 1896, was a trenchant indictment of religious trends, especially in the cities, but he did not go on to give more than a vague outline of a better urban church order.

Nearly everybody admits the existence of serious social disorders, and nearly everybody is trying to account for them. . . .

It is not very many years since society in this country was quite homogeneous; the economical distinction between capitalist and laborer was not clearly marked, for most capitalists were laborers and most laborers were capitalists; the social distinction was not emphasized; there was really but one social class. But our material progress has given full scope to the principle of differentiation; the wage-workers are now distinctly marked off from employers and capitalists; labor itself has become highly specialized, and even the old mechanical trades are split into fractional parts through the use of machinery; industrial groups are numerous, separate, disparate; the lines of social distinction are sharply drawn.

When the wheels of progress are whirling at such tremendous speed, the centrifugal force acts powerfully. Anyone can see that progress, under a competitive régime like ours, must tend to the separation of men, and to the creation of a great many diverse and apparently unrelated elements. Under this process men tend to become unsympathetic, jealous, antagonistic; the social bond is weakened. The first condition of healthy competition is the mobility of labor, so they tell us: but the more mobile are the laboring masses, the less social do they become; people move so often that there is not much neighborly affection. The feeling of a common interest which is the cement of the social order has largely disappeared from large sections of society. . . .

Do not understand me to speak of this as an evil tendency; it is no more evil than the centrifugal motion of the planets is an evil tendency. That would be evil, no doubt, if it were not matched and balanced by the centripetal motion. If the one force were not harnessed with the other, we should soon have no solar system; each individual planet would go whirling off into the blackness of darkness. But the tendency is all good when its proper counterpoise is there; the co-ordination of the two gives us the music of the spheres. And this tendency to social differentiation is not evil, it is one of the elements of progress, if only its proper counterpoise is present. It is a good thing to have society separated into industrial and social groups. It is a good thing to have knowledge specialized, so that each man may know a few things well. But this is only on condition that his knowledge be made serviceable to his fellows, and theirs to him. It would not be a good thing if each one knew only one thing, though he knew it ever so well, if nobody could share his knowledge with anybody else. What makes this special knowledge valuable is the spirit of community by which it is shared.

So it is a great gain to humanity to have industry specialized if the unity of the spirit is not broken in the process. But this calamity, unhappily, is precisely what we are suffering. The forces that divide and differentiate have not been balanced by the forces that unite and integrate. Therefore we are driving toward chaos. And nothing can keep us from wreck but a great reinforcement of the powers that make for unity. Social integration is the crying need of the hour. What can be done to bring these scattered, diverse, alienated, antipathetic groups of human beings into a real unity? How can all these competing tribes and clans, owners of capital, captains of industry, inventors, artisans, artists, farmers, miners, distributors, exchangers, teachers, and all the rest, be made to understand that they are many members but one body; that an injury to one is really the concern of every other; that all for each and each for all is the only law of common life?

. . . Are there no forces, embodied in institutions, whose tendency it is to create and invigorate that consciousness of community out of which all coherent social construction must come?

The State, we might be inclined to say, is such an agency. . . . It does often rise above its meaner self, and manifest the spiritual unity which we all desire to see; but great changes must take place in the prevailing political conceptions before much help can be looked for in this direction.

We have, however, in society, an agency which is expressly intended to perform this very service of social integration. You have been waiting for me to speak its name. It is the Christian Church. The precise business of the Christian Church is to fill the world with the spirit of unity, of brotherhood; to arrest and countervail those divisive and repulsive forces of which we have been speaking; to promote the unity of the spirit in the bonds of peace. The business of the Christian Church is to preach and realize here in the earth the Kingdom of Heaven; and the Kingdom of Heaven, ever since the angels first proclaimed it, has been known to be a kingdom of peace and good-will. The foundation of its fellowship is the royal law, "Thou shalt love thy neighbor as thyself," and the new commandment of our Lord, "That ye love one another as I have loved you." Who is my neighbor? He is any man in need whom you can reach and help; the fact that he is a Jew while you are a Samaritan; that he is an Armenian or an African or even an Englishman, while you are an American; that he is a Catholic while you are a Protestant, or a capitalist while you are a laborer, makes no difference at all; he is your brother; when you say, "Our Father which art in heaven," that word "our" throws your fraternal arm around him and draws him to your side; you do not pray at all, your prayer is meaningless, unless it takes him in, and wishes all good things for him as well as for yourself.

All this is of the very rudiments of the doctrine we profess when we call ourselves Christians. The Christian Church exists in the world for the realization of relations like these among men. To break down all barriers that keep men apart; to demolish the middle wall of partition between Jews and Gentiles,—ay, and between all jealous, hateful, warring nationalities; to realize a state of society in which there shall be no antipathies of race or rank, neither barbarian nor Scythian, neither bond nor free, neither aristocrat nor plebeian; to fulfil the prophecy which was made concerning our Master that "he should gather together in one the children of God that are scattered abroad,"—this is the mission of the Christian Church. The true integrating force in society is a spiritual force; it is the mind that was in Jesus; it is the spirit of Jesus Christ in the hearts of men. When this is present, in all its fullness and beauty, individualism loses its divisive power and becomes the servant of the community. And it is the mission of the Church of Christ to be the incarnation and manifestation of the life of Christ; to believe in it, to live it, to reveal it, to fill the world with those ministries of kindness and gentleness and helpfulness which the love of Christ inspires. This is the power—so far as I know it is the only power—by which these disintegrating and destructive influences can be counteracted, and the life of society preserved.

Is the Church accomplishing this mission? Manifestly it is not; for the very thing of which we are complaining is that the work of social integration is not done. Yet we must be careful to do no injustice here. Ardent and strenuous souls, who discover the shortcomings of the Church, and deplore them, are quite too apt to overlook and belittle the work that she is actually doing. There has never been a time, since the days of the apostles, when the Church of Christ was not exerting a powerful influence in behalf of unity and brotherhood.

To-day, in all the world, the Gospel that is read in its assemblies, the hymns that are sung, the prayers that are offered, set forth the duty of kindness, the beauty of fraternity, the blessedness of peace. No one can imagine what this world would be if this stream of sacred influence were not steadily poured into its turbid currents. Even in those congregations where there is most to deplore and censure, there is still a great deal done to check rapacity, and to make men think more kindly of their fellow men. The churches are doing a vast amount of practical charity—doing it in a quiet way, without sounding any trumpets in the streets—a far larger amount of this kind of work, in my judgment, than is done by all other agencies put together. And it is done in delicate and kindly ways, so that the recipients are neither humiliated nor pauperized by it. I hear the church berated, very often, by people who show by their criticisms, that they have not been inside of a church for twenty-five years and know no more of what it is about than if they lived in Jupiter. Still, after making all these concessions, the fact still remains that the Church has come far short of its high calling. It is doing, ordinarily, a great deal better work than the people who carp at it are doing; but it is leaving undone a very large part of what it ought to do. . . . And what are the causes of her failure? Why has she lost her power to keep in the community the unity of the spirit in the bonds of peace?

In the first place the Church has lost her own unity. The principle of differentiation has done its divisive work within her communion with fearful consequences. There was room for the operation of this principle even here, in a healthful way. Varieties of doctrine, of ritual, of character might well have been developed. It is not an evil thing that we have the different types of teaching and of administration which now exist. It is good to have the pietistic fervor of the Methodist and the intellectual vigor of the Presbyterian, and the liturgic beauty of the Episcopalian, and the ethical thoroughness of the Liberal Christian and the staid simplicity of the Quaker; all these worketh that one and the selfsame Spirit, dividing to each man severally as he will; but it is not good to have these set over against one another as exclusive and antagonistic sects. These hateful schisms have rent into fragments the Body of Christ. Here, to begin with, in our Western Christendom, is the great and fatal division between Catholic and Protestant, which is, in itself, a great gulf fixed between those who worship the same Lord, a gulf almost impassable; and there are hundreds of thousands of people in this country to-day who are devoting a good part of their time and strength to widening and deepening the chasm. The great majority of people of these two branches of the Christian Church will scarcely own one another as Christians; they hardly ever enter one another's churches—many of them, indeed, believe that to do so is a sin; and it is not uncommon for those on the one side of this line of division to entertain the most horrible suspicions and to circulate the most blood-curdling reports concerning the sinister purpose of those on the other side. In the great work of social integration now confronting us there is positively no single task more difficult, more discouraging, than that of bringing these two great branches of the Christian Church into neighborly relations. The chronic inflammation which has been produced by three centuries of wars and persecutions and alienations seems to be almost irreducible. I will bring no accusations of prejudice against the Roman Catholics, for I am a Protestant; but I must say that the determination of millions of Protestants to believe evil and only evil, and that continually, of their Roman Catholic brethren is one of the most melancholy signs of the times. And these prejudices are always most intense in those neighborhoods where there is nothing but hearsay and imagination to feed them. I received a letter not long ago from a physician in a country town of Ohio inquiring whether it was really true that such and such infernal deeds had been done by the Roman Catholics of Columbus.

Harrowing tales of this tenor were in circulation among his neighbors; and although, as he said, there was not, so far as he knew, a single Roman Catholic in his town, the people of that hamlet were lying awake nights for fear the Catholics were coming to burn their houses and butcher them in their beds.

Even among Protestants the sectarian animosities are often intense. In the pushing zeal of propagandism all principles of comity are disregarded; one denomination shrinks not even from destroying the property of another by thrusting in its enterprises where it is clear that one or the other of the competitors must go to the wall. The question of uniting the community in fraternal bonds is about the last question that your loyal denominationalist will ask; his problem is to divide the flock and get as many as he can into his particular fold. . . .

Then the administration of the churches has often been such as to foster pride and exclusiveness and class distinctions. We must be careful here to avoid exaggeration. It is sometimes said that the working-classes have become alienated from the churches. From some of them, not from all of them. The great Roman Catholic church, in all lands, finds ample room for them in all its costliest sanctuaries. Nor have they departed from all of our Protestant churches. We have eight Congregational churches in my own city; in five of them, certainly, the great majority of the members belong to the working-classes. You will find hundreds of churches in all our great cities of which this is true. A great deal of rubbish is retailed from platforms and in newspapers on this subject. What is true is this, that there are *a great many* churches, especially in the aristocratic quarters of the cities, which they do not attend, and where they are not wanted; churches in which the spirit of caste does certainly prevail; churches in which the competitive methods of financiering give the best places to the largest purses, and make the position of the poor man quite intolerable. The sin and shame which we have to confess is not that all our churches are such—that is a slander; but that some of them are such, when of such there ought to be none. The fact that a great many churches in the cities are administered as if they were private clubs, for the benefit of the genteel classes, is the fact that we have reason to deplore.

I fear that we must also say that there are a good many churches in which the tendency is strong to take a class view of all social questions; to regard the grievances of the laboring poor as wholly imaginary and their complaints and uprisings as evidences of depravity; to take sides, rather positively, with the employing class, in every struggle with the laboring class. Manifestly a church in which this sentiment prevails is not in a position to work for the reconciliation of the separated classes. It has itself become one of the elements of alienation—one of the parties to be reconciled.

Such, then, are some of the lamentable facts that we discover when we turn to the Church as the rightful leader in the work of social integration. We find that the Church is greatly disabled for the performance of this work. We find that she who ought to be the weaver of peace in the social household, has herself become in too many cases, the breeder of strife and division. We find that she to whom was spoken the parting benediction of her Lord, "Peace I leave with you; my peace I give unto you," has made but a poor use of this benign legacy. For surely, if the Church of Jesus Christ had but entered into this inheritance, had but realized the significance of her high calling, had but girded herself for the work of promoting peace on earth and good-will among men, the troubles that now disturb our social life would be unknown. And I am constrained to bear witness that the chief blame for the strife of classes, for the social dislocations and divisions which are so serious and alarming, must be laid at the door of the Christian Church. To her was given the commission to keep the peace, and she has not kept it. To her was given the power to counteract those unsocial tendencies which have been created by the rapid differentiation of our industrial life, and she has been found wanting. I do not say that she has done nothing; I insist that with all her faults she has done much; that her inconsistencies have not altogether quenched the light that was given her to hold aloft; but I say that when you compare what she has done with what she might have done, and ought to have done, the showing is pitiful. And if to-day, with anointed vision, we could discern the form of One like the Son of man walking among those golden candlesticks whose light burns so dimly, we should see upon His face some shadow of the sorrow that blurred the stars that night in Gethsemane. Where is the prophetic voice that can call to this Church, pottering with her non-essentials, fussing with her phylacteries, going through her pious motions, tithing the mint and anise and cumin of her vain distinctions, and rouse her to the tremendous charge that God has given her to keep?

What, then, is the first duty of the Church of this day? It seems to me that it is the duty of recognizing and realizing her own unity. . . .

And this union is not and cannot be a matter of mere pious sentiment, it must be a matter of active co-operation. There is no worse hypocrisy on the face of the earth than much of the sentimental unity with which the sects are wont to regale themselves now and then in union meetings, when they sing pleasant songs together and talk of the blessedness of fraternity and then go out and violate all laws of comity and all principles of decency in their fierce competitions. This unity must be visible to all the world, else it is valueless.

Where shall we begin to realize it? Right where we are. It is no great national movement for the consolidation of denominations that we want: that task is hopeless. The men who are the custodians and engineers of the denominational machinery would be leaders in that enterprise and they are apt to be the last men who wish for its success. It is in the local community, the city or the village, that this work must begin.

It is here, if anywhere, that the fact of unity will be discoverable. What is the Church? Where is the Church? . . .

The different congregations of this Church in your town or city are surely more closely and vitally joined together, if, indeed, they are truly Christian congregations, than any one of them can be joined to any other congregation in another town or city. The ties that bind each of these to its nearest neighbors must be nearer and more real than those which bind it to some congregation of similar name to its own in some distant city. It may be that one of these congregations in your city could co-operate with other congregations in other cities for some useful purposes; but the interests with which such co-operation are concerned are remote and insignificant compared with the interests that are common to them as members of the one Church of their own municipality. The actual fellowship, the actual co-operation in Christian work must be here in the one Church to which they all belong. Your city is the parish of this Church, and the enterprise of occupying this parish and cultivating it, by harmonious and efficient labor is one which must require the united and consentaneous activity of the whole Church. This Church has no right to split itself into fragments and scatter its forces all over the field, carrying on its work in desultory, haphazard, unmethodical ways, having no consultations and no common understandings; much less has it the right to countenance or permit the strifes and competitions by which workers get in each other's way and neutralize each other's efforts. If there is but one Church in your city that Church must know itself as one, and must do works meet for unity. Those who are of Christ can unite; to say that they cannot is infidelity and blasphemy. And this is the first duty of the Christians of every city, to discern and manifest the fact of their unity. There will be many diversities among them, but if the mind of Christ is in them the things about which they differ will be trifling compared with the things in which they agree. And when these Christians come together, loyal to their common Lord, mindful of His prayer that they all may be one, Protestant and Catholic giving one another the right hand of fellowship and magnifying the truths that they hold in common; Liberal and Orthodox kneeling together to pray "Thy Kingdom come"; all men of good-will giving voice to their good-will; all the sons of peace blessing one another in the name of the Lord, some good foundation will be laid for that good work of social integration which the Church has so imperfectly done. . . .

PART TWO

THE DOWNTOWN CHURCHES

5. THE CHOSEN ROLE OF
THE DOWNTOWN CHURCH

Address at Trinity Church, New York,
Ascension Day, 1871

BY MORGAN DIX

---

*Trinity Church was chartered in New York City in 1697. As
its members moved uptown and its property increased in value,
Trinity had several times to reconsider its role in the city's
religious life. Morgan Dix (1827–1908), the son of John A. Dix,
United States Senator and later Governor of New York, became associate minister of Trinity in 1855, and was rector for
nearly fifty years. A man of conservative disposition, he was
much more inclined, as this document shows, to celebrate the
current virtues of Trinity than to imagine that new roles would
be desirable. For a less flattering view of Trinity's accomplish-
ments in the middle years of the nineteenth century, see the
first pages of Document 9. The views of Trinity's social role
held by muckraker Ray Stannard Baker are found in Document 6.*

Though Trinity was probably the most celebrated downtown

From Morgan Dix, *Address (Ascension Day, 1871)* (New York: American Church Press Co., 1871), pp. 3–17.

church, congregations in many cities, of many denominations, and at different times, experienced similar trials. Clarence A. Young, THE DOWNTOWN CHURCH *(Lancaster, Pa.: Intelligencer Printing Co., 1912) is a good general study of the Protestant experience. For the Catholic Church, see such representative studies as Henry J. Browne,* ST. ANN'S ON EAST TWELFTH STREET, 1852–1952 *(New York: Roman Catholic Church of St. Ann, 1952) and D. H. Fosselman,* TRANSITIONS IN THE DEVELOPMENT OF A DOWNTOWN PARISH *(Washington: Catholic University of America, 1952), dealing with St. Patrick's in Washington, D. C.*

After due consideration, I have determined to speak to you this morning, my dear brethren and friends, in a very informal address. It is true that we keep the high feast of our Lord's Ascension; yet this day is also our parish festival, and there are circumstances which give it a peculiar interest. It is, as many of you remember, the twenty-fifth anniversary of the consecration of the edifice in which we are now assembled, the third which has stood on this site[1]; the thoughts suggested by that reflection, though not unsuited to expression, could hardly be made the material of a sermon. Your indulgence is therefore craved for what may sound like discursive remarks.

I repeat it; a quarter of a century has passed away, since, by the Right Rev. Samuel A. McCoskry, D.D., in the presence of a great congregation of clergy and laity, this church was solemnly set apart and separated from all unhallowed, worldly, and common uses, for the glory and worship of Almighty God. The vicissitudes which it has seen already are remarkable,

---

[1] The 1st Church was begun A. D. 1696, finished A. D. 1697, enlarged A. D. 1737, and destroyed by fire A. D. 1776.

The 2nd Church was built A. D. 1788, and pulled down to make place for the present one A. D. 1839.

The 3rd Church was begun A. D. 1839, completed in the Spring of 1846, and consecrated on Ascension Day, May 21st., of that year.

considering the shortness of the time. Its erection, through the wise and provident liberality of the Corporation of Trinity Church, according to the plans and under the direction of Richard Upjohn, the honored and respected father of American architects (to whom God grant many more years of usefulness among us), marked an epoch in the history of church-building in this country: it also formed the commencement of a development in worship, in ritual observance, in musical culture, and in ecclesiastical art, which daily grows in breadth and favour, and of which we now see and hear some of the most precise indications. And yet the results already achieved came slowly; not without effort are such things accomplished. This church though but twenty-five years old, has seen days of gloom, through which scarce any light was shining. There was a time, indeed, when men thought and said that a great mistake had been made in building so large and stately a temple as this, in a part of the city in which no congregation could ever be gathered. Judging from what they saw, they even pronounced it "a petrifaction of a past age;" and we who can recollect those days, may well admit that there seemed to be cause for the disheartening remark. The edifice stood here, like a vast, empty shell. On the Lord's Day, what with a choir hidden away in the organ gallery, and with one or two figures of lonesome clergymen reading prayers in the over-large chancel, and some hundred or two of worshippers, or half that number on an afternoon, it looked like a forsaken place. There was neither parish school nor industrial school; and the Sunday scholars were taught in the church. The grounds were ill kept, neglected, and overrun with weeds. Little interest was felt in the building, beyond that which invests any stately pile of masonry standing where it is of no use except as an ornamental feature in the view. Those were the days of shadow, to be followed by a marvelous change. A revival has occurred, very wonderful in its way, and very instructive. Look at the contrast now; and give thanks to Almighty God for it, not forgetting the work zealously done here by His servants. This is, indeed, a gala-day with us; it is the anniversary of the parish; but what you see and hear is not a mere affair of show and spasmodic excitement, nor a fading pageant which leaves no substantial result. On the other hand, it is only one day of gladness in the midst of many of honest, hearty, and successful toil. The church, which was once regarded as little better than a useless pile of stone, is now a centre of life, activity, and far-extended influence; it is a power which the whole neighborhood feels; much work is done here, and more efficiently, I suppose, than ever before. We have a Sunday-school of between 400 and 500 scholars, an industrial school, a music school, and a daily parochial school of high grade, conducted by efficient and accomplished teachers. Lots have been recently purchased, at the corner of Church and Thames streets, on which a large building is to be immediately erected, for the accommodation of all the departments of an educational and charitable work. There is no church in the city, apparently, more attractive to our people than this. It numbers its communicants by hundreds; its confirmation classes are always large; the attendance is steady and regular; and on high feast days, it is impossible to accommodate the crowds who resort hither, to take part in the solemn Services.[2] The up-town churches

---

[2] From statistics, carefully prepared, and from count by persons employed for that purpose, a reliable estimate may be formed of the extent of the influence exerted by this Church. It might be likened to a tide-way, through which, from year's end to year's end, great floods of people drift, seeing, hearing, observing, and remembering. Many take their first impressions of our ritual and services from what is presented to them here; and hundreds bear away, to distant regions, religious ideas and spiritual aspirations awakened or quickened in these hallowed courts. It is thought, that the number of persons, other than the regular congregation, who, in the course of one twelve-month, attend divine service here, cannot fall much below 40,000. Our churches in the lower part of the city present the sight of a constantly changing body of worshippers; they are mission stations, in the strictest sense of that term. On high feast-days, after the church is full, the people who go from the doors, unable to enter, are numerous enough to fill another church of the same size. Last Christmas Day, the crowd was so great that the doors could not be closed; the people stood, in compact mass, in aisles, and porches, and out into the open air of winter as far as anything could be heard or seen.

have been stimulated to more attention to their own ritual, by the example set in this place; and far beyond the limits of the city and the diocese, nay, through the whole land, does that salutary influence extend which is ever flowing forth from this stately temple.

Such are the contrasts of this first quarter of a century. The history forms the justification of those who built the church. It shows us another thing; that our down-town churches must be kept where they are, in their old places. We must maintain them and enlarge them if necessary, increase their efficiency, beautify, adorn, and make them attractive. How few of these old fanes are left! Look at this city of New York. It is not the spirit of Catholic Christianity which has left us bare of churches all through this region, and, tearing down the consecrated shrines, has sent far off the priest and the altar, the Gospel and the preacher thereof. These great and populous districts about us are abandoned and left to Mammon, Sin, and Care. The spirit which has wrought the change is that stunted and cramped temper of congregationalism too common among us. When the idea of Catholicity is lost; when churches are regarded as the property of migratory individuals; when they are the private chapels and oratories of their wealthy pew-owners; when the priests are but the chaplains of a few families whose names they keep in a little visiting book; when it is forgotten that the Church has a mission to the population in general, and when the priest no longer realizes that he has any duties or relations to the ignorant, the ungodly, and the unhappy around his doors; then must such changes come as those which have occurred in New York. Had it not been for our parish, the desolation below Houston street would have been complete, and the town would have taken on the look of heathendom with the loss of all signs of God's Presence among men. And if the guardians of this trust should at any future time be unfaithful to their duty, such results might yet follow. Sometimes we are tempted to sell our churches or ancient burial-places and remove to more attractive quarters of the town; we are told, that such a board or such a company will give so much for this front on Broadway, or for dear old St. Paul's and its sacred ground; we are told that these are worth so many millions.[3] No, gentlemen; it will not do.

TRINITY RECTORY, New York,
Dec. 17th, 1869.

DEAR SIR:—

I have received your note of the 16th inst., informing me that a desire has been expressed by members of the Board of Brokers, of the New York Stock Exchange, to lease the grounds of Saint Paul's Chapel for business purposes, and asking me whether a proposition of this kind or an offer to purchase the said grounds, would be entertained by me as Rector of Trinity Church or by the Church Wardens and Vestrymen of the Parish. You add that, although you are not authorized to make any direct proposition, you feel certain that the Board of Brokers would be glad to acquire the grounds, either by purchase or lease.

Although I cannot speak positively for the Church Wardens and Vestrymen, yet I think I may safely say that their consent to such a disposition of the venerable chapel and its ancient burying ground could not, by any proposals whatever, be obtained. For myself I have to state, that I could not under any circumstances which I can at present imagine as existing, give the slightest consideration to the offer; deeming the grounds of Trinity and Saint Paul's to be as sacred a trust as any ever committed to me, and holding that their preservation, unharmed and undesecrated, is a solemn duty to God, to the living, and to the dead.

With great respect, I remain, very truly yours,

MORGAN DIX

There are things which are worth more than money, and which your millions cannot buy. We have duties to Man and to

---

[3] Some time ago I received a letter from a gentleman of this city, asking whether we would sell Saint Paul's churchyard. As my answer found its way, without my knowledge, into the public journals, I make no apology for printing it here, as an illustration of what was said on this point.

God. "Man doth not live by bread alone." We must stay here, and work on, and keep up the old shrines, lest the face of the land be desolate.

But while we maintain these churches on their ancient and consecrated sites, we must also see to it that they be worth keeping, and, in all respects, such as may profit the age. A church standing where this does, should be a church for the people; its Services should have a dignity and freedom, a breadth and fulness, apt to influence and affect men from generation to generation; its religious order and aspect should be such as "all sorts and conditions" might respect and venerate; its teachings should be broad and general like the Gospel of Christ, not the utterances of some school of this changeful age, but "comfortable words," such as all dying men might hear with gladness to their soul's health. Now that the pride and the show, the class-notions and caste-prejudices, of the fashionable world, have ebbed away from these places, and none are left here but the workers and the sinners, the toilers of land and sea, the neglected and forgotten of gay society, these old shrines should speak with a voice which the lost sheep of the house of Christ may understand. Let us keep our churches; but let us keep them as what may truly be called Catholic churches, homes of the common people, and sanctuaries for men of all classes and conditions.

There are people in this world who live and die in an atmosphere of the narrowest of sect-ideas. There are parishes as carefully shut up into themselves as if there were none beside them in the world. There are cliques of religious persons who think that they have all the true spirituality and vital piety that can at present be found among us. There are dioceses which have one cast throughout, and in which nearly every man is stamped with a particular brand. Amidst all this congregationalism and sectism, how the heart yearns for nobler and more generous things! How it desires to see more of the "Catholic Church!" It craves a religion to which no man's name was ever fastened, and which has more in it than any one brain or heart can hold; a religion essentially the same in any age, in the first, the tenth, the nineteenth, or the ninety-and-ninth; a religion which can last, grand and enduring; not to be readily defaced and eviscerated by a Luther or a Calvin, or uncomplainingly stuffed out and padded with new dogmas by a so-called infallible Pope; but, like the Lord Himself, the same yesterday, and to-day, and forever. Such is the religion which we would fain have taught in these holy places; not class-religion, nor school-religion, nor sect-religion, but a wide, warm and all-enfolding system; a religion for pilgrim man, the toiler, the sinner, who has a heart for love, an eye for beauty and glory, an ear for harmonies, a moral sense for righteousness, a conscience for duty, and a soul for faith; who changes not, however the world may change; a religion such as that which was heard in the deep tones of the Nicene Creed, and threw its heart-devotion into the all-but inspired forms of the great liturgies of the past, themselves, like the holy Gospels, not for a day but for all time.

There is a freedom about this church which they who frequently come hither must have felt and enjoyed. It is a gift to the people. Its stately architecture pleases the eye and refreshes the spirit of many a wayfaring man; its bells, pealing sweetly, send their cheering sounds through the adjacent homes of multitudes of the humble and poor, and are even heard by the mariners and others who are ever coming and going along the paths of the great deep. The trees and flowers around us bloom and blow for no class, but for every one who can be made happier by a look at deep green foliage and the soft splendours of the painted blossom and leaf. Yonder doors stand open, all day long, to men of every name; whoever he be that wends outside, with burden heavy to bear, here is he welcome to enter and rest if he will, and pray his pilgrim prayer to God. The Services, as now performed in this house, are dignified, affecting, and impressive; they befit the state and position of our parish, and commend themselves directly to wise and understanding minds and devout hearts. I know of nothing sectarian or narrow in this temple of God Almighty; if there be any such thing, it is not here with our approval or consent. And thus may things remain; thus would we have it to be with our down-town chapels and churches, whose mission is chiefly to the poor and lowly; not to the poor as a class,—for class-religion is an abomination before Heaven—but chiefly to them, because they abound here, and they are also children of God. Our mission is to the people; let us go to them with words which any people of any age can understand and may be expected to appreciate and accept.

And would that the "murmurings and disputings" of Christ's People might cease! Would that men could be persuaded to cast off the tight lacing of prejudice, burst the bands of sect, and live in unity and godly love! What religious body could lead the way in a movement toward better things more frankly than our own church? and where could a point of departure be found more auspicious than this, in the outer waste and desolation of what once looked like a Christian city? Our Church must hold great varieties of men within her motherly arms; she must tolerate great diversities of thought and taste. We must have laws, of course, but not too many; laws good for all, beneficial, equal, made to help growth, not to check it. If any one deem those laws oppressive, let him seek, by legal measures, their amendment or repeal; but while they stand, let them be obeyed. No man is free to break, at will, the laws which he has sworn to keep; yet, for our comfort and safety let the laws be few, and as general as is consistent with good order and security. Above all, let no man have the power to make his whim a law to his brother, or to force his opinion on another as a rule of action; let bishop, priest, deacon, and layman, be on an equality here, protected from each others' wrong, at peace, and in canonical liberty. This is the only hope for us; freedom, within the limits set by just and equal laws.

Think what ills have come of the crazy running a-muck with individual opinion, and insisting that everything else shall clear the way to make room for its enthronement as supreme. The sect-principle; the idea of "separation for opinions"; what dis-integration has it caused in Christendom, what destruction has it wrought among souls! The history of Protestant Christianity may profitably be taken as a warning to agitators of our day; analyze it, and you find, everywhere, the same dreary and interminable process of division and sub-division for opinion's sake. There was a time when the Church of England was one church, comprehending the whole nation, and, as a matter of course, including men differing very widely about many points of doctrine and practice. In the process of events, when each school thought more highly of its own special opinions than of the unity of great masses of the faithful on the strong basis of historical and traditional Catholicism, men arose, making enor-mous noise and uproar, now on this question and now on that, asserting that they and they only were orthodox, claiming sub-mission to their individual theories, insisting on them as con-taining the marrow of the gospel, seeking to force their own ideas on their brethren, and demanding alteration and revision of the Prayer Book till it should either be made to convey their interpretations of the truth as it is in Jesus, or at least present nothing contradictory to them. Whereupon followed opposition, recrimination, confusion, and strife, in the midst of which developements fanatics and enthusiasts led off their fol-lowers into separation and schism, founding what they called new "churches" for the better enjoyment and propagation of the pet notion or opinion, itself, perhaps, a mere human idea, at the best no more than one item in the great, wide, all-comprehending revelation to us through the Gospel. Each new sect, of the scores which crowd upon and crush one another, driving the devout into dismay and giving to the ungodly his best argument, has come to the birth that way; every fresh schism now formed or impending, may be reduced to that miserable explanation of separation from Catholic Unity for the sake of some opinion, magnified inordinately by men of ardent temper, and held to be of more importance than all other things together. But why do I speak of Protestantism? Let him who will rise up, and do mock honor to the great mother of schisms, old Rome; since there is none like her, for this sectarian mind; she, who is the very mistress and incomparable artist in this work. What a history is hers, from that fatal day in which her letters of excommunication, placed on the trembling shrine of Saint Sophia, clave asunder the body of Christ! And how true to the spirit of that act has she been, through the last three or four hundred years, from time to time contracting, and shrinking within narrower and narrower limits, for the sake of opinions! In the 16th century, she made up her mind to cut a great part of Europe adrift, though she might have held it, because her system demanded consolidation by stringent measures and a more exclusive Creed; and thus whole races and nations were crowded out and lost to her forever. Again, and as if it were but yesterday, a new instance of her policy is given; the dogma of infallibility is pressed on the unhappy frame, which expostulates, and cries aloud, and protests by the mouths of its wisest and most learned prelates, yet without avail; Italy and the Curia, true to Roman principle, force this last cup to the lips of better Catholics; the civilization of Europe, in verbal rebellion, is flouted and contemptuously flung off; this marvellous age, with its arts and learning, its wisdom and its profound longings for spiritual health, its sorrows and sins and shadowy grandeur of light and darkness, all, all must be sacrificed and cast away, that a human opinion, based,—as Roman scholars and theologians tell us,—on not so much as a shred of historical evidence, may be forced on a cramped and tortured constituency as an article of faith. Here is sectarianism indeed, full blown, and putting to shame all the achievements of which Protestantism has hitherto boasted. I see the grey head of Döllinger, first of Catholic scholars and divines in Germany, a man whom all the wise and good might honor, that venerable and dignified head smitten by such lightnings as they are yet able, in the feebly burning furnaces of the Vatican, to forge; and the spirit sinks at the announcement, which his excommunication too clearly makes, that the walls of Rome like those of the haunted chamber in the legend, have contracted once again, that she throws off more and more of her own baptized children to the grasp of infidelity, and that the terms of communion with her henceforward shall be harder than ever before.[4] This is Sectarianism in full, rank bloom; precisely like that which has made of Protestantism the warring, wrangling, death-struck chaos that it is. Here is the same dreary scene, of one set of men setting upon another set of men and driving them out, in order that some pet opinion, some vain and inept notion, may be lifted up into a dogma; that one man's meat may be forced down another man's throat against his will; that where there is freedom to-day, bondage may overtake us to-morrow; and that the tenet or the whim of a clique and a faction may rule and reign with that authority which God's Word only can give over the consciences of men.

Is there any danger lest this wretched history may be repeated in our own branch of the Church? Is there any disposition, among ourselves, on either side, to proscribe opinions which the average mind of the day does not regard as sound, and to worry and annoy, by a hundred arts and appliances, the men who hold them? Are there, for instance, bishops to be found, in our own venerable and venerated House, who would impose their particular views, their theological ideas, or their individual tastes and preferences on their unhappy, and, at present, helpless, clergy, under the sounding but delusive title of "godly admonitions?" Are there men, young or old, who, though, like Joseph, "fruitful boughs," laden with works of

---

[4] [Döllinger, a distinguished German Catholic Biblical scholar, broke with the Church after the first Vatican Council had proclaimed the dogma of papal infallibility. He was excommunicated. Ed.]

piety and charity, and worn down with labors for Christ and the Church, have yet, like him, been sorely shot at by the archers, because of their views on points upon which we, at least, (however it fare with liberty in Rome,) are free to think, (though how long we may be, God knoweth.)? When I hear of men, whom because of their opinions, some of their elder brethren would fain *crush* in the Church, or *drive* out of it, albeit they neither violate rubric nor break canon, I ask whether the principle of Sectarianism has any standing among ourselves? Are we, only, sound, in this respect, while all the rest of Christendom seems more or less infected? There may be reason for gravely revolving these questions. Intolerance and persecution ever drive men into schism, and schism may end in death. Pray God we keep ourselves clear; and, even as it is with our great country, which, last discovered of the nations, opens its broad fields, with liberal freedom, to the oppressed, the disconsolate, and the unhappy of every clime, offering them a home and a place of rest, so let us pray that it may be with our beloved Church, thus far the home and haven of our souls; let her, in her system present some "better thing" to the perplexed children of God; let her give them, what seems to be nowhere in sight in these days, a Catholic Religion, broad enough for all who will agree to accept the Holy Scriptures, the General Councils of the undivided Church, and all true and authentic historical traditions, as a basis on which men, though differing very widely indeed in matters of opinion, in taste, in theory, and in ideas of worship and work, may yet stand, hand in hand, and heart to heart, loving as brethren, deferring to one another, mutually securing each other's liberty, in things which are not vital and have not been ruled by the whole Church, and waiting patiently till the good Lord Himself shall cast the light we need on things about which the best and the most conscientious cannot altogether agree.

And thus our thoughts are led upward to Him, Whose glorious Ascension we celebrate to-day. Christ is risen from the dead; He is also gone up on high; and we praise Him, we bless Him, we worship Him, we glorify Him, we give thanks to Him, for His great glory. Let us remember, while the full volume of praise, swelled by so many voices and such a flood of "all kinds of music" fills this house, let us remember, that He has the nature of all mankind, that He maketh intercession for all, that He watches us all from above, where, lifted up, He draws the world to Himself more powerfully than the moon the tides. Let us remember His relations to us all, and ours to each other, as brethren in Him, the First of the many brethren. Why should we be hard on each other, aggressive, repulsive, exclusive, suspicious, and prone to coerce? Why, reversing the apostolic rule, should we do all things *with* murmurings and disputings? Can we ever have an unworldly spirit and a generous love? We ought to be unworldly; because He has gone away out of this world long ago, and our souls ought thither to ascend and dwell where our Saviour is. We ought to be earnest, loving, and devoted; remembering that what He began on earth and is continually doing in heaven, is done, not for some few of us, nor for a class or sect, nor for people who think in one particular way, but for us poor toilers, sufferers, and sinners together. Let us ask then, that our hearts may dwell in heaven whither he is gone up; that our hands may be prompt and busy in all works of loving service, and that we follow His example in this world where He once dwelt; until, having run with patience the race set before us, we come, in peace, to the day, when all that are in the graves shall come forth, and they also that are alive and remain shall be exalted, and men shall likewise ascend to heaven and be forever with the Lord.

6. THE DOWNTOWN CHURCH
ARRAIGNED

A Study of Trinity—The Richest Church in America, 1910

BY RAY STANNARD BAKER

By 1900, objections against the downtown churches had been systematized into a coherent indictment. To its members it was alleged to offer only a round of meaningless formalisms. For the benefit of those outside the church it maintained a series of unimpressive and uninfluential missions. Meanwhile it managed its property with the single interest apparently of maximizing its profit; when Trinity went to court to avoid having to improve sanitary facilities in the tenements it owned, it contributed to the impression that the most important social role of the downtown church was that of the soulless landlord. Charles E. Russell published a series of muckraking articles in EVERYBODY'S *on Trinity's tenements. But where Russell wrote in Socialist anger, Ray Stannard Baker wrote with the sadness of a man who believed intensely in the importance of developing the religious life of the city. His description of Trinity, ap-*

From Ray Stannard Baker, *The Spiritual Unrest* (New York: Stokes, 1910), pp. 1–48.

*propriately, constituted the first essay in a volume on American
religious life, entitled* THE SPIRITUAL UNREST. *Baker (1870–
1946) had begun as early as 1907 to write, under the pseudo-
nym of David Grayson, a series of essays about the higher amiability of rural life. He later became an assistant of Woodrow
Wilson, edited Wilson's papers, and wrote Wilson's biography
in eight volumes. He told of his own life in* NATIVE AMERICAN:
THE BOOK OF MY YOUTH *(New York: Scribner's, 1941) and*
AMERICAN CHRONICLE *(New York: Scribner's, 1945).*

Trinity Church, which bears the enviable (or unenviable) distinction of being rich—the richest church in America—has
been curiously under attack during recent months. Newspapers and magazines have presented its affairs in a light more
or less unfavorable; its shortcomings have been discussed in
not a few pulpits even in the Episcopal Church; the Legislature
of the State of New York has been asked to consider its conduct as a corporate body; and finally, its distinguished rector
and vestry have been summoned in the courts, and proceedings
have been instituted which have been bitterly contested.

Is not this an extraordinary situation in which to find a
great religious institution? Is it not strange that the public
should be questioning the moral standards (for it comes to
that) of the most notable church in America?

Let not, however, such questioning astonish us: it is neither
unexpected nor unusual. That challenging of entrenched and
wealthy institutions which has been proceeding so briskly for
the past half dozen years has finally reached the last resort of
conservatism: the church. Trinity, as everyone knows, lifts a
presiding finger at the head of Wall Street. From its bronze
doorway one can easily see the chief offices of the Standard
Oil Company and the Steel Trust, and all about are the mighti-
est banks, insurance companies and other moneyed institutions
of this half of the earth. Each in its turn—trusts, railroad com-

panies, insurance companies—has been questioned, attacked, discussed in legislatures, haled into the courts. To each of these institutions democracy has put its blunt queries (is putting them to-day):

Are you serving the people, or, are you serving your own selfish interests? What are you doing that you should be retained as the approved tool of civilization?

Nor should it surprise us to find that democracy stands knocking at last at the closed doors of Old Trinity, nor to hear it asking:

What, then, have *you* done with the talents we gave you? Have *you* been a faithful servant?

I shall here set down the facts regarding Trinity Church; nothing that I could write, indeed, would illuminate more clearly the prevailing condition of spiritual unrest in this country, nor present more graphically the dilemma of the church in our modern life.

What, then, is this Trinity Church?

WHAT IS TRINITY CHURCH?

Every human institution has one supreme function: to serve the people in one way or another. A railroad corporation serves by carrying freight and passengers; a church serves by promoting the true spirit of religion. In order to perform its service to the people properly, a railroad corporation is provided with certain tools—depots, a road-bed and rolling stock, and a church has its spired building, its music, its preaching, its schools. A church is not religion: it is a mere human agency for fostering religion. It may contain the Ark of the Covenant, or it may not. When the people, then, arise to criticise the church, they are not attacking religion, but rather the public service of the institution which assumes to promote religion. It is as proper to ask of a church as of a railroad company: Is it doing its work efficiently?

Like many of the great trusts and corporations, Trinity has

become inordinately wealthy. No church in the world, perhaps, has so much property and such a varied and costly equipment. The value of its property is beyond $50,000,000. Of this about two-thirds is distinctly church property, untaxed: for Trinity parish not only owns the magnificent church which stands in the midst of the spacious and beautiful (and enormously valuable) old churchyard at the head of Wall Street, but it owns and conducts nine other churches some of them nearly as large as Old Trinity itself. It also owns a number of church houses, school buildings, a hospital, and a cemetery, all of which are included in its list of untaxed church property. This vast machinery of service is controlled by Trinity parish, a corporation similar to other business corporations, except that the directors are known as vestrymen, the general manager as Rector, and the stockholders as communicants. Like many other corporations, Trinity has a large income-producing investment outside of its actual operating plant. About one-third of its property—to the value of over $16,000,000 (assessed value, as given in the Trinity report, $13,646,300)—is in rented lands and tenements. In short, it is a big business corporation: calling it a church does not change its character.

One of the deepest, if not the deepest, need of men is religion; hence from the beginning of time men have encouraged and built up institutions to respond to that need with service. No other human institution has been so sedulously fostered or so lavishly maintained as the church. One of the very first things that our forefathers did upon coming to America was to set up churches: and one of the earliest churches so set up in New York Colony was Trinity. It was established in 1697—two hundred and thirteen years ago. It was fostered then, and it has been encouraged since, exactly like any other public service corporation—only with a greater degree of generosity. In the early days of railroading, for example, the people were so eager to extend the service of transportation throughout the country that they gave to railroad corporations vast grants or "bonuses" of land, they presented them with free franchises conveying special rights and privileges, and they even exempted railroad property from taxation.

TRINITY OBTAINS A FRANCHISE

In exactly the same way Trinity Church was built up. In 1697 a franchise was granted to Trinity to build a church "situate in or near the street called Broadway," and it was to be "for the use and behoof of the inhabitants from time to time inhabiting or to inhabit within our city of New York, in communion of our protestant church of England." Eight years later came the "bonus" or grant of land, then called the Queen's farm, which extended picturesquely along the Hudson River on the west side of Manhattan Island. This tract, now densely covered with human habitations, was then practically uninhabited. Since then for over two hundred years that part of the property used for church or educational purposes has not been taxed. It has been calculated that the remitted taxes on Trinity Church property for the last two hundred years— the free gift of the people of New York regardless of creed— would amount to many times the present total value of the property of Trinity.

For many years Trinity acted literally according to the provisions of its franchise. It gave money and land freely to other struggling churches; assisting them first as chapels and as soon as they were strong enough to stand alone, Trinity gave them its blessing and made them independent. St. George's, Grace Church, and other important churches began thus with help from Trinity.

But the city of New York began to grow: the Queen's farm, at first of little use to Trinity, became more valuable. Other churches were organized, and, as usual, where large property values are at stake, a difference of opinion began to arise as to who should control it.

The original grant had been made, as I have shown, to all

"of the inhabitants of our said city of New York" in communion with the Church of England. Naturally other churches than Trinity thought they should have a share of the property: but Trinity would not release its grip. And in 1814, the vestrymen of Trinity succeeded in getting a law passed by the New York Legislature which at one stroke limited the control of the property to "members of the congregation of Trinity Church, or of any of the chapels belonging to Trinity corporation." This was the first step in a long process of centralizing and narrowing the control of the property.

After 1814 the policy of the great church began to change. Instead of serving all the inhabitants it devoted less and less of its income to the building up of outside churches and spent more and more on its own services. Instead of helping a chapel to become independent and self-governing, it established chapels and kept absolute control of them. In 1814 it had only two dependent chapels—St. Paul's and St. John's; to-day it has nine.

All this time the property of Trinity was growing more valuable. The Queen's farm had been cut up into blocks and lots; whole streets had built up with fine residences and places of business. The rental income of Trinity corporation increased enormously. Of course Trinity Church did absolutely nothing to earn this income, except to hold the title of the land: the people of New York who moved into and developed that part of the city were the real producers of the income.

BEGINNING OF THE MOVEMENT UPTOWN

As the money began to pile up, Trinity bethought itself how to spend it. Many of its well-to-do members were moving uptown, so the corporation appropriated what was then (1852) the enormous sum of $230,000 to build Trinity chapel in West Twenty-fifth Street, together with a beautiful residence for the clergy. That act brought forth a storm of protest. It was shown that Trinity had deserted mission work in the lower part of the city where the mass of the people lived, where its own property was located, and diverted the money to the building of a church for the uptown rich. These rich people, of course, might have built a chapel of their own; the poor people downtown whose rentals helped to make Trinity rich could not afford to build churches. The glaring injustice of such an act brought about an inquiry by the legislature, and William Jay, a son of the great chief justice, and one of the most prominent citizens of New York (he was the grandfather of the William Jay who is at present senior warden of Trinity Church), wrote a stinging letter to the Rector of Trinity, in which he said:

"Wealth is naturally defiant, and so long as you can lengthen your rent roll and multiply your thousands, and purchase submission and obsequiousness, you may afford to look down with supercilious indifference on the complaints and disaffection of those who are impotent to injure you. But sir, there are signs in the political horizon which threaten a coming tempest which may level the proud pinnacles of Trinity in the dust."

Mr. Jay also charged that Trinity was using its wealth not "for the permanent benefit of the church" but for building up the influence of the "high church" party in the Episcopal Church, there being at that time a heated conflict going on between the two factions in the church. Said Mr. Jay:

"Her wealth has in this city, in the opinion of many, been lavished in ostentatious buildings, rather than used in promoting true piety and religion; and the parochial reports have given ground for most unfavorable comparison between the number of communicants and the amount of benevolent offerings in Trinity and her chapels, and various other churches in the city."

Trinity continued to grow richer. In 1890 the corporation went still further uptown, following the rich, and built the magnificent church of St. Agnes in West Ninety-second Street, at a cost of about $500,000. In the meantime it had built one large chapel down-town—St. Augustine's, in Houston Street—

and afterward it acquired another, St. Luke's, on the lower West Side.

HOW TRINITY HAS CONTROLLED
ITS GREAT PROPERTY

How has Trinity controlled all of this great property? It is controlled, like that of the life insurance companies, by a board of directors, here called the vestry. The vestry is elected by the stockholders—here called communicants, but not all the communicants by any means are voters. Originally, under the law of 1814, every member of Trinity or its chapels had a vote; but the process of narrowing control has here also been going on. Under a law passed in 1867 (supported in the legislature by Trinity) churches are granted certain powers to establish free chapels. Under this law five dependent chapels were organized having no voice in the affairs of Trinity Church. Not one of the chapels in the poorer districts now has a vestryman; in fact, Trinity corporation is controlled by the two rich chapels: St. Agnes and Trinity Chapel, all the vestrymen being selected from these two chapels and from Old Trinity.

One of the most remarkable conditions brought out in the Hughes investigation of the life insurance companies was the fact that their boards of directors were practically self-perpetuating bodies. Nominally they were elected by the policy holders and stockholders: but as a matter of fact few policy holders were ever present, and the elections were controlled absolutely by the men in power.

Such is the case with Trinity corporation. Though there are many hundreds of communicants entitled to vote at the Trinity elections, comparatively few ever attend. At one election the twenty-two members of the vestry were elected with a total of twenty-three votes. The vestry has been in effect a self-perpetuating body, controlling an enormously valuable property, making no public reports at any time, and oblivious to criticism either from within the church or without.

What was the result of the control of such a self-perpetu-ating, irresponsible board of vestrymen who could be reached by no criticism?

It was very little different from the result in other corpora-tions. Perhaps it was, if anything, worse, because there was less accountability on the part of the board of directors (vestry). An Insurance Department at Albany made at least a pretense of supervising the insurance companies; but there was no Church Department at Albany—no one on earth who had any power to demand any sort of an accounting from Trinity corporation. And unlimited power over vast unearned prop-erty in the hands of a few men who are not accountable to anyone can work out in only one way—whether the men are organized under a churchly name or not.

And what is that result?

THE DISEASE OF UNEARNED PROPERTY

A curious, insidious, benumbing disease seems to afflict those who control unearned property. Subtle psychological changes take place within them. One might expect such men to say to themselves: The people have endowed us with special fran-chise privileges; they have granted us land to work with; they have built up this land and increased its value; they are paying us a large yearly income; they have remitted our taxes for over two hundred years. We therefore owe them the most en-thusiastic service, and the frankest accounting of our steward-ship. Do they say this? Not at all. By the curious psychological change to which I have referred, they come to act as though the property which they control was in reality their own. They resent any questions regarding it; they spend the income where and how they like; they make no accounting to anyone.

But these men of the vestry of Trinity are high-class men. All of them are educated men, some belong to very old fam-ilies, some are famous, nearly all are wealthy. Many are con-nected with various good works (see their names in the Chari-ties Directory). All of the twenty-two (except the controller and the clerk) contribute their services, they receive no salary. Not one of them can be suspected of profiting by so much as a penny from the business transactions of Trinity parish. I suppose, indeed, the same thing can be said of the directors of life insurance companies, railroads and banks—who are also high-class men. Indeed, many of these rich vestrymen of Trinity are actually in the directories of great business corporations (see their names in the "Directory of Directors"); they are part and parcel of the current methods of doing business.

In the life insurance investigations what were some of the discoveries made? It was disclosed that the business was extravagantly conducted; that inordinately high salaries were paid; that gorgeous and expensive offices were maintained; that the men in control made conditions highly comfortable for themselves and their friends. A curious parallelism exists between the life insurance companies and Trinity.

People ordinarily expect to pay something, make some self-sacrifices for their religious advantages. Some of the most heroic stories in the world are told of the sacrifices of men and women to build up places of worship, but the congregations of Trinity parish get their religious advantages practically for nothing. According to the financial statement issued recently by Trinity (the first public report in over fifty years) it cost $340,870 to maintain the ten churches and the schools of Trinity for one year. Of this vast sum the members of all the churches contributed just $18,210 (in pew rents). All the remainder of the expense was met from the rental income from the property owned by Trinity. In other words, the poor people and other tenants on Trinity lands have paid not only for the support of the chapels in the poorer part of town, but they have built the rich uptown churches and are paying practically all the running expenses. Communicants in Trinity worship in churches which they have not built, and to the support of which they contribute practically nothing. They are, in short, religious paupers.

It is true that the congregations of Trinity churches contributed during the year $94,000 for special charities—but none of this money went to church support, and even if it had been so applied it would not have begun to liquidate the cost of operating the churches.

Music alone cost Trinity last year (including care of organs) $63,000, or over three times as much as all the members contributed to the entire support of the church. There have been many complaints of the Trinity tenements (of which more later), but at least they pay for a great deal of fine music—also for twenty-eight clergymen at a cost of $101,674 and for thirty-two sextons and engineers at $26,555. I find an item of "fuel and light for churches" of $12,280. The total contributions of Trinity communicants for church purposes ($18,000) will pay *that*, and some to spare.

As in the life insurance companies, salaries range high, the Rector is said to receive the highest salary of any clergyman in America, $15,000 a year, and some of the vicars receive $8,000 each—more than the salary of a United States senator. Besides the salaries many of the clergy also receive free residences (on partially untaxed property), so that they have no rent to pay—a big item in New York City—and when they retire they are generously pensioned!

It was found in the life insurance companies that, although keen business men conducted the operations, some of the real estate owned yielded a very low income. The same is true of Trinity. It costs just short of $50,000 for salaries and office expenses in conducting the real estate business of Trinity, and yet the net income last year on $16,000,000 worth of real estate was only about $376,000 (gross $752,000)—or a little more than two per cent. Tenement house property in New York is ordinarily expected to pay from five to six per cent. net, and other rented property not less than four per cent. Judging even from a strict business point of view, then, Trinity corporation is certainly open to severe criticism. The management of a private estate which could show earnings of only two per cent. would speedily be turned out, but Trinity, not making public reports, no one could know how the vestry was conducting its trust.

WHAT OF THE TENEMENTS

I come now to the tenements. A great deal has been written and said of these tenements during the last twenty-five years. Many years ago the Trinity houses were occupied by rich or well-to-do people, but to-day they are crowded with wage-earners of all sorts and of many nationalities. While other parts of the city were built up to new buildings, these old houses on Trinity property have largely remained, although, in recent years, Trinity has put up a number of new business buildings and warehouses. There is no more barren, forbidding, unprogressive part of the city than the Trinity blocks south of Christopher Street. Trinity has sat still and waited for the increase of the value of its land.

Well, old buildings are old, and the city has been progressing in nothing more than in tenement house reform—in short, in its views of the responsibilities of the city to the poor and unfortunate. A distinctly higher standard of social morality has been built up in New York in the last twenty-five years. And in its work of improving conditions in the crowded districts of Manhattan Island the city authorities have repeatedly collided with Trinity corporation. The first clash came in 1887. A law had been passed requiring that running water should be furnished on each floor of tenement houses. In most of the Trinity houses the tenants had to go down stairs and out of doors to get their water supply. When the demand was made on Trinity to obey the law, the vestry objected and began a bitter fight in the courts, which finally reached the Court of Appeals. Of course this costly litigation was not paid for by the vestrymen or even by the communicants of Trinity. This legal battle was financed out of the rentals of the very people who were to be benefited by the new law.

However, it was an epoch-making case, the decision of which will long be quoted, for it decided that the state can compel a private owner, for the good of the public to alter a house at his own expense. But the church had to be driven to the new moral standard by the courts. Here is the way in which Judge Peckham, afterwards appointed to the Supreme Court of the United States, laid down the law to Trinity:

"We may own our property absolutely and yet it is subject to the proper exercise of the police power. We have surrendered to that extent our right to its unrestricted use. It must be so used as not improperly to cause harm to our neighbor."

But Trinity's long-fought legal battle had succeeded in delaying the enforcement of the law from 1887 until 1895—eight years. In spite of itself, however, Trinity helped along the cause of better homes for the poor in a way it little intended. The very bitterness of its legal struggle against making improvements served to turn public attention even more closely to housing conditions in lower Manhattan. In 1894 the famous tenement house commission, of which Richard Watson Gilder was chairman, was appointed. Investigation showed that hundreds of tenements had no toilet conveniences in them, but that so-called "school-sinks," or open water closets in the back yards, were used by all the tenants, and that thousands of men, women and children were sleeping in dark holes of rooms in which there were no windows opening to the outer air— breeding places, indeed, for tuberculosis.

In 1901 a law was passed through the efforts of the Tenement House Commission of which Robert W. De Forest was president abolishing "school-sinks" and dark inside rooms in tenements. Trinity waited; this time the law was tested in the courts by another landlord, and it was not sustained until 1904. What did Trinity then do? Where it could not avoid compliance with the law, necessary changes were made, but in many cases it slid out of making improvements through a provision which defines a tenement house as any building occupied by more than two families. In some of the old houses where there had been more than two families, Trinity reduced the number to two, and thus by getting out from under the tenement law, was able to refrain from making the repairs demanded.

TRINITY FIGHTS IMPROVEMENTS

Trinity has always been against improvement; it has always had to be lashed to its moral duty by public opinion or by the courts, or by fear of legislative action. Even when the city was seeking for land for the children's play-ground at Clarkson and Houston Streets on the West Side, it had to enter into a long and costly fight in order to get the land from Trinity corporation.

As to the condition of the Trinity tenements I made a careful investigation of many of them. They are not so bad as I expected to find, no worse than those owned by other landlords in the same neighborhood. In general, they are better— and why shouldn't they be? Why should such ancient tenements have been allowed to remain at all? In general, the rents are low, and in many cases they have not been raised in twenty-five years. And this much must be said to the credit of Trinity; none of its property is rented for saloons or for immoral purposes. There are only two places on Trinity land where liquor is sold, and in those cases the property is under a lease which cannot be controlled by Trinity.

Over and over again, when complaints have been made of Trinity houses, the vestry has said:

"We are not responsible; the land is leased and the building is owned by the lessee. We cannot control it."

And yet when the leases expire, it has been, in the recent past, a custom of Trinity to release for two years to the owner of the building. Of course no such owner can afford to make repairs when he may lose his building in two years and he does as little as possible. Trinity thus gets its land rent, the landlord gets his house rent—and the tenant who pays the bills gets just as bad a place to live in as the Board of Health will permit.

It is difficult, indeed, to see how a group of men individually so intelligent and honorable should collectively exhibit so little vision, so little social sense, so little justice. Whether judged as good morals or as good business, the results have been lamentable and disheartening.

Complaint has been widely made (especially in New York City) that the church was losing its hold on the people, that people do not go to church as they once did nor take the interest in religious affairs that they should. Has the position of Trinity with its low standards of social justice and morality had anything to do with that tendency? When the public and the courts, and the legislature, have to castigate a church to higher moral standards, why should the people go to church for instruction? What inspiration has the church to give? Spending $63,000 a year for music and $340,000—mostly taken from the poor—to support its churches, it has been willing for many years, until brought to a realization of its duty by the force of law, to let at least some of its poor sleep in disease-breeding dark rooms and suffer for the want of sanitary conveniences. How, under such circumstances, can it preach a lowly Savior and the love of man to man?

WHAT TRINITY DOES WITH ITS MONEY

Perhaps I have now dwelt sufficiently upon the business side of Trinity. I come now to the service which it performs. However extravagant or corrupt the administration of life insurance companies had become, the Hughes investigation showed that they yet performed a service; they paid losses.

So Trinity performs a wide and varied service. Every Sunday in all the ten churches the usual religious services are held, and there are also the usual Sunday Schools and week-day meetings. I have attended, at various times, most of the Trinity churches. Some of them are well attended, some not so

well; and the audiences are just about what one finds in the
ordinary New York church.

Besides the regular worship there are also the usual missionary and philanthropic societies, sewing classes, kindergartens and many clubs for young people. One of the interesting
and valuable activities of St. Paul's Chapel is a working girl's
club which furnishes a meeting and luncheon place in one
of the church buildings. But perhaps the most extensive single
department of the activity of Trinity outside of its strict religious work is the day schools. There are seven regular day
schools connected with seven of the churches—somewhat similar to the parochial schools of the Roman Catholics. A manual
training, cooking and drawing school is maintained in Washington Square and there are three night schools. All this work
is free to pupils, the only obligation being that the children
shall attend Sunday School. The work follows closely that of
the public schools, save that a certain amount of religious instruction is also given. School work cost the parish last year
$63,755.

What does Trinity do for churches and charities outside of
its own parish? As I said before, the congregations of Trinity
contributed $94,000 last year for various charities and benevo-
lences. But Trinity corporation itself, which was chartered to
minister to all the inhabitants of New York in communion with
the Episcopal Church, contributed only $46,579 to churches
and charities outside of the parish—or less by some $17,000
than it paid for music in its own churches. It also made one
loan of $5,000 to help a church outside of the parish. One of
the regular expenses of every Episcopal church is the appor-
tionment made for the general mission work of the church.
Old Trinity was supposed to pay $10,000. It never met this
amount: three years ago the general church reduced the ap-
portionment to $2,500, so that Trinity would pay, but never
until last year did it meet even this amount. It has, indeed,
been notorious among the churches of New York for shirking
its missionary obligations.

TRINITY LOSING IN MEMBERSHIP

Judged by its own statistics, Trinity has lost ground. It has been unable to maintain its membership, in spite of the vast sums of money expended, the costly music, the activities of an army of workers. Old Trinity in 1898 had 1,767 communicants; in 1908 it had 1,340—a loss of 427 members in ten years. The figures for the combined church and chapels (except one, acquired since 1898) are scarcely less encouraging. In 1898 the total was 7,220; in 1908 it was 6,939—a loss of 281 members in ten years.

Now, I am acutely conscious, having made this dry, catalogue-like report of the work of Trinity, with its statistics and its cost, that I have not told the whole story of service. I appreciate fully the difficulty of measuring spiritual values. The work of an insurance company or a railroad can be measured more or less accurately by statistics. Not so, a church—even though the clergy themselves are content to appeal to statistics of membership to prove their efficiency. Often I have stepped into the dim coolness of Old Trinity from the roar of Broadway on a busy day and found men and women kneeling in silent prayer. Who shall measure the value to individual human souls of such a place of refuge and worship? Or who, indeed, can compute the incalculable influence of the quiet old churchyard itself—the beauty of it, the calm of it—with its suggestion of eternal values in a place where men are furiously pursuing immediate gain? Nor can any one of us pass judgment upon the service of the individual workers in Trinity—the clergy, the vestrymen, the sisters.

And yet it is not at all a question as to whether Trinity is doing spiritual service. Of course it is. But should it not do far more? Have its leaders that breadth of vision without which the people perish? Has it power of leadership in our common life? Is it making the best use of its tremendous opportunities, its enormous wealth?

These are fair questions; questions which, indeed, the most

earnest men within the Church itself are asking. They are questions which the public at large has a right to ask.

With the idea, then, of presenting the specific facts, I have studied, somewhat carefully, the methods in two or three of the Trinity churches. And I wish here to show how the work is done.

In the first place, the people in the churches have nothing whatever to say as to the conduct of their own affairs. Everything is provided for them by the self-perpetuating autocracy which controls the property; their music is paid for; their ministers are hired by Trinity. The people have nothing at any point to say. Last November a whole congregation—that of St. John's Chapel—was informed one Sunday that the church would shortly be closed, and all the people were told that they could go to another church. No one had been consulted, there had been no chance of protest or explanation; the chapel, which had been open for one hundred and two years, was ordered closed. But of St. John's more later.

Even in the rich chapel of St. Agnes, when Dr. Manning was promoted to be Rector of Trinity, the new vicar was chosen by the vestry before the congregation had ever heard him preach. Thus every detail of the machine is managed, not by the people, but by the benevolent autocracy at the top.

USING MONEY TO PROMOTE RELIGION

Consider, for a moment, the work of one of the chapels in the poorer part of town. I give these facts hesitatingly, because the clergy are earnest men working in the deadening toils of a system which destroys inspiration and quenches brotherly enthusiasm—and yet the truth must be set down. A large proportion of the people connected with that chapel get something out of it in cash or in material benefits. And I say this advisedly, knowing that many individuals love this chapel and receive spiritual advantages from its work. Every member of the choir, of course, is paid a regular stipend. To encourage the Sunday School officers one hundred dollars in cash is distributed among them every year. Last Christmas, that day of spontaneous giving, the corporation appropriated $750 for decorations, a tree, and gifts for the people. The Sunday School is made up largely of the children who are being educated (free) in the day and night schools conducted by the chapel, and are therefore *compelled* to attend Sunday School. And it may be said, further, that the day school pupils are also encouraged by prizes—so they, too, get something out of it.

Besides these regular payments, the dispensation of charity of various sorts undoubtedly assures the connection of not a few people with the church. It is one of the emphasized rules of this chapel that "assistance is given only to persons that are regularly enrolled members of the chapel cure."

This particular chapel has a staff of twenty-six clergy, teachers, lay-workers and sextons regularly hired, and a choir of twenty-four members—a total of fifty paid workers. Yet I have been in that chapel during services when there were not fifty people in the congregation. Think of it! With land and buildings worth $300,000 and an operating cost (I could not get the exact figures) of probably not less than $50,000, although it is in a neighborhood swarming with people, this is the use to which it is put! A little money—very little—is collected from the congregation for charities, but not one cent is paid by the people of the church for the support of the work. It is pure charity.

Do not think that the people in the neighborhood who see this sort of work do not know exactly what is going on. No people are more sensitive to real values, or quicker to see the difference between charity and brotherly love, than these people of the tenements. Charity is indeed often necessary, but it requires the genius of love to bestow it properly. One woman, a member of a Trinity Chapel—one of the clean, self-respecting, hard-working sort, an example and a light in her neighborhood—gave me this point of view in so many words:

"There is too much giving. Most of the people go there to get something; they don't expect to help. The tendency is to pauperize the people and cheapen the real meaning of religion."

No, the people are not fooled.

When I asked a clergyman in Trinity why so much was given to these people and so little required of them, I was told:

"Why, they are poor; they can't help."

"THEY DESPISE THE PENNIES OF THE POOR"

He said that the church had discontinued certain of its collections because the people gave only pennies! He thought they should be discouraged in making such small offerings! "They despise the pennies of the poor."

From this very chapel I went down to Baxter Street—not far away—and visited a Catholic Church—the Church of the Most Precious Blood. It is a large new church, with a lively, able priest at the head of it. It is attended exclusively by Italians—the poorest people in the neighborhood, and yet that church has been built complete in fifteen years out of the pennies of poor people, and it is supported to-day by their offerings. I am not here entering into a discussion of the Roman Catholic system; I am merely pointing out that poor people can and do contribute to religious work, when that work really means something to them.

Nor need I make a comparison only with the Roman Catholics. I have a still better example: a Protestant church on the lower West Side, not far from two of Trinity's chapels, St. John's and St. Luke's, and ministering to the same sort of people. I refer to the Spring Street Presbyterian Church, the work of which is like the shadow of a rock in a weary land. The Spring Street Church ministers wholly to wage-earners, the average wage of the membership being less than ten dollars a week—and the highest wage of any member being eighteen dollars a week. While both the Trinity chapels still have a few well-to-do people in their congregations, the Spring

Street Church has none at all. And yet, while Trinity paid last year $20,000 to operate St. John's Chapel, Spring Street Church was wholly self-supporting. When the Rev. H. Roswell Bates, its minister, went to the church eight years ago, he told the feeble congregation that he would enter the work only upon condition that every expense (including his own salary) was met by the people of the community. The members got together and resolved to work as they never had before. Some of them went without eggs and butter all the first year, others walked to their work to save car fare, in order to help raise the amount necessary. And the church has grown rapidly both in membership and in influence. Last year the congregation contributed $4,900 and maintained an active and enthusiastic work for six hundred and thirty-five members. The church has become a marvelous source of power in the community; everybody works for somebody else; everybody gives, rather than gets. They have now built up a neighborhood Settlement House next the church, where there are many clubs, classes, a kindergarten, a day nursery and the like, largely conducted by volunteer workers. Money from the outside is contributed to help maintain the settlement work, but the church is supported wholly by the congregation.

While the Spring Street Church supports its work for 635 members with $4,900, Trinity pays $20,000 for 487 communicants at St. John's chapel. And this is not making an unfavorable comparison of St. John's as against other Trinity chapels: for the work of St. John's, cost for cost, is probably more profitable than at most of the other chapels. At St. John's the music cost $6,000—more than the entire cost of the work at the Spring Street Church. St. John's has six paid clergymen and lay workers, while the Spring Street Church has three.

STORY OF ST. JOHN'S CHAPEL

In what I have said about St. John's, let me not blame the clergy. They were earnest young men; they had to labor against the paralysis of the Trinity system, and in spite of that they had been broadening their work. They had increased the number of communicants of the chapel, and they had built up guilds and classes of various sorts. I wish to make this point particularly, because I come now to the story of St. John's Chapel. As every one knows, Trinity attempted to close St. John's Chapel in the fall of 1908 and precipitated a storm of agitation.

St. John's Chapel is one of the oldest churches in New York; a beautiful building, once in a fashionable quarter of the city, now surrounded by warehouses and tenements. One Sunday in November, 1908, the curate in charge read a notice from the pulpit to the effect that the vestry had ordered the church closed on February first, and that the congregation would be expected to attend St. Luke's Chapel—a mile further north. It came like a thunderbolt out of a clear sky. Trinity corporation, probably looking about to reduce expenses, had thus, by executive order, cut off a chapel with four hundred and eighty-seven communicants, and a Sunday School of three hundred and twenty-one members, in a neighborhood where many of its tenements were located, and from which it drew nearly all of its income. Its excuse was that the work, considering the changing character of the neighborhood, and the influx of foreigners, no longer paid, that the money could be better expended elsewhere (perhaps on the rich churches uptown), that the congregation of St. John's could easily go to St. Luke's and the work of both chapels could go forward together.

A storm of protest at once arose. A petition from the members of St. John's was presented to the vestry respectfully asking that their committee be granted a hearing and the St. John's Chapel be not closed. It was ignored. The members then presented a second petition, in which they said:

"The request accompanying our former petition, that a committee appointed by the members of St. John's chapel be granted a hearing, has been ignored. We have no representative on the vestry. Years ago, five of the vestrymen were members of St. John's Chapel, but owing to the movement of wealthy people to uptown districts, the vestry seems now to be largely selected from members of the Chapel of St. Agnes, located on West Ninety-second Street, leaving us with no representation. Bishop Potter, a friend of St. John's Chapel, and the late Rector, the Rev. Dr. Dix, who dearly loved it, are no longer with us; and our beloved Vicar, who has ministered to us for more than thirty years, is absent on account of ill-health. The present rector has been in the city of New York but a few years, during which period he has resided in the upper part of the city; and we believe he has not had occasion to become familiar with conditions existing in the neighborhood of St. John's Chapel. Since he has been rector we have not seen him at any of the services of St. John's Chapel, and the first and only communication we have received from him was the notice which was read from the pulpit that the doors of the church would be closed February first, 1909."

AN APPEAL TO THE BISHOP

The committee also appealed to the Bishop of the Diocese, Bishop Greer, and finally offered on behalf of the congregation to take over and support the church themselves. Still Trinity corporation did not budge.

Then the public began to stir. A notable memorial was presented to the vestry on behalf of St. John's; it was signed by the most distinguished citizens of New York, among them President Roosevelt, Secretary Root, Mayor McClellan, Ex-Mayor Seth Low, Joseph H. Choate and others.

Other memorials were presented by the New York Art Commission and the Fine Arts' League. The Municipal Art Commission asked "respectfully and earnestly" that the corporation might further consider "whether in the public interest St. John's Chapel, as a landmark of the early religious and social life of the city, and as a work of art, might not be permanently preserved and maintained as a place of worship."

One of the most impressive and powerful appeals was a poem written for the New York *Evening Post* by the late Richard Watson Gilder. It was called "Lines on the Proposed Demolition of St. John's Chapel." It is published here:

LINES ON THE PROPOSED DEMOLITION
OF ST. JOHN'S CHAPEL

By Richard Watson Gilder

Guardians of a holy trust
Who, in your rotting tenements,
Housed the people, till the offense
Rose to the Heaven of the Just—
Guardians of an ancient trust
Who, lately, from these little ones
Dashed the cup of water; now
Bind new laurels to your brow,
Fling to earth these sacred stones,
Give the altar to the dust!
Here the poor and friendless come—
Desolate the templed home
Of the friendless and the poor,
That your laurels may be sure!
Here beside the frowning walls
Where no more the wood-bird calls,
Where once the little children played,
Whose paradise ye have betrayed,
Here let the temple low be laid,
Here bring the altar to the dust—
Guardians of a holy trust!

And finally, Trinity spoke. Three defensive statements were made, one by Trinity corporation itself, one by Bishop Greer, and one by Dr. Huntington, rector of Grace Church. It is significant that neither the Bishop nor Dr. Huntington had ever investigated the condition of the people of St. John's nor the work being done there, yet they defended the action of

Trinity as being "in the interests of the Christian religion," to quote from Dr. Huntington. The *Churchman* says of these three statements:

"But the distinguishing characteristic of the three statements is that nothing is said of the people in St. John's parish, of their rights, of their hopes or of their souls. Even the appeals that have been made in their behalf have been ignored. What religion means under such conditions, the public are left to guess."

Not having investigated, neither these men nor the Rector of Trinity, could know the real love with which many of the members of St. John's clung to their chapel. Here is the brief story of one of the communicants:

"I have been a regular member and contributor of St. John's Chapel, in good standing, for more than twenty-five years. The religious life largely of my immediate family has been connected with St. John's Chapel. My only brother was confirmed there and he died twenty-two years ago and his funeral services were held there. My sister was a communicant at St. John's Chapel; she was confirmed there, and was married in that church. My mother was confirmed there; she died about fourteen years ago, and her funeral services, also, were held in that church. In that church I met my wife, who was baptized and confirmed there, and our marriage ceremony was performed in that church, and our two children have been baptized there, and one of them, my boy, is at present a choir-boy in St. John's Chapel. My wife and I have both taught Sunday School in St. John's Chapel, and my wife is now and has been for some time a delegate to St. Augustine's League from that chapel."

The plain fact is that Trinity did not care for the people. And it was not really until the agitation had grown to such an extent that legislative and judicial action were threatened that Trinity began to move. Then it was too late to prevent the whole matter from being carried into the courts. The people of St. John's based their case on the declaration that under the charter of 1814 they were voters in Trinity parish and that the closing of St. John's and the relegation of the membership to the free-mission chapel of St. Luke's deprived them of their franchise rights, and they demanded redress from the courts. A temporary injunction was immediately issued ordering Trinity to keep St. John's Chapel open for religious services. The litigation, however, is likely to be long continued and very bitter. On the side of the people the cost of the cases will have to be raised by general subscription where money is not plentiful; but it will cost the vestrymen personally not one cent; they will use the ready money of the church— which comes out of the rentals from the very neighborhood served by St. John's Chapel. Their chief lawyer is himself a vestryman, paid by the vestry.

RESULTS OF THE AGITATION AGAINST TRINITY

Several excellent results, however, have come out of the agitation. First, Trinity corporation has shown the first evidence in its history that it feels any responsibility to the public. It has issued a public report defending its position in closing St. John's Chapel, and giving its first financial statement in over fifty years. It has also declared its purpose of doing away with the old tenements as rapidly as possible and improving the land with new buildings. It has also decided to open St. John's Chapel on week-days, and provide noon revival services for the people of the neighborhood.

I have talked with many of the people connected with Trinity in various capacities. I found them all disturbed— indeed, astonished, perplexed, and unable to account for the extent and violence of the public agitation. One of them said it was "jealousy of the wealth of Trinity"; another blamed the clergy of St. John's; another laid it up to "agitators." They did not seem to understand, to have any grasp of the new spiritual impulses which are permeating our common life—the new democracy, if you will—and they are yielding just as they have in the past, grudgingly, without vision. They are paralyzed by their own wealth and the pride of their traditions. They would like to improve things—a little—but they do not see that the whole aristocratic, feudalistic system upon which they are operating belongs to a past age, that religion is not charity, but justice and brotherly love. They are not ready to make the self-sacrifice necessary, in the highest sense, to save the life of their church.

It is, indeed, not at all surprising to hear the clergymen of rich and doctrine-bound churches strike the note of disheartenment. They themselves often work hard, with a passionate earnestness of devotion, but they do not get spiritual results. The church is not holding its own; people avoid the church. The clergy wonder why; they ask vainly, "What is the matter with the church?" It even seems to some of them that religion itself is decaying.

But religion is not decaying; it is only the church. More religion is to be found in our life to-day than ever before, more hearts respond to its inspiration; it is found among common men and women everywhere. As ever, it demands, not observances, nor doctrines, nor a habitation in magnificent temples—but self-sacrifice and a contrite heart.

Thus earnest men in Trinity find their efforts paralyzed by wealth and tradition. They are very far away from life, these poor men of Trinity; they have not felt the thrill and inspiration of the new time. By and by they will find it impossible to listen to beautiful and costly music, which they have not paid for, without thinking of the people of the tenements, and of the men and women and the little children there who must work long hours at low wages, and out of whose small earnings comes the money to pay for that music. And they will see the absurdity of taking from the people of the tenements and giving nothing back—save empty homilies. "It will become a matter of wonder that there should ever have existed those who thought it admirable to enjoy without working, at the expense of others, who worked without enjoying."

PART THREE

TRANSPLANTED RURAL CHURCHES

7. THE OLD FAITH REASSERTED

Cleansed by the Blood, 1882

BY LEWIS R. DUNN

---

*The strength of the evangelical persuasion that many country
people brought with them to the city was the absolute conviction that the duty of the churches was simply to preach
"Christ and Him Crucified." Dunn (1822–1898), a Methodist
minister of the Newark Conference, served his people by occasional forays against such threats as Popery and Free Thought.
But his greatest contribution was the eloquence with which he
inveighed against the "wisdom" of the world, and with which
he hailed the "folly" of the Cross. He used no metaphors to
explain away the historical fact that Christ had shed his blood
for mankind. (Two of his best-known sermons were "The Blood
and the Testimony" and "The Blood-Washed Throng.") It is
characteristic of the kinship between this kind of emphasis
and the growing "Holiness" movements, that an excerpt of
"Cleansed by the Blood" was reprinted in* THE GUIDE TO HOLI-
NESS, 87 *(February, 1891), 34–37. It is also evidence of the alienation city dwellers of rural origin felt for their new surroundings that many of Dunn's sermons were delivered at Camp
Meetings held in places like Round Lake, New York, or Pitman
Grove, New Jersey, or Vermilion, Ohio.*

From Lewis R. Dunn, *Sermons on the Higher Life* (Cincinnati:
Walden and Stowe, 1882), pp. 68–87.

Text: *"The blood of Jesus Christ his Son cleanseth us from all sin."* I John 1:7.

The words of our text contain one of the most remarkable and, at the same time, one of the most heart-cheering announcements ever made to our sin-stricken humanity. They present before us the only foundation of our hope of pardon, purity, and eternal life. All along the ages men have been groaning under the burden and the bondage of sin, and sighing for deliverance from its guilt and power. The earth has been darkened with the smoke of innumerable altars, and crimsoned with the blood of countless victims. But in the midst of this universal unrest this blessed evangel breaks upon our ears. No one can or dares to say, "I have no sin," "I have not sinned." But all can say, "I am redeemed." "There is a fountain of blood in which I can wash away my sin." So these two great facts on the manward side, and these two great facts on the Godward side stand confronting each other: "I have sin;" "I have sinned"—"the blood of Jesus Christ his Son cleanseth us from all sin;" and "if we confess and forsake our sins he is faithful and just to forgive us our sins and to cleanse us from all unrighteousness." Here, then, is the amplest and freest provision for the pardon of our sins and the washing away of our impurities and defilements. These two great facts will now engage our attention: The blood of Christ the Son of God, and its cleansing power.

I. The Blood of Christ.

1. In all the ages the blood of beasts and birds, and especially of men, has been regarded as of peculiar, and, in multitudes of instances, as *of sacred, value.* The blood of the murdered Abel assumed a voice, and called out from the ground for vengeance. In the original grant made to Noah concerning the use of animal food, the eating of blood was expressly forbidden. "But flesh with the life thereof, which is the blood thereof, shall ye not eat." And this command was re-enforced with the most solemn and fearful penalties attached in the

Sinaitic laws. Again, from the very infancy of time the law of blood for blood, and life for life, was a governing principle among the nations. So God speaks of it to his ancient people: "And surely your blood of your lives will I require; at the hand of every beast will I require it, and at the hand of man. At the hand of every man's brother will I require the life of man. Whoso sheddeth man's blood, by man shall his blood be shed." And mark the reason for this: "For in the image of God made he man."

Madame de Stael has well said, "Nothing in effect can obliterate from the soul the idea that there is a mysterious efficacy in the blood of the innocent, and that heaven and earth are moved by it." There seems to be no physiological reason for the forbidding of the use of the blood of birds and beasts, nor is it easy to present clearly a moral reason for it; it is evidently founded upon the idea of the sacredness of blood and its efficacy.

2. This was God's *chosen sign or symbol* in the deliverance of his people from Egyptian bondage. On that dark and terrible night, when the destroying angel was to pass over the doomed land, and there was not to be an Egyptian home but in which there would be one dead, there was only one way of deliverance for Israel. They were ordered, in each family, to slay a lamb without blemish, and to take the blood in a basin and sprinkle it upon the upper door-post and the two side posts of their dwellings. And it was promised to them for a token, that when "I see the blood I will pass over you, and the plague shall not be upon you to destroy you when I smite the land of Egypt." In other words, the blood of the lamb was the redemption of the first-born of Israel. It is in reference to this fact that Paul says: "For even Christ, our Passover, is sacrificed for us."

3. The blood of the victims slain under the Mosaical dispensation was declared to be an *atonement* for the soul. "For the life of the flesh is in the blood, and I have given it unto

you upon the altar to make an atonement for your souls; for it is the blood which maketh atonement for the soul." (Lev. xvii, 11.) This, doubtless, was emblematical of the great fact that the race was to be redeemed by the blood of Christ. So the blood of beasts and birds was kept constantly streaming. It was blood, blood, blood. The altars were constantly flowing with it, and the pavements and walls of the temple were ever crimsoned with it. On the great day of atonement, and of the Passover, as well as at Pentecost, thousands of sheep and oxen were slain, and their blood caught by the priests and poured upon the altar, so that the secret channels, so recently discovered, must have often "gurgled with blood." The apostle tells us, Heb. ix, 18–22: "Neither the first tabernacle was dedicated without blood. Moses took the blood of calves and goats and sprinkled both the book and all the people. He sprinkled with blood the tabernacle and all the vessels of the ministry. And almost all things are by the law purged with blood; and without shedding of blood there is no remission."

Nor was this idea peculiar to the Jews. Nearly all the Ethnic religions were sanguineous. All have demanded sacrifices of animals and birds, and some of men, women, and children. In the Egyptian mythology it is said that "the sun-god mutilated himself, and that from the stream of his blood he created all things." It is said of Belus, the supreme deity of the Babylonians, that he "cut off his own head that the blood flowing from it might be mixed with the dust out of which men were to be formed." The Carthaginians, at the crisis of their struggle with Rome, devoted to the anger of their gods four hundred of the sons of their principal nobles. Thus human sacrifices, which originated among the Semitic nations, passed among the Greeks and other peoples. Human sacrifices were not abolished from Rome until about 400 B. C. We all know that the religion of the Aztecs demanded that human hearts, taken dexterously from the breasts of living human beings, should be laid upon the altar of their war-god. With these general facts before us, I advance to consider

4. The historical fact that *Christ shed his blood in Geth-semane and on Calvary,* and the evangelical *interpretation* of that fact. The statement is made in the Gospels that Christ, in the garden, "being in an agony, his sweat was, as it were, great drops of blood falling down to the ground;" that is, his sweat was tinged and colored with his blood. So in Pilate's court-yard, under the scourging, he must have lost much blood. It doubtless trickled down his face when the thorny crown was pressed upon his brow. So when the spikes were driven through his hands and feet, on the cross, the blood must have flowed freely. And when the soldier pierced his side, "forthwith came out blood and water." Thus the fact is most clearly as well as inferentially stated, that Christ's blood was shed.

Now the inquiry arises, Why was his blood shed? And the whole of revelation is employed in answering it. It says that it was *necessary;* made necessary on account of sin. So the divine ordination was that "without shedding of blood there is no remission." And the Son of God declared, "The Son of man must suffer many things and be put to death."

Again, Christ's act was *voluntary.* He declared, "I have power to lay down my life, and I have power to take it again." And when he was arrested by the temple guard he said to his over-zealous disciple, "Thinkest thou that I can not now pray to my Father, and he shall presently give me more than twelve legions of angels?" Thus it will be readily seen that Christ might have prevented his death if he had chosen so to do. But he voluntarily "humbled himself and became obedient unto death, even the death of the cross." Furthermore, before he entered upon his work Christ clearly foresaw the sufferings and death he must endure. And these things were present to his mind during every period of his ministry. All along his ministry he told his disciples what he must suffer. At the Last Supper he said, "This cup is my blood of the New Testament, shed for many for the remission of sins." He said to the Jewish people, "And I, if I be lifted up, will draw all men unto me."

And the evangelist explains by saying, "This he said, signifying by what death he should die." Here, then, in brief is the fact as presented before us in the Gospel.

But this is not all. If Christ's death was voluntary, it was either a *suicide* or a *sacrifice*. No man has the right voluntarily to give up his life when he has the power to prevent its destruction, unless it is done vicariously, for his country, his family, his friends, or in the interests of humanity. Now it is clearly evident that Christ had the power to prevent his death. But he did not do it. His Father did not do it. True, he prayed in Gethsemane, "If it be possible, let this cup pass from me." Thrice that prayer was uttered, but there was no response. The heavens were silent to his plea. Did I say there was no response? Yes, there was an angel sent from heaven to strengthen him, not to take away the cup, but to help him drink it. Then, on the cross, he cried out, "My God! my God! why hast thou forsaken me?" And yet, weak, faint, feeble, dying, no response was made to that piteous cry. Wonderful scene! Seemingly a strange paradox! He died voluntarily, and yet he *must* die. If his death, then, was not that of a suicide, it was a vicarious *sacrifice*. So God's Word declares it to be a sacrifice for the sins of the world.

All this is in accordance with the teachings of the Pauline, Petrine, and Johannic epistles. Paul says, "In whom we have redemption through his blood, even the forgiveness of sins." "Whom God hath set forth to be a propitiation through faith in his blood." He speaks also of the "Church of God, which he hath purchased with his own blood." John says, in the text, "The blood of Jesus Christ his Son cleanseth us from all sin." In writing from Patmos he breaks forth in the grand anthem of praise: "Unto Him that loved us and washed us from our sins in his own blood." He also represents to us the whole of the Church triumphant as singing, "Thou wast slain and hast redeemed us to God by thy blood." And Peter says, "Ye were not redeemed with corruptible things, as silver and gold, but with the precious blood of Christ, as of a lamb without blemish and without spot."

Thus we see that the salvation, the cleansing from all sin, is not because of Christ's teachings or of his spotless example or his wonderful life or his more wonderful death, that death being considered simply as that of a martyr, but *by his blood.* Well does Krummacher ask: "What avails the blood of Christ?" "It avails," he answers, "what mountains of good works heaped up by us, what columns of the incense of prayer, curling up from our lips toward heaven, and what streams of tears of penitence gushing from our eyelids, never could avail: 'The blood of Jesus Christ his Son cleanseth us from all sin.' One will say: "Helps us to cleanse ourselves, perhaps?" No, cleanseth us. "Furnishes the motive and the obligation for us to cleanse ourselves?" No; it *cleanseth* us. 'Cleanseth us from the desire to sin?' No, cleanseth us from *sin* itself. "Cleanseth us from the sin of inactivity in the work of personal improvement?" No; from *all* sin. "But do you say the blood does this?" Yes, the blood. "The doctrine of Christ you must mean?" No, his *blood.* "His example it is?" His blood, *his blood.*

II. We now come to the inquiry, "Why is it said that *this blood has such cleansing power?*" I answer:

1. Because it is *something more valuable* and *efficacious* than the sacrifices of the law, or the blood of a mere man. So the text says. It is "the blood of Jesus Christ, his Son." Hence it is the blood of a divine being. Indeed, in a most important sense, it was divine blood. The union of the Godhead with the humanity of Christ stamped his blood with an infinite merit and value. The apostle presents the contrast between the sacrifices of the law and the sacrifice of Christ in the most vivid manner when he says: "For if the blood of bulls and goats and the ashes of a heifer, sprinkling the unclean, sanctifieth to the purifying of the flesh; how much more shall the blood of Christ, who through the Eternal Spirit offered himself without spot to God, purge your conscience?" What comparison is there

between the blood of the lambs offered in daily sacrifice and "the Lamb of God, who taketh away the sin of the world?" All the blood poured upon Jewish altars could not take away sin; but Jesus' blood cleanseth from all sin.

2. It has made provision whereby all men may be *completely purified* from their sin and guilt. The provision is of infinite merit, sufficient for a universe of sinners.

If sinners were more in number than sands upon the shores of the ocean, or leaves on the trees of the forest, or blades of grass on hill-top or meadow, or atoms in the universe, here is blood of sufficient power to cleanse them all and save them all. O, there is no limit to the extent or to the efficacy of the provision! No one of all the race is excluded. All may come to this fountain of blood, and wash away all their sins.

But it is objected to this that "our religion is a sanguineous religion, and hence an offense to all intelligent persons." Atheists and skeptics of every grade join in this cry. And freereligionists, within the last quarter of a century, have uttered the loudest and most vehement cries against it. One of their journals, speaking of a collection of evangelical hymns—and especially of that grand hymn of Cowper's, "There is a fountain filled with blood"—says: "We like every thing about the book but the theology, which is stuffed into the hymns in all possible ways, and which sticks out in the most offensive forms, even where we least expect it. Scores of hymns are so saturated with 'the blood of Christ' that the sanguineous currents seem to drip into every line." Mr. Beecher, who to all intents and purposes is on the same line with them, said not long ago of the language of the text: "That thought of blood never did me the least good in the world. [I'm afraid it never did.] The idea of blood is not to my taste—it pertains to the old sacrifices; the sheep or animal was killed, and priest, people, and every thing was spattered with the blood. I do not use that text." It is a pity he does not.

Again, it is asked: "What connection is there between the

blood of Christ and the cleansing of the soul from sin and guilt?" "How does the blood of Christ cleanse from all sin?" Has it never occurred to those who ask these questions that similar language is often employed in reference to the interests of the Church and the nation? How often is it said, "The blood of the martyrs is the seed of the Church"? When Kossuth was in this country he said, in one of his addresses, "It has always been the fate of liberty to be baptized in blood." We speak frequently that "the price paid for liberty, by which freedom from tyranny, oppression, and bondage is enjoyed, is blood." We say that our Revolutionary fathers bought our liberties with their blood, and that our soil is consecrated to liberty by that blood. More appropriate still is the language we use when we say that "the foul blot of slavery was washed from our national escutcheon by the blood of hundreds of thousands of our brothers, who were slain in the recent war of the Rebellion." If, then, we may justly and truly say that the blood of our forefathers bought our liberties; and that the blood of our sons and brothers washed out the deep and damning blot of slavery from our land, why should it be thought so strange if the Word of God declares it, and we love to repeat it in sermon and in song: "The blood of Jesus cleanseth us from all sin?"

Is it not true that the history of every nation is written in blood? that the literature of every nation is steeped in blood? that the national songs of every land are vocal with the cry of blood? Thus the great law of vicarious suffering and sacrifice is as old as the world, and as universal as our humanity. And in all these instances referred to the idea is that it was because blood was shed that nations are free; that foul, loathsome stains were washed out by it; and that richest blessings are enjoyed because it was shed. So the Word of God, from its Genesis to its Apocalypse, is ever speaking of blood. And it is everywhere said, in type and symbol, in sacrifice and Gospel, that, because Christ shed his blood, not only are pardon and salvation proffered, but actually enjoyed; that not only are defilement and impurity provisionally washed away by the shedding of his blood, but actually cleansed by the application of that blood, by faith on the part of the sinner as the instrument, and by the Holy Ghost as the almighty and efficient agent.

The Word of God tells us of the seven-fold value of this blood. We have redemption in it; we are justified by it; we are washed from our sins in it; we are brought nigh to God by it; Christ has made peace by his blood; he sanctifies the people with it; and the saints overcome by it.

But the text further says:

3. It cleanseth from *all sin.* Various are the kinds as well as the degrees of sin. There is original and actual sin. There are aggravated and presumptuous sins. There are sins of ignorance and sloth. And there are secret and open sins. So with the degrees of sin. They are multiplied. There are great and small sins. There are the openly wicked, and the mere moral, or ungodly man. There are sins which strike terror into a community, and the world shudders at their atrocity; there are others which do not lie so heavily upon the conscience, and do not so seriously affect our fellows. But all willful sin is damning. "The soul that sinneth, it shall die." But here is a provision for all sin. No spot is so deep, or dark, or loathsome, but this blood can wash it all away. Even the blood-stains upon the hand of a Macbeth—which "all great Neptune's ocean" could not wash away, but which, itself, would "incarnadine all the multitudinous seas, and make the green, one red"—this blood of Jesus could wash away.

> If all the sins which men have done,
>   In thought, in will, in word, or deed,
> Since worlds were made, or time begun,
>   Were laid on one poor sinner's head,
> The stream of Jesus' precious blood
> Could wash away the dreadful load.

4. The provision is not only *ample and free,* it is also *present.* It "cleanseth us." This is an ever-present act. It does not say, *hath* cleansed us, or *will* cleanse us; but *cleanseth* us. It is not a single completed act, to last for a life-time, as the act of our justification, resulting from the atonement; but a continuous act—daily, hourly, momentarily cleansing. Frances Ridley Havergal says: "It was that one word, 'cleanseth,' which opened the door of hope and joy to me. I had never seen the force of the tense before, a continual present, always a present tense, not a present which the next moment becomes a past. It goes on cleansing, and I have no words to tell how my heart rejoices in it. Not a coming to be cleansed in the fountain only; but a remaining in the fountain, so that it may and can go on cleansing. One of the intensest moments of my life was when I saw the force of that word, 'cleanseth.'"

5. *The conditions* of the reception of this cleansing are presented before us in this verse: "If we walk in the light, as he is in the light." It is only the justified and regenerated believer who can thus walk in the light of God, in the light of his favor, in the light of his reconciled countenance. While thus walking in the light there is a revelation to our consciousness of the remains of sin in our hearts, of existing evils from which we are not yet fully saved. And not only so, there comes to us, through the teachings of the Word and the illumination of the Holy Spirit, a revelation of our privilege in Christ Jesus. Thus both the necessity and the possibility of being cleansed from all sin are clearly shown to us. If, under these revealings, the soul will rise up and lay hold of its privilege, it will know the blessedness of this truth by an experience of it in its consciousness.

Two great benefits of walking in the light are here presented before us:

1. *Fellowship with God.* This may be realized by a regenerate soul, even while struggling against remaining corruptions. These occasion no condemnation while we are longing for de-

liverance from them, and seeking, by the use of all means within our reach, to have them washed away. Our heavenly Father does not withdraw his presence or his favor from these struggling ones. No. He walks with them and talks with them. And the nearer they get to him, and the closer their walk is with him the more do they see the holiness of his character and the loathsomeness and vileness of their own. The light is thus revealing, and if we are walking in it how soon it will lead us to the opened fountain where sin is all washed away. It is the greatest of all follies to lower the standard of justifying and regenerating grace in order to exalt that of heart-purity. No, the higher the soul rises in these conditions, the more fully it walks with God, the nearer it is to the conscious realization of the cleansing from all sin. And how blessed this fellowship is, even in the regenerate soul, no tongue can tell, no language can express.

2. It is only while walking in the light and having fellowship with God that this cleansing of the blood *can be fully realized.* No unpardoned sinner can experience this; no backslidden professor can come into this condition at once. There are certain conditions which must exist before this is enjoyed. An unjustified man does not, can not, walk in the light of God; a backslider in heart or in life can not thus walk. The sinner must be pardoned and regenerated, and the backslider must be thoroughly reclaimed before the cleansing from *all* sin is possible.

That this state is clearly distinct from that of justification and regeneration is evident, according to the opinions of the most learned interpreters. Alford says: "This [being cleansed from all sin] is plainly distinguished from the forgiveness of sins, distinguished as a further process, as, in a word, sanctification, distinct from justification." Dr. Ebrard says: "The correct interpretation of the Greek word translated 'cleanseth,' by which it is understood to refer to the sanctifying efficacy of the blood of Christ, has of late been generally admitted. Cleansing must, therefore," he says, after giving several reasons for this view, "signify here the sanctifying activity of God dwelling in the believer, and this view is confirmed by the additional clause, 'from all sin.'" Lange says: "The Greek word translated 'cleanseth' can not refer to forgiveness of sins, for in verse 9 it is expressly distinguished from it. The apostle speaks here not of the remission of the penalty of sin, of the removal of guilt, but of the removal of sin itself, of being made free from sin. The subject-matter is sanctification, not justification or regeneration." Dr. Düesterdick says: "From another point of view the death of Christ is the victory over sin itself, and his blood is the purifying factor by which sin itself, still dwelling in those who have been justified, is to be washed away."

These quotations might be multiplied, and no doubt can be entertained of the correctness of these interpretations. Alford adds to the words already quoted from him: "This meaning, however much it may be supposed that justification is implied or presupposed, must be held fast here." And here we propose to hold fast. To this Mr. Wesley and the greatest intellects that have been associated with his societies have held fast. And it is only by holding fast here that any Church can lay full claim to having and teaching apostolical doctrine.

The cleansing from all sin, then, is sanctification, is purity, is holiness, and is the privilege of every believer *walking in the light of God*. This is the condition of faith for this purity, and this purity is the condition of oneness with the Father and his Son Jesus Christ, and with the whole body of believers in Christ. The rule in the Church of God is, and will be, the more heart-cleansing, the more unity. Further, while the word "cleanseth" may, and evidently does, mean an on-going process, it also clearly means a *present* process. It cleanseth *now*. This is the great fact which faith is to grasp. If the soul is now walking in the light and longing to be cleansed from all sin it may now believe this fact and realize it in the depths of its consciousness just as clearly, aye, and even more so, as it realized forgiveness of sins when it first believed in Christ for pardon. There is no room for ambiguity or equivocalness here. It is just as true as that God lives and that Christ has died. And when once this fact is grasped it is so easy afterwards to believe and realize it. It also brings great relief to the mind to know that the same blood which cleanseth when we believe, *keeps* us clean by continuance in believing. As long as we breathe we live; as long as we believe we are cleansed.

We shall never see the period when we shall not need the blood. We need it every day, hour, and moment of our earthly history. When we are dying, and through all eternity, our purity, our blessedness, will be connected with the blood of Christ. Saints, blood-washed and glorified before the throne, amid the effulgent glories of the heavenly world, never forget two great facts: first, that they have sinned; and, secondly, that the blood of Christ has cleansed them from all their sins. This is the burden of the song which they sing forever before the throne.

This is the song of the ages, and will be the song of eternity. Christ, "the lamb slain," shedding his blood "from the foundation of the world." This is "salvation's source" always. Patriarchs, prophets, priests, and kings, apostles and martyrs, saints of all ages, are saved through the blood. Not saved because they had not sinned, because they were not depraved, weak, sinful men, but saved from their sins through the blood of the Lamb. And so they all join in this universal song. This chord may be "struck by the plectrum year after year, century after century, from eternity to eternity, and its vibrations will ever be resonant and thrilling, yet sweet and Æolian." No age bounds this provision. No condition of color, clime, language, or nationality is a barrier to its realization. Everywhere, at all periods, among all classes, immortal beings may be cleansed by this blood and become witnesses of its cleansing power. The witnesses of this fact are, indeed, multiplying. The song is even now arising from all parts of the earth. The heaven of heavens is ringing with the shout. Thus the universe is vocal with it. So John in vision heard it. "I beheld and I heard the voice of many angels round about the throne and the living ones and the elders, and the number of them was ten thousand times ten thousand, and thousands of thousands, saying, with a loud voice, Worthy is the Lamb that was slain to receive power and riches and wisdom and strength and honor and glory and blessing. And every creature which is in heaven and on the earth and under the earth, and such as are in the sea, and all that are in them, heard I saying, Blessing and honor and glory and power be unto Him that sitteth upon the throne, and unto the Lamb forever and ever."

> O may we bear some humble part
>   In that immortal song;
> Wonder and joy shall tune our heart,
>   And love command our tongue.

But if we would join that song we must experimentally know the fact which it celebrates. We read of the cleansing power of this blood, our songs of praise are burdened with it, we pray that we may enjoy it, but we fail to believe, with an appropriating faith, in the cleansing power. Many think the disease of their heart is so obstinate, their condition so peculiar, their surroundings so adverse, that they can not enjoy continuously this cleansing of the blood. But it is idle and vain to laud the efficacy and power of a medicine which is always baffled by the power or obstinacy of the disease. No assertion in song or sermon or prayer will be credited which acknowledges that on account of our weakness, frailties, or sins, the cleansing blood must fail to make us holy. Put that blood to the test to-day. *Now,* while you read, and you will feel, you will know how powerful it is to cleanse. Then you will join the song of the Church on earth. "Unto Him that loved us and washed us from our sins in his own blood, and hath made us kings and priests unto his God and Father; to him be the glory and the dominion forever and ever. Amen."

8. THE GHETTO CONGREGATIONS

OF THE IMMIGRANTS

The Question of Nationality, 1889

BY ANTON H. WALBURG

When the first representatives of a European immigrant group arrived in an American city, they frequently disappeared into the various "American" churches to be found there, or else lapsed into churchlessness. But after a sizable contingent had come, they usually founded a congregation of their own. Not just liturgy and theology, but custom and, above all, language reinforced a cherished sense of continuity with the past. American cities of the late nineteenth century were stippled with foreign congregations—Norwegian Lutheran, German Baptist, Polish Catholic, and Lithuanian Jewish, for example.

Most American churchmen were pleased at first by a development which promised at once to satisfy the immigrants and to free "native" churches from the obligation of accommodating strange and uncouth newcomers. Even Catholic bishops, committed to a system of territorial parishes, usually made efforts to create national parishes in which all the Poles, or Germans, or French of the city might gather. In return, ethnic

---

From Anton H. Walburg, *The Question of Nationality in Its Relation to the Catholic Church in the United States* (Cincinnati: Herder, 1889.)

*leaders came to believe that the religion of their group de-
pended upon the continuing segregation of their congregations. Though it now seems ironic that it was possible to find
in a single city Lutherans, Catholics, and Jews all arguing,
for example, that the true faith could be expressed only in
German, there was nothing fanciful in the perception that the
bonds holding their congregations together were as much cultural as religious.*

*Still, the situation of these congregations was inherently
unstable. As new immigrant groups arrived, an ethnic church—
say a German Catholic parish—might be faced with demands
to provide at least some services in Polish or Italian. Even
more ominously, toward the end of the century voices began
to be heard contending that Catholicism, or Lutheranism, or
Judaism would never really prosper in America, and certainly
would never meet the challenge of the cities, unless they re-
nounced their self-segregation and "Americanized" their congregational life. Not surprisingly, the ethnic churches did not
take kindly to such demands.*

*Anton H. Walburg (1840–1910) was a Roman Catholic priest,
pastor of St. Augustine's Church in Cincinnati, the city where he
had been brought up. Colman Barry's* THE CATHOLIC CHURCH
AND GERMAN AMERICANS *(Washington: Catholic University
Press, 1953) describes the sharpening antipathies between German Catholics and a group of Irish-American Catholics who
gloried in the title of "Americanists." Walburg was by inclination a moderate, and he did his best in* THE QUESTION OF NA-
TIONALITY *to find middle ground. Willy-nilly, however, his
pamphlet testifies to the passionate hostility of ethnic congregations to proposals to renounce the consolations of the ghetto.*

The founders of our government made this country a home
and an asylum for the poor and the oppressed of all nations.

Immigration was invited, the boon of citizenship was extended to all, and foreigners shared equal rights and privileges with the resident or native population. In consequence there was a vast influx of foreigners into this country; and the foreigners brought with them their languages, and their national tastes, prejudices and usages. It was impossible for them to divest themselves at once of their national peculiarities, to jump into the American nationality, and to become thorough, full-fledged Americans immediately. They naturally retained, and, in some measure, tried to perpetuate, their distinctive national characteristics. . . .

The Germans are naturally a religious people. Even the infidel and indifferentist must admit that Christianity has struck deep in the German heart and woven itself into the inner life of the nation as one of its essential and most influential principles. The genius and the temperament of the German nationality have a decidedly religious tendency, and there is perhaps no nation so religiously inclined as is the German. . . .

The faith of the Catholic Germans shone with such undiminished lustre in all the trials and persecutions they suffered in the last century, that they can truly be said to belong to the best Catholics of the world. . . .

It was fortunate that, at an early date, a large German immigration set in to the United States, which furnished such excellent material to the young and growing Church in America. These German immigrants were poor and destitute, ignorant of the language of the country. It was a hard struggle to support themselves and their families, yet they saved from their scanty earnings and denied themselves the necessaries of life to build churches and schools. With indomitable determination and perseverance they overcame all obstacles until their efforts were crowned with success. The hardships, the sufferings, the privations they endured in accomplishing this, attest the sincerity of their faith and their devotion to religion. The seed sown amid such unremitting care and ceaseless toil, produced an abundant, glorious harvest. There are at present in this country 1,500,000 German Catholics, 2,100 priests, 1,200 churches, and 145,000 children attending the German Parochial Schools. One of these schools, St. Joseph's School of Cincinnati, O., has sent out the large number of thirty-seven priests. It can be said without fear of successful contradiction, that this grand record can not be excelled by any other school in the United States. When the writer of this, who claims the distinction of being the first native of German descent in this city who was called to the holy priesthood, attended this school, all branches, excepting Geography and English Reading, were taught in the German language. The present pastor, who has been there nearly forty years, can not speak a correct English sentence. . . . Can any Catholic say, Cut down this tree laden with the richest fruit and engraft on it the withered, distorted sprig of Americanism? Great God! . . . Should he not rather say, Make these schools more intensely, thoroughly German, cultivate this soil if you wish to build up the Church in America? . . .

With regard to Americanism we make a distinction. There is a true and a false Americanism. . . . As virtue is the principle, and the chief support of a Republic, true Americanism aids and encourages whatever promotes the growth of virtue and morality. It makes no distinction between natives and foreigners, considering all born free and equal, all entitled to the enjoyment of life, liberty, and happiness, and extends the hand of welcome to all nations. There is an analogy between true Americanism and the Catholic Church. She, too, invites all to enter her fold, is established for all nations, and all times, and makes no distinction of color, rank, condition, or nationality. . . .

The American nationality, properly so-called, is the Anglo-Saxon or the Anglo-American nationality, the descendants of early settlers who came from England. . . . Although the Irish, the German, and other nationalities, proved to be valuable accessions to our population, yet our forefathers were English, and the rank and position we hold among nations is due to the Anglo-American nationality, which is therefore entitled to the honor and glory of being called the American nationality. . . .

Nevertheless the American nationality, when tried by the test of true Americanism, will in many respects be found wanting. It is often the hotbed of fanaticism, intolerance, and radical, ultra views on matters of politics and religion. All the vagaries of spiritualism, Mormonism, free-loveism, prohibition, infidelity, and materialism, generally breed in the American nationality. Here, also, we find dissimulation and hypocrisy. While the Irishman will get drunk and engage in an open street fight, and the German drink his beer in a public beer-garden, the American, pretending to be a total abstainer, takes his strong drink secretly and sleeps it off on a sofa or in a club-room. Who are trusted employees, the public officers, that enjoyed the unlimited confidence of the people, and turned out to be hypocrites, impostors, and betrayers of trusts? As a rule they are not Irish or Germans, but Americans. Who are the devotees at the shrine of mammon? Who compose the syndicates, trusts, corporations, pools, and those huge monopolies that reach their tentacles over the nation, grinding down the poor and fattening in immense wealth? They are not Germans or Irish, but Americans. Who are the wild and reckless bank speculators, the forgers, the gamblers, and the defaulting officials? They are not Irish or Germans, but Americans. Read the list of the refugees to Canada and you will find it made up of American names. We meet here also all species of refined wickedness. The educated villain, the expert burglar, the cool, calculating, deliberate criminal, generally belongs to the American nationality. Where the foreigners are corrupt they have in a great measure been corrupted by the example of Americans. A republic that is not based upon morality and religion, where virtue is depressed, is ripe for an ignoble grave.

The Anglo-Saxon nationality has always been in England

and in this country the bulwark of Protestantism and the main-stay of the enemies of the faith. It is so puffed up with spiritual pride, so steeped in materialism, that it is callous, and imper-vious to the spirit and the doctrines of the Catholic religion. It is true there are eminent converts in England and a few in this country; but they have no followers; the bulk of the people are as remote as ever from entering the Church. . . . Religion seems to make no impression upon them; they are as hostile as ever to the Church, and, though they perhaps wish it well as doing its share to keep the turbulent foreign element in check, they have not the remotest idea of becoming Catholics themselves. And now we are asked to assimilate with this ele-ment, to adopt its usages, customs, feelings, and manners. That can not but prove detrimental to the Church. Are we going to lead our simple, straightforward, honest Germans and Irish into this whirlpool of American life, this element wedded to this world, bent upon riches, upon political distinction, where their consciences will be stifled, their better sentiments trampled under foot?

But, it will be said, religion will keep them from rushing to this end, will sustain them in the path of virtue and rectitude. Nonsense! Denationalization is demoralization. It degrades and debases nature. A foreigner who loses his nationality is in danger of losing his faith and character. When the German immigrant, on arriving in this country, seeks to throw aside his nationality and to become 'quite English you know,' the first word he learns is generally a curse, and the rowdy element is his preference to the sterling qualities of the Puri-tans. . . . It has been observed, that the most noisy, disorderly, unruly class are the native, would-be American, Germans, and often, for that matter, too, the young Catholic Germans. . . .

Protestantism pervades the nature, the character, and the literature of the English language, and greatly impairs its power and fitness for the proper and full expression of Catho-lic thought and feeling. This is illustrated by the use of the second person singular in addressing the Deity. In the German language, for instance, the word *'thou'* is customary between parents and children, and intimate friends, and conveys a meaning of affection and familiar companionship. When the Protestant, who looks upon God as the Supreme Lord and Ruler of the universe, says, *'Thou* great and glorious God,' the phrase is natural and appropriate; but to the Catholic, who conceives God under the sublime and lovely ideal of a good kind father, and Jesus Christ, of a dear friend and brother, the words, 'I love *thee,* O God,' sound strange and unnatural. These words in German convey a depth of feeling which the English language is inadequate to express. And, in praying to the Blessed Virgin, 'We fly to *thee* weeping and sorrowing,' how strained this phrase seems to express our confidence in that motherly love and tenderness, beaming upon us, ready to shield and guard us, and to console our drooping hearts. Let any one, thoroughly conversant with both languages, take, say a chapter of St. Thomas à Kempis, and read the same in English and German, and he will readily perceive from which he derives the greater spiritual satisfaction, unction, and devotion. The English classic writers are Protestant, and our best Catholic writers, who are converts, such as Cardinal Newman, Cardinal Manning, Father Faber, and Dr. Brownson, naturally retain, in the culture of their taste and the formation of their style, a coloring of their early Protestant training.

The Church has made marvelous progress in this country. This has, however, not been brought about by Americanizing the heterogeneous elements of our incoming population, but by sustaining and keeping alive the languages and the nationalities of the foreign elements. Though not so flattering to our vanity it might prove more profitable to us to examine the losses we have sustained instead of rejoicing over the gains we have seemingly made. . . . [Based on estimates of immigration into America] there ought to be about 18,000,000 Irish

Catholics, about one-third of the Germans, say nearly, 5,000,000, Americans, Poles, Italians, etc., 2,000,000,—total 25,000,000.

According to Hoffmann's Directory the number of Catholics for the present year, 1889, is 8,157,676.

This shows a loss of two-thirds of the Catholic population to the faith. The loss of this immense number can, in a great measure, be attributed to the fact that they have been Americanized, that they have lost their nationality, and with their nationality their religion. According to a census gathered by Father Enzleberger, we have 1,500,000 German Catholics, and our loss from the above estimates is therefore 3,500,000.

The comparative census for Cincinnati in the years 1840, 1850, and 1880, is as follows:

	Churches		Population	
	Irish	German	Irish	German
1846	4	3	12,117	25,912
1850	5	7	13,616	30,628
1880	9	21	15,077	46,157

This shows an astonishing increase in the number of German churches and the German Catholic population, which is owing to the fact that the Germans have retained their language and nationality, even though many of them have joined the English-speaking congregations.

A similar result is observed in the German Protestant churches. In the year 1842, a certain Frederick Rammelsberg maintained that the German language would soon die out in this country and that everyone should speak English. He established an English-speaking congregation among the German Lutherans. And what was the result? While his church scarcely survives, the German-speaking Lutheran churches have increased from five at that time to twenty-five at the present time. . . .

Dr. William H. Egle, Historian of Central Pennsylvania, in

his 'Notes and Queries,' gives numerous instances where Irish Catholic families,—even whole Catholic settlements,—forsook their faith, and became Methodists, Baptists, Presbyterians, etc. Further investigation would show that they Americanized, that they were no longer Irish, and therefore no longer Catholics. . . .

From the foregoing we can conclude that religion and nationality go hand in hand, that religion sustains nationality, and nationality is an aid to religion. We have seen, that where the Irish, German, and French were isolated, their language and nationality encouraged and fostered, they were kept true to the faith, and that they generally lost their faith in proportion as they were Americanized. . . .

It is doubtful whether the object of the originators and supporters of the movement to strengthen and perpetuate the German nationality in the Church in this country can be attained. This nationality has deserved well of the Church, dotted the land with churches, schools, and institutions, and is therefore justified in making lawful efforts to prolong its life and maintain its existence. The Germans stand second to none as loyal, faithful, children of the Church, and it seems unjust to reprove them for showing signs of vitality and arousing their energies in the great cause for which they have so successfully labored. When, in the course of time, the German nationality should come to an end, and when its days are numbered by the years that are past, may the children of the American pioneers, who follow them in another, the American nationality, cherish and preserve as the richest legacy, the spiritual title-deed of their holy religion.

No foreign nationality can permanently maintain itself in this country. It is, of course, natural that immigrants should wish to find again their fatherland in this land of their adoption, but they will Americanize in spite of themselves. The American nationality will finally prevail. It assimilates the children of foreigners, and is strengthened by contributions from foreign sources. Foreign nationalities will be absorbed by it and flow in the current of American life.

However, the transition from one nationality to another, is always a dangerous process, and it will not do to hasten it and to force foreigners to Americanize. For the present we should remember that the American nationality counts for little or nothing in the American Church, and if it is ever to be converted, it must be done by the clergy and population already Catholics. The most efficient portion of our Catholic body are of foreign birth and training, and will be for some time to come. However we may work for non-Catholics, we must carry with us the sympathies and affections of the Catholic body. This body is composed of various nationalities with peculiarities of languages, habits, and prejudices. If these are opposed, and the national sensitiveness wounded, they may become irritated and indifferent, and lose their affection for the Church. We cannot move much in advance of the public sentiment of our own body. We must hold a tight rein, check the impatience to Americanize, and, though there may be some wrangling among conflicting nationalities, if we move slowly we will finally land in the American nationality with the Catholic body under full control and faithful to the Church.

The Church is not trammeled by nationalities and is adapted to all nations. She does not take part in the idiosyncracies, in the antagonism and war, of races. All are placed on a footing of equality, and a Hindoo or a Hottentot can be as good a Catholic as a Frenchman or an Italian. The various nationalities, with their differences of race, color, manners, habits and usages, form a beautiful mosaic in her glorious temple.

The American nation is yet to be added as another rich gem in her crown. It is true we are one hundred years old. But what is one hundred years in the life of a nation, or the life of the Church? We are still laying the foundation of national greatness and prosperity; the Church is still sowing the seed that is to penetrate the living mass of American society, and subject it to the truth and sanctity of the Gospel. Let us then continue to sow, it may be in tribulation and sorrow, that future generations may reap in joy a rich and abundant harvest. . . .

PART FOUR

ADAPTATIONS

9. THE NEIGHBORHOOD

CHURCH EULOGIZED

Henry Ward Beecher and His Church, 1867

BY JAMES PARTON

From the perspective of the middle of the twentieth century, it is perhaps hard to think of Brooklyn as a suburb, and of Henry Ward Beecher as a harbinger of a successfully modern Christianity. But in the years just after the Civil War a celebrated biographer and journalist, James Parton (1822–1891), could draw a very sharp contrast between the stultifying trend in downtown churches, and the vigor and promise of Plymouth Church. No doubt Parton was too much the free spirit to typify churchgoers of his time, but his enthusiasm for Beecher's church was echoed by many witnesses.

Is there anything in America more peculiar to America, or more curious in itself, than one of our "fashionable" Protestant churches,—such as we see in New York, on the Fifth Avenue and in the adjacent streets? The lion and the lamb in the Millennium will not lie down together more lovingly than the Church and the World have blended in these singular es-

From James Parton, *Famous Americans of Recent Times* (Boston: Ticknor and Fields, 1868), pp. 347–372.

127

tablishments. We are far from objecting to the coalition, but note it only as something curious, new, and interesting.

We enter an edifice, upon the interior of which the upholsterer and the cabinet-maker have exhausted the resources of their trades. The word "subdued" describes the effect at which those artists have aimed. The woods employed are costly and rich, but usually of a sombre hue, and, though elaborately carved, are frequently unpolished. The light which comes through the stained windows, or through the small diamond panes, is of that description which is eminently the "*dim*, religious." Every part of the floor is thickly carpeted. The pews differ little from sofas, except in being more comfortable, and the cushions for the feet or the knees are as soft as hair and cloth can make them. It is a fashion, at present, to put the organ out of sight, and to have a clock so unobtrusive as not to be observed. Galleries are now viewed with an unfriendly eye by the projectors of churches, and they are going out of use. Everything in the way of conspicuous lighting apparatus, such as the gorgeous and dazzling chandeliers of fifteen years ago, and the translucent globes of later date, is discarded, and an attempt is sometimes made to hide the vulgar fact that the church is ever open in the evening. In a word the design of the fashionable church-builder of the present moment is to produce a richly furnished, quietly adorned, dimly illuminated, ecclesiastical parlor, in which a few hundred ladies and gentlemen, attired in kindred taste, may sit perfectly at their ease, and see no object not in harmony with the scene around them.

To say that the object of these costly and elegant arrangements is to repel poor people would be a calumny. On the contrary, persons who show by their dress and air that they exercise the less remunerative vocations are as politely shown to seats as those who roll up to the door in carriages, and the presence of such persons is desired, and, in many instances, systematically sought. Nevertheless, the poor are repelled. They know they cannot pay their proportion of the expenses of maintaining such establishments, and they do not wish to enjoy what others pay for. Everything in and around the church seems to proclaim it a kind of exclusive ecclesiastical club, designed for the accommodation of persons of ten thousand dollars a year, and upward. Or it is as though the carriages on the Road to Heaven were divided into first-class, second-class, and third-class, and a man either takes the one that accords with his means, or denies himself the advantage of travelling that road, or prefers to trudge along on foot, an independent wayfarer.

It is Sunday morning, and the doors of this beautiful drawing-room are thrown open. Ladies dressed with subdued magnificence glide in, along with some who have not been able to leave at home the showier articles of their wardrobe. Black silk, black velvet, black lace, relieved by intimations of brighter colors, and by gleams from half-hidden jewelry, are the materials most employed. Gentlemen in uniform of black cloth and white linen announce their coming by the creaking of their boots, quenched in the padded carpeting. It cannot be said of these churches, as Mr. Carlyle remarked of certain London ones, that a pistol could be fired into a window across the church without much danger of hitting a Christian. The attendance is not generally very large; but as the audience is evenly distributed over the whole surface, it looks larger than it is. In a commercial city everything is apt to be measured by the commercial standard, and accordingly a church numerically weak, but financially strong, ranks, in the estimation of the town, not according to its number of souls, but its number of dollars. We heard a fine young fellow, last summer, full of zeal for everything high and good, conclude a glowing account of a sermon by saying that it was the direct means of adding to the church a capital of one hundred and seventy-five thousand dollars. He meant nothing low or mercenary; he honestly exulted in the fact that the power and influence attached to the possession of one hundred and seventy-five thousand dollars were thenceforward to be exerted on behalf of objects which he esteemed the highest. If therefore the church before our view cannot boast of a numerous attendance, it more than consoles itself by the reflection, that there are a dozen names of talismanic power in Wall Street on its list of members.

"But suppose the Doctor should leave you?" objected a friend of ours to a trustee, who had been urging him to buy a pew in a fashionable church.

"Well, my dear sir," was the business-like reply; "suppose he should. We should immediately engage the very first talent which money can command."

We can hardly help taking this simple view of things in rich commercial cities. Our worthy trustee merely put the thing on the correct basis. He frankly *said* what every church *does*, ought to do, and must do. He stated a universal fact in the plain and sensible language to which he was accustomed. In the same way these business-like Christians have borrowed the language of the Church, and speak of men who are "good" for a million.

The congregation is assembled. The low mumble of the organ ceases. A female voice rises melodiously above the rustle of dry-goods and the whispers of those who wear them. So sweet and powerful it is, that a stranger might almost suppose it borrowed from the choir of heaven; but the inhabitants of the town recognize it as one they have often heard at concerts or at the opera; and they listen critically, as to a professional performance, which it is. It is well that highly artificial singing prevents the hearer from catching the words of the song; for it *would* have rather an odd effect to hear rendered, in the modern Italian style, such plain straightforward words as these:—

> Can sinners hope for heaven
> Who love this world so well?
> Or dream of future happiness
> While on the road to hell?

The performance, however, is so exquisite that we do not think of these things, but listen in rapture to the voice alone. When the lady has finished her stanza, a noble baritone, also recognized as professional, takes up the strain, and performs a stanza, solo; at the conclusion of which, four voices, in enchanting accord breathe out a third. It is evident that the "first talent that money can command" has been "engaged" for the entertainment of the congregation; and we are not surprised when the information is proudly communicated that the music costs a hundred and twenty dollars per Sunday.

What is very surprising and well worthy of consideration is, that this beautiful music does not "draw." In our rovings about among the noted churches of New York,—of the kind which "engage the first talent that money can command,"—we could never see that the audience was much increased by expensive professional music. On the contrary, we can lay it down as a general rule, that the costlier the music, the smaller is the average attendance. The afternoon service at Trinity Church, for example, is little more than a delightful gratuitous concert of boys, men, and organ; and the spectacle of the altar brilliantly lighted by candles is novel and highly picturesque. The sermon also is of the fashionable length,—twenty minutes; and yet the usual afternoon congregation is about two hundred persons. Those celestial strains of music,—well, they enchant the ear, if the ear happens to be within hearing of them; but somehow they do not furnish a continuous attraction.

When this fine prelude is ended, the minister's part begins; and, unless he is a man of extraordinary bearing and talents, every one present is conscious of a kind of lapse in the tone of the occasion. Genius composed the music; the "first talent" executed it; the performance has thrilled the soul, and exalted expectation; but the voice now heard may be ordinary, and the words uttered may be homely, or even common. No one unaccustomed to the place can help feeling a certain incongruity between the language heard and the scene witnessed. Everything we see is modern; the words we hear are ancient. The preacher speaks of "humble believers," and we look around and ask, Where are they? Are these costly and elegant persons humble believers? Far be it from us to intimate that they are not; we are speaking only of their appearance, and its effect upon a casual beholder. The clergyman reads,

> Come let *us* join in sweet accord,

and straightway four hired performers execute a piece of diffi-cult music to an audience sitting passive. He discourses upon the "pleasures of the world," as being at war with the interests of the soul; and while a severe sentence to this effect is coming from his lips, down the aisle marches the sexton, showing some stranger to a seat, who is a professional master of the revels. He expresses, perchance, a fervent desire that the heathen may be converted to Christianity, and we catch ourselves saying, "Does he mean *this* sort of thing?" When we pronounce the word Christianity, it calls up recollections and associations that do not exactly harmonize with the scene around us. We think rather of the fishermen of Palestine, on the lonely sea-shore; of the hunted fugitives of Italy and Scotland; we think of it as something lowly, and suited to the lowly,—a refuge for the forsaken and the defeated, not the luxury of the rich and the ornament of the strong. It may be an infirmity of our mind; but we experience a certain difficulty in realizing that the sump-tuous and costly apparatus around us has anything in common with what we have been accustomed to think of as Chris-tianity.

Sometimes, the incongruity reaches the point of the ludi-crous. We recently heard a very able and well-intentioned preacher, near the Fifth Avenue, ask the ladies before him whether they were in the habit of speaking to their female attendants about their souls' salvation,—particularly those who dressed their hair. He especially mentioned the hair-dressers; because, as he truly remarked, ladies are accustomed to converse with those *artistes,* during the operation of hair-dressing, on a variety of topics; and the opportunity was excellent to say a word on the one most important. This incident perfectly illustrates what we mean by the seeming incongruity between the ancient cast of doctrine and the modernized people to whom it is preached. We have heard sermons earnestly read, which had nothing in them of the modern spirit, contained not the most distant allusion to modern modes of living and sinning, had no suitableness whatever to the people or the time, and from which everything that could rouse or interest a human soul living on Manhattan Island in the year 1867 seemed to have been purposely pruned away. And perhaps, if a clergyman really has no message to deliver, his best course is to utter a jargon of nothings.

Upon the whole, the impression left upon the mind of the visitor to the fashionable church is, that he has been looking, not upon a living body, but a decorated image.

It may be, however, that the old conception of a Christian church, as the one place where all sorts and conditions of men came together to dwell upon considerations interesting to all equally, is not adapted to modern society, wherein one man differs from another in knowledge even more than a king once differed from a peasant in rank. When all were ignorant, a mass chanted in an unknown tongue, and a short address warning against the only vices known to ignorant people, sufficed for the whole community. But what form of service can be even imagined, that could satisfy Bridget, who cannot read, and her mistress, who comes to church cloyed with the dainties of half a dozen literatures? Who could preach a sermon that would hold attentive the man saturated with Buckle, Mill, Spencer, Thackeray, Emerson, Humboldt, and Agassiz, and the man whose only literary recreation is the dime novel? In the good old times, when terror was latent in every soul, and the preacher had only to deliver a very simple message, pointing out the one way to escape endless torture, a very ordinary mortal could arrest and retain attention. But this resource is gone forever, and the modern preacher is thrown upon the resources of his own mind and talent. There is great difficulty here, and it does not seem likely to diminish. It may be, that never again, as long as time shall endure, will ignorant and learned, masters and servants, poor and rich, feel themselves at home in the same church.

At present we are impressed, and often oppressed, with the too evident fact, that neither the intelligent nor the uninstructed souls are so well ministered to, in things spiritual, as we could imagine they might be. The fashionable world of New York goes to church every Sunday morning with tolerable punctuality, and yet it seems to drift rapidly toward Paris. What it usually hears at church does not appear to exercise controlling influence over its conduct or its character.

Among the churches about New York to which nothing we have said applies, the one that presents the strongest contrast to the fashionable church is Henry Ward Beecher's. Some of the difficulties resulting from the altered state of opinion in recent times have been overcome there, and an institution has been created which appears to be adapted to the needs, as well as to the tastes, of the people frequenting it. We can at least say of it, that it is a living body, and *not* a decorated image.

For many years, this church upon Brooklyn Heights has been, to the best of the visitors to the metropolis, the most interesting object in or near it. Of Brooklyn itself,—a great assemblage of residences, without much business or stir,—it seems the animating soul. We have a fancy, that we can tell by the manner and bearing of an inhabitant of the place whether he attends this church or not; for there is a certain joyousness, candor, and democratic simplicity about the members of that congregation, which might be styled Beecherian, if there were not a better word. This church is simply the most characteristic thing of America. If we had a foreigner in charge to whom we wished to reveal this country, we should like to push him in, hand him over to one of the brethren who perform the arduous duty of providing seats for visitors, and say to him: "There, stranger, you have arrived; *this* is the United States. The New Testament, Plymouth Rock, and the Fourth of July,—*this* is what they have brought us to. What the next issue will be, no one can tell; but this is about what we are at present."

We cannot imagine what the brethren could have been thinking about when they ordered the new bell that hangs in the tower of Plymouth Church. It is the most superfluous article in the known world. The New Yorker who steps on board the Fulton ferry-boat about ten o'clock on Sunday morning finds himself accompanied by a large crowd of people who bear the visible stamp of strangers, who are going to Henry Ward Beecher's church. You can pick them out with perfect certainty. You see the fact in their countenances, in their dress, in their demeanor, as well as hear it in words of eager expectation. They are the kind of people who regard wearing-apparel somewhat in the light of its utility, and are not crushed by their clothes. They are the sort of people who take the "Tribune," and get up courses of lectures in the country towns. From every quarter of Brooklyn, in street cars and on foot, streams of people are converging toward the same place. Every Sunday morning and evening, rain or shine, there is the same concourse, the same crowd at the gates before they are open, and the same long, laborious effort to get thirty-five hundred people into a building that will seat but twenty-seven hundred. Besides the ten or twelve members of the church who volunteer to assist in this labor, there is employed a force of six policemen at the doors, to prevent the multitude from choking all ingress. Seats are retained for their proprietors until ten minutes before the time of beginning; after that the strangers are admitted. Mr. Buckle, if he were with us still, would be pleased to know that his doctrine of averages holds good in this instance; since every Sunday about a churchful of persons come to this church, so that not many who come fail to get in.

There is nothing of the ecclesiastical drawing-room in the

arrangements of this edifice. It is a very plain brick building, in a narrow street of small, pleasant houses, and the interior is only striking from its extent and convenience. The simple, old-fashioned design of the builder was to provide seats for as many people as the space would hold; and in executing this design, he constructed one of the finest interiors in the country, since the most pleasing and inspiring spectacle that human eyes ever behold in this world is such an assembly as fills this church. The audience is grandly displayed in those wide, rounded galleries, surging up high against the white walls, and scooped out deep in the slanting floor, leaving the carpeted platform the vortex of an arrested whirlpool. Often it happens that two or three little children get lodged upon the edge of the platform, and sit there on the carpet among the flowers during the service, giving to the picture a singularly pleasing relief, as though they and the bouquets had been arranged by the same skilful hand, and for the same purpose. And it seems quite natural and proper that children should form part of so bright and joyous an occasion. Behind the platform rises to the ceiling the huge organ, of dark wood and silvered pipes, with fans of trumpets pointing heavenward from the top. This enormous toy occupies much space that could be better filled, and is only less superfluous than the bell; but we must pardon and indulge a foible. We could never see that Mr. Forrest walked any better for having such thick legs; yet they have their admirers. Blind old Handel played on an instrument very different from this, but the sexton had to eat a cold Sunday dinner; for not a Christian would stir as long as the old man touched the keys after service. But not old Handel nor older Gabriel could make such music as swells and roars from three thousand human voices,—the regular choir of Plymouth Church. It is a decisive proof of the excellence and heartiness of this choir, that the great organ has not lessened its effectiveness.

It is not clear to the distant spectator by what aperture Mr.

Beecher enters the church. He is suddenly discovered to be present, seated in his place on the platform,—an under-sized gentleman in a black stock. His hair combed behind his ears, and worn a little longer than usual, imparts to his appearance something of the Puritan, and calls to mind his father, the champion of orthodoxy in heretical Boston. In conducting the opening exercises, and, indeed, on all occasions of ceremony, Mr. Beecher shows himself an artist,—both his language and his demeanor being marked by the most refined decorum. An elegant, finished simplicity characterizes all he does and says: not a word too much, nor a word misused, nor a word waited for, nor an unharmonious movement, mars the satisfaction of the auditor. The habit of living for thirty years in the view of a multitude, together with a natural sense of the becoming, and a quick sympathy with men and circumstances, has wrought up his public demeanor to a point near perfection. A candidate for public honors could not study a better model. This is the more remarkable, because it is a purely spiritual triumph. Mr. Beecher's person is not imposing, nor his natural manner graceful. It is his complete extirpation of the desire of producing an illegitimate effect; it is his sincerity and genuineness as a human being; it is the dignity of his character, and his command of his powers,—which give him this easy mastery over every situation in which he finds himself.

Extempore prayers are not, perhaps, a proper subject for comment. The grand feature of the preliminary services of this church is the singing, which is not executed by the first talent that money can command. When the prelude upon the organ is finished, the whole congregation, almost every individual in it, as if by a spontaneous and irresistible impulse, stands up and sings. We are not aware that anything has ever been done or said to bring about this result; nor does the minister of the church set the example, for he usually remains sitting and silent. It seems as if every one in the congregation was so full of something that he felt impelled to get up and sing it out. In other churches where congregational singing is attempted, there are usually a number of languid Christians who remain seated, and a large number of others who remain silent; but here there is a strange unanimity about the performance. A sailor might as well try not to join in the chorus of a forecastle song as a member of this joyous host not to sing. When the last preliminary singing is concluded, the audience is in an excellent condition to sit and listen, their whole corporeal system having been pleasantly exercised.

The sermon which follows is new wine in an old bottle. Up to the moment when the text has been announced and briefly explained, the service has all been conducted upon the ancient model, and chiefly in the ancient phraseology; but from the moment when Mr. Beecher swings free from the moorings of his text, and get fairly under way, his sermon is modern. No matter how fervently he may have been praying supernaturalism, he preaches pure cause and effect. His text may savor of old Palestine; but his sermon is inspired by New York and Brooklyn; and nearly all that he says, when he is most himself, finds an approving response in the mind of every well-disposed person, whether orthodox or heterodox in his creed.

What is religion? That, of course, is the great question. Mr. Beecher says: Religion is the slow, laborious, self-conducted EDUCATION of the whole man, from grossness to refinement, from sickness to health, from ignorance to knowledge, from selfishness to justice, from justice to nobleness, from cowardice to valor. In treating this topic, whatever he may pray or read or assent to, he *preaches* cause and effect, and nothing else. Regeneration he does not represent to be some mysterious, miraculous influence exerted upon a man from without, but the man's own act, wholly and always, and in every stage of its progress. His general way of discoursing upon this subject would satisfy the most rationalized mind; and yet it does not appear to offend the most orthodox.

This apparent contradiction between the spirit of his preaching and the facts of his position is a severe puzzle to some of our thorough-going friends. They ask, How can a man demonstrate that the fall of rain is so governed by unchanging laws that the shower of yesterday dates back in its causes to the origin of things, and, having proved this to the comprehension of every soul present, finish by *praying* for an immediate outpouring upon the thirsty fields? We confess that, to our modern way of thinking, there is a contradiction here, but there is none at all to an heir of the Puritans. We reply to our impatient young friends, that Henry Ward Beecher at once represents and assists the American Christian of the present time, just because of this seeming contradiction. He is a bridge over which we are passing from the creed-enslaved past to the perfect freedom of the future. Mr. Lecky, in his "History of the Spirit of Rationalism," has shown the process by which truth is advanced. Old errors, he says, do not die because they are refuted, but *fade out* because they are neglected. One hundred and fifty years ago, our ancestors were perplexed, and even distressed, by something they called the doctrine of Original Sin. No one now concerns himself either to refute or assert the doctrine; few people know what it is; we all simply let it alone, and it fades out. John Wesley not merely believed in witchcraft, but maintained that a belief in witchcraft was essential to salvation. All the world, except here and there an enlightened and fearless person, believed in witchcraft as late as the year 1750. That belief has not perished because its folly was demonstrated, but because the average human mind grew past it, and let it alone until it faded out in the distance. Or we might compare the great body of beliefs to a banquet, in which every one takes what he likes best; and the master of the feast, observing what is most in demand, keeps an abundant supply of such viands, but gradually withdraws those which are neglected. Mr. Beecher has helped himself to such beliefs as are congenial to him, and shows an exquisite tact in passing by those which interest him not, and which have lost regenerating power. There *are* minds which cannot be content with anything like vagueness or inconsistency in their opinions. They must know to a certainty whether the sun and moon stood still or not. His is not mind of that cast; he can "hover on the confines of truth," and leave the less inviting parts of the landscape veiled in mist unexplored. Indeed, the great aim of his preaching is to show the insignificance of opinion compared with right feeling and noble living, and he prepares the way for the time when every conceivable latitude of mere opinion shall be allowed and encouraged.

One remarkable thing about his preaching is, that he has not, like so many men of liberal tendencies, fallen into milk-and-waterism. He often gives a foretaste of the terrific power which preachers will wield when they draw inspiration from science and life. Without ever frightening people with horrid pictures of the future, he has a sense of the perils which beset human life here, upon this bank and shoal of time. How needless to draw upon the imagination, in depicting the consequences of violating natural law! Suppose a preacher should give a plain, cold, scientific exhibition of the penalty which Nature exacts for the crime, so common among church-going ladies and others, of murdering their unborn offspring! It would appall the Devil. Scarcely less terrible are the consequences of the most common vices and meannesses when they get the mastery. Mr. Beecher has frequently shown, by powerful delineations of this kind, how large a part legitimate terror must ever play in the services of a true church, when the terrors of superstition have wholly faded out. It cannot be said of his preaching, that he preaches "Christianity with the bones taken out." He does not give "twenty minutes of tepid exhortation," nor amuse his auditors with elegant and melodious essays upon virtue.

We need not say that his power as a public teacher is

due, in a great degree, to his fertility in illustrative similes. Three or four volumes, chiefly filled with these, as they have been caught from his lips, are before the public, and are admired on both continents. Many of them are most strikingly happy, and flood his subject with light. The smiles that break out upon the sea of upturned faces, and the laughter that whispers round the assembly, are often due as much to the aptness as to the humor of the illustration: the mind receives an agreeable shock of surprise at finding a resemblance where only the widest dissimilarity had before been perceived.

Of late years, Mr. Beecher never sends an audience away half satisfied; for he has constantly grown with the growth of his splendid opportunity. How attentive the great assembly, and how quickly responsive to the points he makes! That occasional ripple of laughter,—it is not from any want of seriousness in the speaker, in the subject, or in the congregation, nor is it a Rowland Hill eccentricity. It is simply that it has pleased Heaven to endow this genial soul with a quick perception of the likeness there is between things unlike; and, in the heat and torrent of his speech, the suddenly discovered similarity amuses while it instructs. Philosophers and purists may cavil at parts of these sermons, and, of course, they are not perfect; but who can deny that their general effect is civilizing, humanizing, elevating, and regenerating, and that this master of preaching is the true brother of all those high and bright spirits, on both sides of the ocean, who are striving to make the soul of this age fit to inhabit and nobly impel its new body?

The sermon over, a livelier song brings the services to a happy conclusion; and slowly, to the thunder of the new organ, the great assembly dissolves and oozes away.

The Sunday services are not the whole of this remarkable church. It has not yet adopted Mrs. Stowe's suggestion of providing billiard-rooms, bowling-alleys, and gymnastic apparatus for the development of Christian muscle, though these may

come in time. The building at present contains eleven apart-
ments, among which are two large parlors, wherein, twice a
month, there is a social gathering of the church and congregation, for conversation with the pastor and with one another.
Perhaps, by and by, these will be always open, so as to furnish
club conveniences to young men who have no home. Doubtless, this fine social organization is destined to development
in many directions not yet contemplated.

Among the ancient customs of New England and its colonies
(of which Brooklyn is one) is the Friday-evening prayer-meeting. Some of our readers, perhaps, have dismal recollections of
their early compelled attendance on those occasions, when,
with their hands firmly held in the maternal grasp, lest at the
last moment they should bolt under cover of the darkness, they
glided round into the back parts of the church, lighted by one
smoky lantern hung over the door of the lecture-room, itself
dimly lighted, and as silent as the adjacent chambers of the
dead. Female figures, demure in dress and eyes cast down,
flitted noiselessly in, and the awful stillness was only broken
by the heavy boots of the few elders and deacons who constituted the male portion of the exceedingly slender audience.
With difficulty, and sometimes, only after two or three failures,
a hymn was raised, which, when in fullest tide, was only a
dreary wail,—how unmelodious to the ears of unreverential
youth, gifted with a sense of the ludicrous! How long, how
sad, how pointless the prayers! How easy to believe, down in
that dreary cellar, that this world was but a wilderness, and
man "a feeble piece"! Deacon Jones could speak up briskly
enough when he was selling two yards of shilling calico to a
farmer's wife sharp at a bargain; but in that apartment, con-
tiguous to the tombs, it seemed natural that he should utter
dismal views of life in bad grammar through his nose. Mrs.
Jones was cheerful when she gave her little tea-party the
evening before; but now she appeared to assent, without
surprise, to the statement that she was a pilgrim travelling

through a vale of tears. Veritable pilgrims, who do actually meet in an oasis of the desert, have a merry time of it, travellers tell us. It was not so with these good souls, inhabitants of a pleasant place, and anticipating an eternal abode in an inconceivably delightful paradise. But then there was the awful chance of missing it! And the reluctant youth, dragged to this melancholy scene, who avenged themselves by giving select imitations of deaconian eloquence for the amusement of young friends,—what was to become of *them?* It was such thoughts, doubtless, that gave to those excellent people their gloomy habit of mind; and if their creed expressed the literal truth respecting man's destiny, character, and duty, terror alone was rational, and laughter was hideous and defiant mockery. What room in a benevolent heart for joy, when a point of time, a moment's space removed us to that heavenly place, or shut us up in hell?

From the time when we were accustomed to attend such meetings, long ago, we never saw a Friday-evening meeting till the other night, when we found ourselves in the lecture-room of Plymouth Church.

The room is large, very lofty, brilliantly lighted by reflectors affixed to the ceiling, and, except the scarlet cushions on the settees, void of upholstery. It was filled full with a cheerful company, not one of whom seemed to have on more or richer clothes than she had the moral strength to wear. Content and pleasant expectation sat on every countenance, as when people have come to a festival, and await the summons to the banquet. No pulpit, or anything like a pulpit, cast a shadow over the scene; but in its stead there was a rather large platform, raised two steps, covered with dark green canvas, and having upon it a very small table and one chair. The red-cushioned settees were so arranged as to enclose the green platform all about, except on one side; so that he who should sit upon it would appear to be in the midst of the people, raised above them that all might see him, yet still among them and one of them.

At one side of the platform, but on the floor of the room, among the settees, there was a piano open. Mr. Beecher sat near by, reading what appeared to be a letter of three or four sheets. The whole scene was so little like what we commonly understand by the word "meeting," the people there were so little in a "meeting" state of mind, and the subsequent proceedings were so informal, unstudied, and social, that, in attempting to give this account of them, we almost feel as if we were reporting for print the conversation of a private evening party. Anything more unlike an old-fashioned prayer-meeting it is not possible to conceive.

Mr. Beecher took his seat upon the platform, and, after a short pause, began the exercises by saying, in a low tone, these words: "Six twenty-two."

A rustling of the leaves of hymn-books interpreted the meaning of this mystical utterance, which otherwise might have been taken as announcing a discourse upon the prophetic numbers. The piano confirmed the interpretation; and then the company burst into one of those joyous and unanimous singings which are so enchanting a feature of the services of this church. Loud rose the beautiful harmony of voices, constraining every one to join in the song, even those most unused to sing. When it was ended, the pastor, in the same low tone, pronounced a name; upon which one of the brethren rose to his feet, and the rest of the assembly slightly inclined their heads. It would not, as we have remarked, be becoming in us to say anything upon this portion of the proceedings, except to note that the prayers were all brief, perfectly quiet and simple, and free from the routine or regulation expressions. There were but two or three of them, alternating with singing; and when that part of the exercises was concluded, Mr. Beecher had scarcely spoken. The meeting ran alone, in the most spontaneous and pleasant manner; and, with all its heartiness and simplicity, there was a certain refined decorum pervading all that was done and said. There was a pause after the last hymn died

away, and then Mr. Beecher, still seated, began, in the tone
of conversation, to speak, somewhat after this manner.

"When," said he, " I first began to walk as a Christian, in my
youthful zeal I made many resolutions that were well meant,
but indiscreet. Among others, I remember I resolved to pray,
at least once, in some way, every hour that I was awake. I
tried faithfully to keep this resolution, but never having succeeded a single day, I suffered the pangs of self-reproach, until
reflection satisfied me that the only wisdom possible, with regard to such a resolve, was to break it. I remember, too, that I
made a resolution to speak upon religion to every person with
whom I conversed,—on steamboats, in the streets, anywhere.
In this, also, I failed, as I ought; and I soon learned that, in
the sowing of such seed, as in other sowings, times and seasons
and methods must be considered and selected, or a man may
defeat his own object, and make religion loathsome."

In language like this he introduced the topic of the evening's
conversation, which was, How far, and on what occasions, and
in what manner, one person may invade, so to speak, the personality of another, and speak to him upon his moral condition.
The pastor expressed his own opinion, always in the conversa-
tional tone, in a talk of ten minutes' duration; in the course of
which he applauded, not censured, the delicacy which causes
most people to shrink from doing it. He said that a man's personality was not a macadamized road for every vehicle to drive
upon at will; but rather a sacred enclosure, to be entered, if
at all, with the consent of the owner, and with deference to
his feelings and tastes. He maintained, however, that there
were times and modes in which this might properly be done,
and that every one *had* a duty to perform of this nature. When
he had finished his observations, he said the subject was open
to the remarks of others; whereupon a brother instantly rose
and made a very honest confession.

He said that he had never attempted to perform the duty in
question without having a palpitation of the heart and a com-

plete "turning over" of his inner man. He had often reflected upon this curious fact, but was not able to account for it. He had not allowed this repugnance to prevent his doing the duty; but he always had to rush at it and perform it by a sort of *coup de main,* for if he allowed himself to think about the matter, he could not do it at all. He concluded by saying that he should be very much obliged to any one if he could explain this mystery.

The pastor said: "May it not be the natural delicacy we feel, and ought to feel, in approaching the interior consciousness of another person?"

Another brother rose. There was no hanging back at this meeting; there were no awkward pauses; every one seemed full of matter. The new speaker was not inclined to admit the explanation suggested by the pastor. "Suppose," said he, "we were to see a man in imminent danger of immediate destruction, and there was one way of escape, and but one, which *we* saw and he did not, should we feel any delicacy in running up to him and urging him to fly for his life? Is it not a want of faith on our part that causes the reluctance and hesitation we all feel in urging others to avoid a peril so much more momentous?"

Mr. Beecher said the cases were not parallel. Irreligious persons, he remarked, were not in imminent danger of immediate death; they might die to-morrow; but in all probability they would not, and an ill-timed or injudicious admonition might forever repel them. We must accept the doctrine of probabilities, and act in accordance with it in this particular, as in all others.

Another brother had a puzzle to present for solution. He said that he too had experienced the repugnance to which allusion had been made; but what surprised him most was, that the more he loved a person, and the nearer he was related to him, the more difficult he found it to converse with him upon his spiritual state. Why is this? "I should like to have this question answered," said he, "if there *is* an answer to it."

Mr. Beecher observed that this was the universal experience, and he was conscious himself of a peculiar reluctance and embarrassment in approaching one of his own household on the subject in question. He thought it was due to the fact that we respect more the personal rights of those near to us than we do those of others, and it was more difficult to break in upon the routine of our ordinary familiarity with them. We are accustomed to a certain tone, which it is highly embarrassing to jar upon.

Captain Duncan related two amusing anecdotes to illustrate the right way and the wrong way of introducing religious conversation. In his office there was sitting one day a sort of lay preacher, who was noted for lugging in his favorite topic in the most forbidding and abrupt manner. A sea-captain came in, who was introduced to this individual.

"Captain Porter," said he, with awful solemnity, "are you a captain in Israel?"

The honest sailor was so abashed and confounded at this novel salutation, that he could only stammer out an incoherent reply, and he was evidently much disposed to give the tactless zealot a piece of his mind expressed in the language of the quarter-deck. When the solemn man took his leave, the disgusted captain said, "If ever I should be coming to your office again, and that man should be here, I wish you would send me word, and I'll stay away."

A few days after, another clergyman chanced to be in the office, no other than Mr. Beecher himself, and another captain came in, a roistering, swearing, good-hearted fellow. The conversation fell upon sea-sickness, a malady to which Mr. Beecher is peculiarly liable. This captain also was one of the few sailors who are always sea-sick in going to sea, and gave a moving account of his sufferings from that cause. Mr. Beecher, after listening attentively to his tale, said, "Captain Duncan, if I was a preacher to such sailors as your friend here, I should represent hell as an eternal voyage, with every man on board in the agonies of sea-sickness, the crisis always imminent, but never coming."

This ludicrous and most unprofessional picture amused the old salt exceedingly, and won his entire good-will toward the author of it; so that, after Mr. Beecher left, he said, "That's a good fellow, Captain Duncan. I like *him*, and I'd like to hear him talk more."

Captain Duncan contended that this free-and-easy way of address was just the thing for such characters. Mr. Beecher had shown him, to his great surprise, that a man could be a decent and comfortable human being, although he was a minister, and had so gained his confidence and good-will that he could say *anything* to him at their next interview. Captain Duncan finished his remarks by a decided expression of his disapproval of the canting regulation phrases so frequently employed by religious people, which are perfectly nauseous to men of the world.

This interesting conversation lasted about three quarters of an hour, and ended, not because the theme seemed exhausted, but because the time was up. We have only given enough of it to convey some little idea of its spirit. The company again broke into one of their cheerful hymns, and the meeting was dismissed in the usual manner.

During the whole evening not a canting word nor a false tone had been uttered. Some words were used, it is true, and some forms practised, which are not congenial to "men of the world," and some doctrines were assumed to be true which have become incredible to many of us. These, however, were not conspicuous nor much dwelt upon. The subject, too, of the conversation was less suitable to our purpose than most of the topics discussed at these meetings, which usually have a more direct bearing upon the conduct of life. Nevertheless, is it not apparent that such meetings as this, conducted by a man of tact, good sense, and experience, must be an aid to good living? Here were a number of people,—parents, business-men, and others,—most of them heavily burdened with respon-sibility, having notes and rents to pay, customers to get and keep, children to rear,—busy people, anxious people, of ex-tremely diverse characters, but united by a common desire to live nobly. The difficulties of noble living are very great,— never so great, perhaps, as now and here,—and these people assemble every week to converse upon them. What more ra-tional thing could they do? If they came together to snivel and cant, and to support one another in a miserable conceit of being the elect of the human species, we might object. But no description can show how far from that, how opposite to that, is the tone, the spirit, the object, of the Friday-evening meeting at Plymouth Church.

Have we "Liberals"—as we presume to call ourselves—ever devised anything so well adapted as this to the needs of aver-age mortals struggling with the ordinary troubles of life? We know of nothing. Philosophical treatises, and arithmetical com-putations respecting the number of people who inhabited Pal-estine, may have their use, but they cannot fill the aching void in the heart of a lone widow, or teach an anxious father how to manage a troublesome boy. There was an old lady near us at this meeting,—a good soul in a bonnet four fashions old,— who sat and cried for joy, as the brethren carried on their talk. She had come in alone from her solitary room, and enjoyed all the evening long a blended moral and literary rapture. It was a banquet of delight to her, the recollection of which would brighten all her week, and it cost her no more than air and sunlight. To the happy, the strong, the victorious, Shake-speare and the Musical Glasses may appear to suffice; but the world is full of the weak, the wretched, and the vanquished.

There was an infuriate heretic in Boston once, whose antip-athy to what he called "superstition" was something that bordered upon lunacy. But the time came when he had a child, his only child, and the sole joy of his life, dead in the house. It had to be buried. The broken-hearted father could not endure the thought of his child's being carried out and placed in its grave without *some* outward mark of respect, *some* ceremonial which should recognize the difference between a dead child and a dead kitten; and he was fain, at last, to go out and bring to his house a poor lame cobbler, who was a kind of Methodist preacher, to say and read a few words that should break the fall of the darling object into the tomb. The occurrence made no change in his opinions, but it revolutionized his feelings. He is as untheological as ever; but he would subscribe money to build a church, and he esteems no man more than an honest clergyman.

If anything can be predicated of the future with certainty, it is, that the American people will never give up that portion of their heritage from the past which we call Sunday, but will always devote its hours to resting the body and improving the soul. All our theologies will pass away, but this will remain. Nor less certain is it, that there will always be a class of men who will do, professionally and as their settled vocation, the work now done by the clergy. That work can never be dispensed with, either in civilized or in barbarous communities. The great problem of civilization is, how to bring the higher intelligence of the community, and its better moral feeling, to bear upon the mass of people, so that the lowest grade of intelligence and morals shall be always approaching the higher, and the higher still rising. A church purified of superstition solves part of this problem, and a good school system does the rest.

All things improve in this world very much in the same way. The improvement originates in one man's mind, and, being carried into effect with evident good results, it is copied by others. We are all apt lazily to run in the groove in which we find ourselves; we are creatures of habit, and slaves of tradition. Now and then, however, in every profession and sphere, if they are untrammelled by law, an individual appears who is discontented with the ancient methods, or sceptical of the old traditions, or both, and he invents better ways, or arrives at more rational opinions. Other men look on and approve the improved process, or listen and imbibe the advanced belief.

Now, there appears to be a man upon Brooklyn Heights who has found out a more excellent way of conducting a church than has been previously known. He does not waste the best hours of every day in writing sermons, but employs those hours in absorbing the knowledge and experience which should be the matter of sermons. He does not fritter away the time of a public instructor in "pastoral visits," and other useless visitations. His mode of conducting a public ceremonial reaches the finish of high art, which it resembles also in its sincerity and simplicity. He has known how to banish from his church everything that savors of cant and sanctimoniousness,—so loathsome to honest minds. Without formally rejecting time-honored forms and usages, he has infused into his teachings more and more of the modern spirit, drawn more and more from science and life, less and less from tradition, until he has acquired the power of preaching sermons which Edwards and Voltaire, Whitefield and Tom Paine, would heartily and equally enjoy. Surely, there is something in all this which could be imitated. The great talents with which he is endowed cannot be imparted, but we do not believe that his power is wholly derived from his talent. A man of only respectable abilities, who should catch his spirit, practise some of his methods, and spend his strength in getting knowledge and not in coining sentences, would be able anywhere to gather around him a concourse of hearers. The great secret is, to let orthodoxy slide, as something which is neither to be maintained nor refuted,—insisting only on the spirit of Christianity, and applying it to the life of the present day in this land.

There are some reasons for thinking that the men and the

organizations that have had in charge the moral interests of the people of the United States for the last fifty years have not been quite equal to their trust. What are we to think of such results of New England culture as Douglas, Cass, Webster, and many other men of great ability, but strangely wanting in moral power? What are we to think of the great numbers of Southern Yankees who were, and are, the bitterest foes of all that New England represents? What are we to think of the Rings that seem now-a-days to form themselves, as it were, spontaneously in every great corporation? What of the club-houses that spring up at every corner, for the accommodation of husbands and fathers who find more attractions in wine, supper, and equivocal stories than in the society of their wives and children? What are we to think of the fact, that among the people who can afford to advertise at the rate of a dollar and a half a line are those who provide women with the means of killing their unborn children,—a double crime, murder and suicide? What are we to think of the moral impotence of almost all women to resist the tyranny of fashion, and the *necessity* that appears to rest upon them to copy every disfiguration invented by the harlots of Paris? What are we to think of the want both of masculine and moral force in men, which makes them helpless against the extravagance of their households, to support which they do fifty years' work in twenty, and then die? What are we to think of the fact, that all the creatures living in the United States enjoy good health, except the human beings, who are nearly all ill?

When we consider such things as these, we cannot help calling in question a kind of public teaching which leaves the people in ignorance of so much that they most need to know. Henry Ward Beecher is the only clergyman we ever heard who habitually promulgates the truth, that to be ill is generally a sin, and always a shame. We never heard him utter the demoralizing falsehood, that this present life is short and of small account, and that nothing is worthy of much consideration except the life to come. He dwells much on the enormous length of this life, and the prodigious revenue of happiness it may yield to those who comply with the conditions of happiness. It is his habit, also, to preach the duty which devolves upon every person, to labor for the increase of his knowledge and the general improvement of his mind. We have heard him say on the platform of his church, that it was disgraceful to any mechanic or clerk to let such a picture as the Heart of the Andes be exhibited for twenty-five cents, and not go and see it. Probably there is not one honest clergyman in the country who does not fairly earn his livelihood by the good he does, or by the evil he prevents. But not enough good is done, and not enough evil prevented. The sudden wealth that has come upon the world since the improvement of the steam-engine adds a new difficulty to the life of millions. So far, the world does not appear to have made the best use of its too rapidly increased surplus. "We cannot sell a twelve-dollar book in this country," said a bookseller to us the other day. But how easy to sell two-hundred-dollar garments! There seems great need of something that shall have power to spiritualize mankind, and make head against the reinforced influence of material things. It may be that the true method of dealing with the souls of modern men has been, in part, discovered by Mr. Beecher, and that it would be well for persons aspiring to the same vocation to *begin* their preparation by making a pilgrimage to Brooklyn Heights.

10. THE NEW OPPORTUNITIES

OF THE MINISTER

Sphere of the Christian Minister, 1869

BY HENRY WARD BEECHER

---

*American Protestantism had for at least a century been shift-
ing its emphasis "from piety to moralism," but the process
was enormously accelerated with the appearance of churches
like Plymouth in an environment so untraditional that new
"problems" continually were forced upon the minister's consideration, and with a congregation so specialized that a minister could consider these problems with a fair certainty of
what solutions would be acceptable. One of the characteristics
of Beecher that made him so attractive to James Parton was
his sensitivity to contemporary intellectual and moral issues. In
the preface to this sermon, Beecher declared that "it was wise
for Puritan divines to preach whole bodies of divinity, set
forth with vast learning, and with a minuteness that would
now be insufferably tedious." But today, "the sermons that will
be read by multitudes are those which bring God's infinite
truth into vital relations with the thoughts, sympathies, enterprises, habits, loves, hatreds, temptations and sins, ideals and*

From *The Sermons of Henry Ward Beecher in Plymouth Church,
Brooklyn* (New York: J. B. Ford, 1869), pp. 305–323.

aspirations of the times. . . ." Beecher, however, did not pro-
pose to be a Jeremiah, at least to his own people, for he went
on, "The true preacher . . . is to be in sympathy, not with
ideas and truths alone, but with living men." By insisting
on the right of the minister to be a prophet, Beecher freed
himself from most traditional theological concerns; but he
stopped well short of violating the bond of sympathy with
his congregation.

"And Paul said unto them, Sirs, I perceive that this voyage will be
with hurt and much damage, not only of the lading and ship, but
also of our lives. Nevertheless, the centurion believed the master
and the owner of the ship, more than those things which were
spoken by Paul." Acts 27:10, 11.

I suppose that we should have done just the same. Paul was a
landsman. What did he know about navigation? He was a
foreigner; and the Roman centurion had no great respect for
Jews. Nobody has respect for persons that are not born in the
nation that they are. He was a captive and that, too, threw
discredit. And now, to intermeddle, or give advice which was
not asked for, seemed ungracious enough. And so the centurion
said—just as you would have said; just as I should have said—
"This is a matter that I would rather take the testimony of
the ship-master and the owner about, than yours." And the
voyage went on, and it all came as Paul had declared; and
he had that sweet opportunity that every body longs for, of
saying, "I told you so." For, after great storms and long ab-
stinence, Paul stood forth in the midst of them, and said, "Sirs,
ye should have hearkened unto me, and not have loosed from
Crete, and to have gained this harm and loss. And now I exhort
you to be of good cheer." For with every one of these discredit-
ing circumstances the manhood of Paul, his sagacity, his remarkable foresight, his aptness at command, and all these
qualities summed up in those others that go to make a leader

among men, so shone out, that, when it came to the extremity, this Roman centurion—who was a man, (and the presumption always is that a Roman centurion was a *man,* and a good man, just and excellent)—at the last marked him. And having had an opportunity of seeing the captain in danger, and the owner in danger, and the crew and soldiers in danger, he picked out Paul. The Jewish captive was the man, and thereafter the centurion did as Paul commanded him. So that Paul, at the end of the voyage, although it was disastrous, commanded the captain, and the owner, and the crew, and the soldiers, and the centurion, and had charge of every thing on board, and finally of the islanders themselves, when they were wrecked. A true man shows that he is true at that very point where other men break down.

There are two points of sensitiveness among men, both of which are illustrated in this history. Men are sensitive to the interference of moral elements with their secular liberty. First, men do not like to have ministers meddle with their business; they know better than ministers do their own affairs, they think. Secondly, men are sensitive to non-professional advice from any body. The assumption is, that there is no man that can understand the affairs of any given sphere or department so well as he that is engaged in it. These two considerations are the germs of my sermon to-night.

1. Men are jealous, and they are indignant often, at clergymen's attempting to meddle with the affairs of society, and with their personal and private affairs. I do not wonder at it. And when clergymen are associated in a class, with arrogant pretensions, men ought to resent their intrusion.

There are two theories on which the clerical profession is organized. The one holds that there is a body of men taken up by God's appointment, and set apart from human life, and endowed with special prerogatives, and given special virtues; and that as a class, they stand above their fellow-men in authority in moral things. But there has never been an order of clergy established in the church or in the state that has not been mischievous, and there never will be. The moment that you establish men into a class, and make them believe that, on account of some divine arrangement, they hold powers superior to those which belong to their own individual personality—that by virtue of their profession they are more and other than their fellow-men—that very moment you vitiate their character, and so vitiate their influence. All members of a hierarchy—that is, an aristocracy of clergy—all members of high ecclesiastical organizations, are to be repelled in their intrusions upon society, because they work, not for society, but for a class in society. This vice is inherent in such organizations. And however much individual men may rise above the temptations of their circumstances, the great body of an aristocracy will work for an aristocracy. The great body of a special class in politics will work for their class; and a body of clergymen will work for themselves. *Esprit de corps* will spring up among them, and the influence of the whole class will be to work for the clergy.

Then there is another theory on which clergymen are built. It is held that a man may, moved by his own good sense, by his own moral aptitudes, become a teacher of moral ideas in a community. He is not endowed with any gifts beside those which belong to any other men of his mark or make. And the fact that he becomes a moral teacher gives him no special divine power. No special grace passes over into him, either by the touch of priestly hands, or through any long channel derived from the apostles. He is what he is by the grace of God in the ordinance of his birth, and in the processes of his education—just that. And he derives just as much power as he can exert—not a bit more, and not a bit less. He is just like another man. Call up a layman that is his equal in intelligence, that is his equal in moral power, with his simplicity, sincerity, and directness, and that layman is just as much as he is. There is nothing in ordination; there is nothing in the imposition of hands. God's ordination lies in birth. That is the grand ordination. And when to that is given afterward the sanctifying influences of the Spirit, in a form which belongs to one just as much as to another, it is a part of the prerogative of universal liberty. It does not belong to, and can not be appropriated by, the clergy, nor any rank or influence in society, nor in the church. When to the original endowment is added the inspiration of God's Spirit, which is given to him and to others, then he is what? He is just what he is—no more and no less—a force in society.

There has been a great deal of jealousy about ministers mixing in public affairs; and if it is directed against the *class*-clergy, I participate in it. None shall surpass me in unwillingness that clergymen should become a class. I will not permit any body to make me a member of a class. I say that I am simply a citizen, and that any thing you have a right to, I have a right to. I will not be separated from you. I will not be taken out of the brotherhood of my fellow-citizens. I am just like you, with the same right to speak, and the same right to exert my influence that you have—no more and no less. And those that protest against a clergyman's meddling with public affairs are the artificers and the architects of a hierarchy. You take just that course that will shove clergymen together in a body, and make them feel that they are holy men; and when by and by they begin to think that they are holy, and something above the average of men, you turn round and curse them for thinking so! You blame them for being what you have made them to be.

A clergyman is a man; he is a citizen; he is a teacher of moral things, without any privilege to teach more than any body else. Any body may teach that can and wants to. And if he tries and succeeds, that is call enough. That is the best evidence that he is ordained to teach. Four hundred thousand angels blowing trumpets for a fool would not give him a right to preach; and without a trumpet, without a call, a man that has got it in him, and loves men, and understands what is for their welfare, and is willing to tell them of it, has a right to preach. The whole matter is as simple as common sense itself.

Therefore, when men are unwilling that clergymen should meddle with public or private affairs, it is true that they should not, if by "clergy" you mean *class*-clergy. It is not true, if you mean ordinary moral teachers. They arrogate nothing to themselves, and are not bound to go in a class. They are members of their own church. They are simply elder brothers in teaching. They are in the community just what every other man is. There is no reason for jealousy in regard to the intrusion of such men. Where they are seeking to apply moral truths to the conduct of affairs, to the character of men, to the processes of business, to the flow of pleasure, there is no reason why they should be denied the privilege or refused a hearing.

A judgment formed by a clear head upon any course from high moral grounds, is likely to be sounder, wiser, and more cogent than judgments which are formed from mere practical grounds. There may be, there often is, what is called speculative judgment, theoretical judgment. Or, as it is sometimes said, men may be *doctrinaires*. And this is thrown into strong antithesis and contrast with practical wisdom.

Now, I hold that moral intuition may be, and often is, wiser than practical experience itself. Nay, the reason why practical experience is continually stumbling and falling at the crisis is, that it lacks the moral element. And a man who can add this to the ordinary wisdom of common men is just the man who—in addition to the judgment which men form by familiarity with the details of their business—has the moral inspiration which shall give him an insight into the relations of men in society, and has a light which shall make him wiser than he could have been by his own practical experience alone. An outsider is very useful to an insider. As the engineer can not steer, being down below among the machinery, he is very much helped by a man that is on the lookout; and men that are buried in the hull of their affairs ought to be thankful if there is any body on deck that can keep a lookout, and tell which way the ship is going.

All kinds of business, all professions, all courses in social life, besides their relationships to other ends and instruments, stand in a yet higher relation to moral law, which is the highest relation of all. They stand in a relation to the moral welfare of the whole community. And we have a right—I have a right; you have a right; every body has a right—with or without ordination, by virtue of our essential manhood, which is the highest ordination, to meddle with the moral relations of every course and calling. There is nothing in society so strong, so high, or set apart with such exclusiveness, that I have not a right to put my probe into it, and search it, and instruct it. And if it does not need instruction, it does no more hurt than rain does a slate roof—for it can run off. If it does need it, and does not take it, it is hurt and lost.

Many and many a voyage has been disastrous because when a Paul said, "Ye will come to harm," the centurion said, "We have the ship-master and the owner, and we will listen to them rather than to this Paul. What does he know about it? We probably know more about our own business than any stranger does." In many and many a case it has turned out that the stranger, whose advice was rejected with scorn, knew more than the ship-master, the owner, and all on board put together.

This has been Christ's quarrel from the beginning. As it was said on one occasion, so it is said now, "What have we to do with thee?" which is the same as saying, What hast thou to do with us? "Art thou come to torment us before our time?" Whenever the stimulating power of divine truth has begun to work upon men's consciences, whenever the light has begun to shine into the darkness, the darkness would not comprehend it. And when Christian teachers begin to apply the larger principles of criticism to the evil courses of society, which almost always revolve in small circles, with limited sight and no foresight, men say, "Ye meddlers, why do you not attend to your business, and let us attend to our business? Stay thou at home and preach the Gospel, and let our amusements alone. Stay thou at home and preach Christ, and not touch grog-shops and liquor-sellers. Stay thou at home, and not meddle with lotteries. Especially do not meddle with caucuses and fiscal managements and maneuvers. What hast thou to do with Wall street? What hast thou to do along the wharves and piers? What hast thou to do with machinists? What hast thou to do with business men? Follow the meek and lowly Jesus." I *do* follow him—precisely that; for he said, "I came not to send peace, but a sword." "For I am come to set a man at variance against his father, and the daughter against her mother, and the daughter-in-law against her mother-in-law. And a man's foes shall be they of his own household." Those that follow Christ do not go about whispering to men, and patting them, and making soft pillows for them to put their heads on, and easy cushions for them to sit down on, and sweet music for them to do their iniquities in. He that follows Christ is not one of these smooth speakers. Do you suppose that these pulpit birds of paradise are the best fitted to save their fellow-men, and do the world good? Far from it. The men especially who follow Christ and his apostles, are the men who turn the world upside down.

While, then, I disavow the rights of the clergy as a body organized for their own interest, and hold them to be a danger-ous class, and the most dangerous class in society, because they are the most conscientious—for when a man has his face set toward wickedness, there is nothing like conscience to ride him to the devil: the more conscientious men are, the more deadly are they in their persecutions, and the more disastrous is their influence on society—while I disavow clerical class-hood, I affirm the rights of individual reason, I affirm the rights of individual conscience, I affirm the rights of the moral teacher, not because he is a minister, but because he is a *man*.

He has a right to go into every part of society. He has a right to give advice. He has a right to whisper, if whispering is the proper method. He has a right to thunder, if thundering is the proper method. And if I do these things, no man can say, "It is none of your business." It *is* my business. Every thing that is done under God's sun is my business. And no man shall say to me, "You are going out of your sphere." My sphere is as broad as the sunlight. No man shall say, "You are intruding." I am *not* intruding. When I stand and look upon those things which are of common interest to you and to me, and say, "Such courses and such a career jar against the universal fellowship, against the general prosperity, against the integrity at large," it is precisely my business.

2. There is a popular impression—and it seems to men like a philosophical truism—that every man understands his own business best; that he need not be meddled with, at least till he asks advice; and that even then no one can counsel him so wisely as one of the same craft. Complaint is often made on that ground, of ministers, that they meddle with things that they do not understand. I think they do, too, when they preach theology! There is an amazing deal of wisdom that will be called rubbish one of these days! But when ministers meddle with practical life, with ethical questions and relations, they are meddling with just what they do understand, or ought to. If they do not understand these things, they have failed to prepare themselves for one of the most important functions to which they could address themselves as ministers.

But look at this matter. Is it true that a man generally understands his own business best? Is it true that, if he needs counsel, he had better take it from some one who is in the same business that he is? I admit that there is a truth in this matter. Familiarity with details, which goes so largely to constitute success in any secular calling, may be supposed to be chiefly confined to those who are engaged in that calling. The printer knows more about the details of printing than I do. The lawyer knows more than I do about the thousand and one details of practice in our courts; of methods of procedure; of rules that have been formed; of precedents that have been established. The machinist understands the fashion of the machine—the principle and working of it, at any rate—better than I do. And in manufacturing interests, men understand the interior of their business better than I do—unless I have made it a matter of special study. So of political economy. So of ten thousand interests in society.

But does it follow that a man understands the general relations of his business to other businesses? Yet that is very important. Does it follow that a man understands the moral relations of his business better than an outsider? Does it follow that a man understands the relations of his business to political economy better than an outsider does? So far from that, experience shows that no man is so blind as a man that is immersed in his own business. It is not often the case that any department of life is reformed of its own accord. Medicine does not reform itself. The reformation is thrown upon it from without. Law does not reform itself. It is the community that compels law to reform. Governments do not reform themselves. De Tocqueville said—and it was true then, it is true now, and it always will be true—"Governments will be as rascally as the people will let them be." It is the light that is brought in from the outside that reforms governments. In some way the general interest of the whole community is concentrated upon some disturbing career, or business, until the men who are engaged therein yield to reformation. The reformation of any calling is seldom developed in the calling itself. It always is forced upon it *ab extra.*

There is nothing, therefore, that is more untrue, than that a man understands his own business best, if by that you mean that he understands it in its largest relations—in its general results to the welfare of society; and more particularly if you mean that he understands his own business best in its moral influence upon himself, upon his fellows, and upon society. Usually, none understand the moral bearing of a business so little as the men who are embarked in it. The broker does not understand the moral relations of brokerage so well as I do, though he understands the details of that business far better than I do. The lawyer does not understand all the workings of the law as well as I do. It is not the machinery, but what it can do, what it works out, that I understand. It does not follow that the miller understands bread better than I do. I know what good bread is as well as he does. He knows more about the process of making flour than I do. The baker knows more about kneading dough, about the time that it should require to rise, and about how long it should be in baking; but when it is done, and I take the loaf, and eat it, then I am as good a judge of bread as he is.

And so it is with the various kinds of business. They bring out results here and there, and the community is made to take the benefit or damage, as the case may be. And men who stand and look on—men who have discrimination, large reflection, clear intuition, and who, above all, judge from a moral standpoint—such men are competent to be critics of every thing that there is in human society. But when, as preachers or teachers, they say, "You had better not loose from Crete," men turn to the captain, or the owner, as if he knew more than they. Let them take their storms. The time will come when you can say to them, "I told you so. You ought not to have loosed, and to have come to all this harm and damage."

Not alone to dwell in generalities, these remarks are abundantly true and abundantly verified in the matter of law and its general procedure. It is not for me, perhaps, to say how a judge shall discharge his function; but it *is* for me to say when he discharges his function wrongly. It is not for me to say what is the special province of an advocate; but it is for me, when I see that a lawyer is violating the fundamental laws of morality, to be his critic. The moment he so conducts his profession that it touches the question of right and wrong, he comes into my sphere. There I stand; and I put God's measure, the golden reed of the sanctuary, on him and his course; and I am his master, if I be a true seer, and a true moral teacher; and I am not meddling. He has brought his business up to me the moment it comes into the sphere of right or wrong. He has brought it to my court, to my tribunal. For the truth stands back of all other courts, and has, in the last estate, to try every course and every procedure. Nothing is good for any individual in society that is not right. In the long run, righteousness is policy. Therefore, although it is not for me to meddle with the ordinary processes of courts, or of the profession of the law, where certain courses and certain practices become damaging to the young, damaging to men at large, damaging by example, and damaging by corruption, it is for me to lay the law of God on them.

There is a Judge that is higher than judges, whose servant I am; there is a law that is higher than laws; there is a court, thank God, a *Superior* court, a *Supreme* court, in which all inferior courts shall yet come to arbitrament, and many of them to damage. And I am not going out of my profession, I am not going one step beyond it, in meddling with these things. When they stink, and the stench comes up into my nostrils, then it becomes my business to deal with them. Why? Because I am citizen. Why? Because I am a man. Why? Because I undertake to judge by the law of God; by the law of conscience; by the law of everlasting rectitude. That gives me my right. It is not because I am a minister—certainly not because I am a priest; for I am not a priest, and do not believe in priests. It is not because I am specially ordained. My mother ordained me. God sent her to be my ordaining power. I do not assume any authority except that which is in reason. I do not arrogate any authority except that which lies in moral appeal. But I do affirm my right to speak, and to speak boldly, and to say to every crooked judge, "Woe be upon thine head!"

and to every trafficking lawyer, "Woe be unto thee!" I do not say that I am sent of God to do it more than any other honest man; but I say that every honest man is sent to do it. And woe be to those men who, knowing what is taking place around them, refuse to join me in denouncing those that are the corrupters of the community in the highest places of it!

I *will not* let it rest. I *will* go back to this subject again and again. I will see it *through*. I have lived to see the victory of many a struggling cause whose advocates were in the minority; and I shall live to see the cleansing of our courts, and to see the hideous names of many of our judges enshrined as are the names of corrupt judges of other nations and other times; and they will be used as new-invented terms of infamy!

The same is true of political economy; of the industries; in other words, of society; of the means and sources and method of its wealth. A moral teacher, it may be supposed, has little in common with these things. It is supposed that a moral teacher is a poor, dapper, nice little man, shut up to a kind of musical service of the sanctuary, where he has to stand like a feeble taper in a golden candlestick, or pipe out his little homily. There may be such men; but I am not one of them! I would not waste my life in any such petty business as that. I hold that a minister has the noblest sphere which is open to any man. He is a clear thinker, a large-hearted man, loving his fellow-men, patriotic to the heart's core, concerned with every thing that concerns men and human society, and interested in whatever properly interests any body else, studying them as far forth as he has an opportunity to study them, exercising his plenary right of manhood, and speaking plainly what he feels deeply. And I look into political economy— that is to say, the courses which industry pursues—not simply in their relations to the public wealth, but also in their relations to that higher and deeper wealth, namely, the conscience—the incorrupt condition of the community. If I were to preach on tariffs, if I were to preach on banks and banking, and on the various kindred subjects, men would say, "What does he know about these things?" If, after they had heard me, it was evident that I did not know any thing about them, it would be pertinent; but if they hear me, and find that I do know as much as they do about such matters, it is impertinent. If I am a minister, and I am rightly informed on these subjects, why should I not preach about them? Have you the prerogative to be selfish? and have not I the prerogative to find you out? Have you a right to be partial? and have I not a right to point out your partiality? Have you a right to conduct the courses of society in such a way that they wear out the road on which millions must walk? and have I no right in humanity to stand and plead for the necessity that the way of the Lord should be cast up, and not the way of Mammon? And do you say that the presumption is that you know your own business, and I do not know anything about it? If I know my own business—and the presumption is that I do—it is to hunt men, and study them!

Do you suppose that, because a man is an apothecary, he does not know how to catch trout? He has studied the nature of trout on purpose to amuse himself. Does it follow that, because a man is an able lawyer, he can not go to the Adirondacks and be a skillful hunter? Experience shows that he can, though he may not have made it the sole business of his life to hunt along the brooks or streams, or in the deep sea. Shall any body say that, not having devoted himself to these things, the probability is that he does not understand them? Do you suppose that I study old musty books when I want to preach? I study *you!* When I want to deliver a discourse on theology, I study *you!* When I want to know more about the doctrine of depravity, I study *you!* When I want to know what is right and what is wrong, I see how *you* do; and I have abundant illustrations on every side!

A true minister is a man among men. A true minister is a man that concerns himself in respect to all the courses of human life, because he is to shed light upon them; because he is to apply the divine rule to human conduct.

If, therefore, any man standing inside of his business, says "What do you know about it?" and turns to the ship-master and the owner, I shall say to him ere long, "I told you that you ought not to have loosed from Crete, and to have come to this loss and damage."

The same is true of the career of commerce, and all the instruments of commerce—of banking; of brokerage; of speculation; of railway management. There are a thousand things in these that a man can not well and perfectly understand who does not devote himself to them. There are a thousand points that I do not meddle with. There are a thousand questions that no man would meddle with who was not inside of these things. These questions themselves are but so many types in a sentence. Society is a great fact; and society is made up of these ten thousand separate letters, as it were, or sentences, or words. And while I may not be able to go into an analytic description of each individual department, I stand and look at the way in which they affect society, and have a word to say as to how they shall steer.

Paul did not say to this man, "You ought to hoist this sail, or that sail." That was not his business. He did not say, "Your stevedore has not laden you right." He left that to the stevedore's superior knowledge. But he did say to them, "You must not make this voyage." He knew that the season was unfavorable; he knew that it was about the time when the equinoctial storms would prevail. He had some knowledge of the great courses of nature as well as other men. And the fact that he was an apostle did not take away his power of judging of these things.

So I stand and say, "There are certain courses in the great commercial world that are sure to bring damage to those that pursue them." And you shall not revile me, saying, "You are nothing but a minister. You are a landsman. You know nothing about sailing." There are certain courses in banking that I know to be atrocious. I know that there are operations in railway management that outrage every law of prudence. I know that where mighty capital is combined, and capitalists are joined together, a fraternity of villains, they shall be able to swamp legislatures, and sweep whole communities to destruction. And when this accumulation of peril begins to globe up and fill the very horizon, I know it is my business to sound the alarm, and to say to men, "There is no prosperity to society so long as such gigantic swindles and frauds as these are going on." And when I do say it, they say to me, "Are you a railroad man?" No, but I am after railroad men. "Do you understand this business?" No, but I understand the men who are in this business. "Is it a part of your parochial affairs to meddle with such matters?" Yes; it *is* a part of my parochial affairs. I am a citizen of the United States; and my parish is the United States; and you are my parishioners; and I see that you are criminals, pursuing culpable courses which violate honesty, and purity, and conscience, and that you are not honorable men, and do not pass for such before God, though you may before men; and it is just my business to tell you these things. And when it is said, "Nobody can give advice in regard to the affairs of any given department unless he belongs to those affairs," I say that a cock does not need to be in bed with you to know that the morning has come, and crow! It is because he is out of doors, and sits aloft, and sees where the sun is coming up, that he becomes the clarion of the morning, and gives you the signal for waking up.

That which is true of these departments is just as true of political affairs. And now we come to a more familiar theme —to the old, old theme, which for twenty years I have been battling here, and which I think is at last given over. It is thought that ministers are incurable, and that they *will* meddle in *public* affairs; and men have almost agreed to let them— fortunately for them! For the process of public administration comes even nearer to us than either of the other elements that I have mentioned.

It is an evil day when patriotism is considered to be too foul for a minister. It is an evil day when the formation of the laws is considered to be a business in which righteous men should not dabble. It is an evil day when the appointment of magistrates and of the chief officers of the commonwealth is considered to be so discreditable that an honorable and pure-minded religious man should not have much to do with it. It is an evil day when the policy of the state, which carries with it the welfare of the whole mass of men—their joy or their sorrow, their weal or their woe—is such that a man of a pure heart can not touch it. And I say that, as long as I love my country, as long as I love the old commonwealth, as long as I am joined in equal fellowship to every man whose heart beats for pleasure or for suffering—so long I am concerned in all these things, and so long I will be concerned in them, and so long I will speak, in and out of prison, in and out of the pulpit, and in and out of papers; rising up or sitting down, going out or coming in. And I will speak, not with the liberty of a minister, but with a higher liberty than that—with the liberty of a *man* and a *citizen*. I take on nothing as a minister. I am not a minister; I am not a priest; I am simply an honest man, speaking to honest men. And I speak of things which concern the state and the country, not because you voted me right to do it, not because the Synod or any other conclave gave me the right; but because it is a right which inheres in my very being. When God said, "Let that man be born," he gave me the right. And I accept it. And I accord it to you, and to every living man who has a head and heart, and the feeling and the courage to use it with boldness in the service of the country.

Therefore, if men say, "What do you understand of the mechanism of politics?" I say, "I am not an engineer. The machinery of politics I know very little about; but I know what courses tend toward everlasting rectitude. I know what courses tend toward intelligence. I know what courses tend toward liberty. I know what courses make men out of men, and what courses make slaves out of men." And I know these things better than men do who dabble in politics. For, when a man nuzzles in the mud, when a man forgets God, and forgets country, and forgets manhood, that he may go down and mould in the lower parts of the earth his nefarious plans, I know more than he does, because I stand out in the upper light. And if he says, "You do not know what I know," that is the reason I know more than he does, and am better qualified to be a teacher of rectitude in public affairs than if I had stultified my moral sense, and blinded myself to the interior elements of public political life.

Ah! it is possible for a man to go through the furnace that Shadrach, Meshach, and Abednego went through; but woe to the man who goes into the furnace if he has not the faith of Shadrach, Meshach, and Abednego! Woe be to the man that goes into the fire until "the form of the fourth" is seen walking with him! Woe be to the man that goes to Albany or Washington unless the Lord goes with him!

Do you say, "Is not this strange to be talking on Sunday night and in a church about these things?" What then! do you not believe that men are corrupt? Do not you believe that the young men are perverted in their ambition? Do not you believe that the bottom is falling out of honesty? Do not you believe that men are falling as far from patriotism, as he fell from virtue, who,

> Nine times the space that measures day and night
> To mortal men,

was hurled,

> With hideous ruin and combustion, down
> To bottomless perdition?

And is there to be nobody to say any thing about these things? Have you a church that is like a boy's toy? and am I to stand and play on my trumpet for the amusement of the nursery? Am I to see humanity damaged to its very core; am I to see the nation shaken to its deepest foundations; am I to see God's cause in imminent peril, and must I *remember that I am a minister,* and not talk about these things? Is that your idea of a minister's business? Is that your idea of fidelity on the part of a minister? Was that the course that made Isaiah and Jeremiah what they were? Was that the course that made Paul what he was? Was that the course that made martyrs and confessors? Was that the course that made every reformer who was hated in his own age and worshiped in the ages that followed?

Do you say that it is not my business to regulate public affairs? I tell you, it is the business of every man to whom God gives the opportunity, the understanding, the courage, and the impulse; and it is my business. And if the centurion says, "I would rather believe the ship-master and the owner," and he goes out, and will not take my advice, it will not be long before I shall have the chance to say to him after the desolating storm, "You ought to have heard my words."

There is a remarkable illustration of this whole matter carried through and enacted in the matter of slavery. For years and years God's teachers in the North declared what was the terrific effect of slavery upon political economy, and people would not believe it. They declared what was the effect of slavery upon the public prosperity, and men would not believe it. They declared what was the effect of slavery upon personal morals and manhood in the South and men would not believe a word about it. They declared what the effect of slavery must be upon the master and the slave; and men would say to them, "You live at the North, and do not understand this matter. Why do not you go South and find out the facts in the case?" We said, "We know the tendency of slavery, and we know the tendency of liberty. We know that in a condition of slavery a man is ignorant and degraded, and that he can not be any thing else. We know, on the other hand, that there is nothing like the prosperity which springs from liberty." And this battle went on: we saying that slavery was violating every law of society, and every element of God's moral truth; and they declaring, "Your testimony is not worthy to be taken. You are not acquainted with our affairs. You do not understand the working of slavery as well as you would if you were in the midst of it."

Now the great drama is played out to the fifth act; and who was right? Who was wrong? Did we not have in the war overwhelming evidence of the evil effects of slavery upon a community? When the pressure came, how the South, with its institution of slavery, was smashed like an egg-shell! And the North with her free labor, and the training which free labor gives, went into the struggle, and came out stronger in every bone, and muscle, and nerve than when she went in. And we are better able to-day to go into such a conflict than we were at the beginning to go into that one. And how has the South come out? Lying along the ground, panting, poor, impoverished, utterly wretched and ruined! Are these the influences of slavery upon political economy? And yet men would not believe that slavery did not make communities rich. It was sucking out the blood of the people; and the war has proved it. Men said, "Slavery does not injure the master;" but did it not turn the hearts of fifteen States full of men away from as good a government as ever kindly permitted them to ride it? Did it not breed treason—and the treason of savagery? And in the process of the war did it not prove that what we call honor was scarce, and that what we call barbarity was rife and diffused far and near?

I hold that it is not possible to bring up a generation of men familiar with slavery, and accessory to it, and have them honest and honorable and incorrupt. I appeal to facts, and put it to you, if in the end slavery did not prove itself utterly weak, and if the communities where it existed were not crushed to atoms when the stress of war was brought to bear upon them. But more than any thing else, it was said that we did not understand the nature of the slave. It was declared that he loved his master so that he would not take his liberty: and then, in the very next breath, it was said that, if he were given his liberty, he would turn round and kill his masters, and wallow in their blood. What are the facts? Although during the war there were districts where there were a thousand black men to one white man, they patiently staid at home, without lifting a finger of violence, and attended the crops, and cared for the family, and performed every duty of their station, when they knew they had the power in their own hands; and yet, when the joyful proclamation of liberty came, with the power to enforce it, in a moment was there found one single man who disdained the boon? Was there found, from the old, praying, white-headed patriarch to the new-born child, one that did not *leap* for liberty? Yet, they said they understood their slaves better than we did. We told them that emancipation would be ennobling to the slave. They said it would leave them worse than it found them. And who were right, they that lived among them, or we that stood at a distance from them and judged them by the average of human nature, and the general principles of God's moral government?

It was said, "If you free the blacks, they will be so lazy that you can not do any thing with them. They will need somebody to take care of them." But it is the confession of all men that, in all those regions where there is distress in the South, the most prosperous class are the blacks. In the malarial portions of the South, the blacks are the most prosperous class. It was the testimony of Dr. Sears that, in the administration of the Peabody Trust Fund, the most of it was used for the establishment of Normal schools for the whites in the various States of the South, because it was felt that *the most destitute and ignorant class must be taken care of first!* And it is true in many parts of the South.

Besides, everywhere there is an appetite for knowledge in these men that people said were brute beasts. And there is a natural tendency now to industry, just as fast and as far as they see that it is safe for them to amass property for themselves. And they are almoners of bounty to the whites in not a few cases. Thousands of masters and mistresses are to-day the pensioners of their old slaves, who keep them from starvation. And who knew the nature of these people best, those that were inside of the sphere of slavery and came in contact with it, or those that were outside of its influence, and judged of it by general moral principles?

It was declared that they were a cowardly set; and when it was proposed to make soldiers of them, it was pronounced to be in vain to attempt it. But when soldiers *were* made of them, and in the battle-charge those men ran away from them who had despised them before, I think they occupied their time in repenting of that heresy, and admitting that there might be some courage in a "nigger," after all! For there is nothing for conviction like a thrust of the bayonet in a man, as he runs from the charge of an army of negroes. It lets out prejudice, and lets in the light! They are brave men, and they make noble soldiers, in every respect equal to white soldiers. They are different in some respects from other races; but the French soldiers differ from the English; and the Yankee soldiers differ from either. At any rate, the black man makes in his way a good soldier.

Who would believe that ten years ago, that eight years ago, I, on general moral grounds, was ridiculed for forming judgments that did not belong to my sphere, and because I expressed my opinion adversely to slavery? Men said, "You had better go down South and see for yourself what the condition of the slaves and their masters is. You will understand the subject, in the nature of things, better than you can while you are so far removed from there." And yet, the judgment of men of the North, on every point, in regard to the negro race, formed on the theory of political economy, on the knowledge of human nature, and on general moral principles, has proved to be more accurate, all the way through, than the judgments of the men that lived among them.

I think this is one of the most remarkable cases that ever came into the world, to show that *not* they that are in business or in any department of it, are the best judges of it, so far as it has relations to collateral interests and general questions of morality.

And this leads me, finally, to say that, judged by this case of the apostle, judged by the whole career of the apostle, and judged by these reasonings, there is no calling on earth that is so many-sided—no calling, let me say, that is so full of all natural life, so full of vitality, as the calling of the true minister of Christ. You take away from him, perhaps, the tiara, and robe, and mystic ordinances; you take away from him his proud pretensions; you take away from him that unconscious arrogance by which he puts himself higher than other men, and claims to be the lord of God's husbandry; and you reduce him to the mere level of a brother, so that he has nothing in the world but just the forces which he brings into a sanctified use, and he is what he is by the grace of God, and his influence is simply that which belongs to his character. It seems as though you had degraded him; but you have not. A man's influence and a man's power do not depend on the clothes he wears. It does not depend upon what position he occupies. It does not depend upon any thing of that sort. Put a man into a golden house, and set him to writing philosophical treatises, and if he has not the head for it, he fails. In the estimation of men he is ranked downward; and none of his exterior circumstances can keep him up.

Go into that little closet-room, not as large as this platform, in which Jonathan Edwards wrote his Treatise on the Will, in a cane-bottom chair, (which a man promised to give me and never kept his word;) and would you say that in that room about eight feet square, with a little miserable table and chair, it was not possible for a man to write an immortal treatise? You would have him sit on a meetinghouse steeple, and write under the broad canopy of heaven. You would have the place where he worked bear some proportion to his magnificent treatise. But what a man can do does not depend upon the place he is in. His head and heart determine this. You may put him where you please; he does not care. It does not make any difference whether a bird sits on the topmost bough, or the lowest bough of a tree; his song fills the air all round about. He sits, to all intents and purposes, wherever his song goes.

Now, a minister stands not entangled in any of these courses of business, and he is better able to judge of the moral effects of those courses, than the men who are in them; and his business is to follow out the right and the wrong connected with them in their infinite developments and applications. He is the friend of all men—even of wicked men—a better friend to them than they are to themselves, flashing light into their bat's-eyes, sounding alarms in their deaf ears, pointing out the road that they refuse to walk in, working for them, working for the community, working for God and for eternity. And when a man lives in this inspiration, do you suppose he fears what men shall do unto him, or what they shall say about him? Is there anything nobler in this life than such an inspiration? All that lies in God's broad hemisphere is his. All that the seasons bring from the equator to the poles is his. All that science develops is his. All that art knows is his. All that there is in beauty; all that there is in power; all that there is in treasure; and all that there is in knowledge—these are his instruments. "The earth is the Lord's, and the fullness thereof;" and he is God's son, sent of his father to do God's work among men. And he may take whatsoever his hands can handle, wherever it is. All things are right, and all things are lawful, to him who is bent on doing good.

Is there, then, any other calling like that of the minister of the Gospel? Is there any other business that is so nourishing? Is there any other business that has in it such intrinsic honor? Is there any other business in which a man can so well afford to go without external praise, when it is interpreted in this large light?

Oh! to bring men back to the All-Lover. Oh! to rebuke iniquity, that it may grow strong unto righteousness. Oh! to make men your enemies, that they may become your lovers. Oh! to wound them, that they may be healed into greater strength; to slay them, that they may live again, and live forever—is there any business that is nobler and more transcendent than this?

While men go delving in the mines of this world, while men pursue their various avocations, I would not say one word of discouragement to them; but when they look with pity upon me, and say, "Because you are a minister your sphere must needs be circumscribed, and you must be a kind of recluse," they understand it not. Higher than any other calling is that which stands between God and man in the spirit of love and fidelity.

If there be those, then, that are in the midst of life, or are entering life, and have had serious thoughts whether it was not their duty to become preachers of the Gospel, but have been held away by some ambitious sister, or some sweetheart, who has had thoughts of public honor and glory; if there be some that have looked wearily at the till and the chest, and have wondered and pondered whether it was best for them to throw away their life in the poverty of the pulpit; if there are any that have heard their companions gleefully marking out their vocation, and magnifying its trials and self-denials, and have sunk back from the prospect that they have before them, let me say to you, All these are deluding influences. I am happier every year of my life than, I had almost said, all the votaries of pleasure; I have remunerations in one year of my life greater than all they have that pursue the phantom of ambition.

I am angry when I hear people talk about the "awful responsibility" of being a minister. People sometimes say to me, "I should think you would shudder when you stand up before your congregation." I shudder? what should I shudder for? Do you shudder when you stand up before a garden of flowers? Do you shudder when you go into an orchard of fruit in October? Do you shudder when you stand up in the midst of all the richness and grandeur of nature? I shudder in your midst? "But the responsibility!" I have no responsibility. I am willing to do my duty; and what more is there than that? I will not stand for the consequences. I will do the best I can. I will say the best things I can every Sunday; I will bring the truth home to you; and I will do it in the spirit of love. Even when I say the severest things, it is because I am faithful to love. "But your care!" I have not a bit of care. I forget the sermon a great deal quicker than you do. "Your burden!" I have no burden. I take up the battle, and I lay the battle aside again as soon as it is over. And I shall sleep to-night as sweetly as any man that is here. And every man that is in the ministry, and is willing to love men, and to be faithful to them, will find joy in it from day to day.

I am the happiest man that lives. You could not tempt me out of this place. Suppose they had offered me the senatorship of the United States, do you suppose I would have accepted it? Never, never! I do not expect to be tried! It is not the style of men that they are after now! They do not look into churches and pulpits for public men, to-day! But were they to do it, there would be no temptation in it. There *could* be no temptation in it. Do you suppose I could be bribed out of the pulpit if Brown Brothers offered me a full half-partnership in their business? Never! There is not money enough in all the Rothschilds' coffers to bring me the happiness that I have in your confidence and generous support, and the liberty which I have of discharging my conscience by free speech in your midst. I tell you, there is a secret in living to do good. There is a secret in fidelity to men's consciences, and in that sympathy which can appeal to God and say, "Thou knowest that I love my country; thou knowest that I love my fellow-men; thou knowest that I love thee, and that my whole life, from core to circumference, and from circumference back to core again, is in this blessed work of reconciling men to God, and thus building them up in Christian virtue and purity." More happiness than you can extract from wealth, or honor, or pleasure itself, you can—I say to every young man who is rightly endowed, and who has a heart that beats for this world —extract from the sphere of the Christian minister. You never will find a nobler sphere than that. If you come for the sake of honor, if you come for the sake of support, keep away; but if you love the work, and are willing to take it through good report and through evil report, there is not on this earth another calling that delights as it does to be an ambassador for Christ, and to be a friend of man among men.

Here is a place where a man, humbling himself, becomes a leader. Here is a place where a man, throwing his life away, finds it. The pulpit is above all other places on the earth. It is higher than the law, higher than the Senate, higher than the Governor's seat, higher than the Presidency. And it is open to all. You can come if you love the business, and here you will find joys that care can not ruffle, and remunerations that time itself can not take from you.

And the best of it is, that when you have had all this, you have had nothing. It is but just a small handful of first-fruits thrown forward. The full reward shall come when God shall gather the little children. And those that I have brought in here—you and I—a great company of us—shall stand to-gether in the presence of the Redeemer, and see the smile of his love and the outstretching of his hands, and feel the beginning of heaven, which we are to enjoy forever and forever.

Oh! call me not away! Tempt me to nothing else! Now, henceforth, and forever let me know Christ for you, for your household, for your commerce, for your political economy, for your public affairs, for the State, for the nation, and the world—Christ, the Healer and the Redeemer.

11. THE GOSPEL OF

SWEET MANHOOD

What Is Salvation? 1872

BY HENRY WARD BEECHER

When Beecher did preach on traditionally religious subjects, he almost invariably blurred the radical disjunctions between God, man, and nature that had been central to Protestant orthodoxy. Occasionally, the warmth of his sentiments and the luxuriance of his rhetoric led him to a sermon like "The Comforting God" (1869), with its very close similarity to modern "peace of mind" writing. In the sermon printed here, he was somewhat more conservative, but his emphasis is strikingly different from that apparent in D. L. Moody, the adventists, and the Pentecostals, for whom documents are given later. In this sermon he is aware of Darwinism, but cannot wholly accept or approve of it. In 1885, he published EVOLUTION AND RELIGION (New York: Fords, Howard, and Hulbert, 1885) to report his final understanding that God might work as easily through evolution as in some single creative act. He was then able to declare, as he could not quite in 1872, that salvation was essentially a process, not a moment of decision.

From *Plymouth Pulpit, Volume 9* (New York: J. B. Ford, 1872), pp. 59–72.

I will read in the first chapter of Ephesians, from the fifteenth verse to the end:

Wherefore I also, after I heard of your faith in the Lord Jesus and love unto all the saints, cease not to give thanks for you, making mention of you in my prayers; that the glory of our Lord Jesus Christ, the Father of glory, may give unto you the spirit of wisdom and revelation in the knowledge of him: the eyes of your understanding being enlightened; that ye may know what is the hope of his calling, and what the riches of the glory of his inheritance in the saints, and what is the exceeding greatness of his power to us-ward who believe, according to the working of his mighty power, which he wrought in Christ when he raised him from the dead, and set him at his own right hand in the heavenly places, far above all principality, and power, and might, and dominion, and every name that is named, not only in this world, but also in that which is to come: and hath put all things under his feet, and gave him to be the head over all things to the church, which is his body, the fullness of him that filleth all in all.

This is Paul's recapitulation of the topics of his prayer for the disciples of Christ. I have selected it because it is eminent in two respects—as giving an exalted view of the work of the divine Spirit in the human soul in this world, and as giving a large and sublime intimation of what religion means in the heart of man. I have selected it, also, as giving, in pre-eminent words which are dim, I might say, with undisclosed glory, a conception of the power of the Lord Jesus Christ to effect in men that character which is so exalted, so rich, so noble, in this transporting vision of the apostle. Two grand ideas unfolded here are the recapitulation, as a statement from the apostle, of what he had been accustomed to do for the followers of Christ since he heard that they had come into discipleship; and of the destiny of man as revealed in Christ Jesus, Christ himself being the supreme influence and power by which that destiny was to be accomplished. Great as the work is, impossible as it seems to nature, and absolutely impossible as it is to unaided human power, being a vision of poetry—almost a rhapsody of transcendental prophecy—yet, when it is coupled with the majesty and might of Christ as representing the fullness of God's loving power, it becomes not only possible, but certain, and is the theme of unbounded joy in anticipation, as it will be the theme of transcendent joy in inheritance.

The development of the human character (a theme most fit at this period of the world's history, when so much is being learned about the past of men, when such humiliating disclosures are being made, and when there is so much that leads men gladly to look away from their origin), is a subject which may well deserve our consideration. The character of man originally is poor indeed. His average condition upon the globe is such as not particularly to attract our admiration. The feebleness of men in every part—in reason, in emotion, in moral sentiment—is apparent. The race as discriminators of that which is right; as knowing how to obey even the lowest cycle of laws, the material; and as knowing how to obey social and civil and spiritual laws—does not present a spectacle which it is pleasant to contemplate. As you rise step by step along these graded cycles of law, the comparison becomes more and more painful. Nor will the best specimens, under the best conditions, and with the longest development, bear too close a scrutiny. For human life is made up of infinite weaknesses. It is partially developed here and there. It yet lies in solitude in many places. As in some parts of a new country there are clearings on which remain the stumps of the original trees, and as these clearings are surrounded by the rank wilderness, so spots here and there in men's nature are partially developed, and the rest lies yet uncultivated.

Now, to look upon the race of men, and to predict that they are to come into a condition in which they shall be perfect in every faculty and harmonious in all their relations, seems like the dream of a poet run mad with hope; and yet such is the destiny that is pointed out in the New Testament ideal of men. Whatever may have been their origin, there is a process by which they are coming up to manhood. Whatever may have been disclosed concerning them, there is a creative method by which they are to become *men*. Whatever may be the discriminations between the different portions of the human race, as to which is highest and which is lowest; whatever may be thought in respect to men as denizens of this world, or as citizens of any part thereof, or as agents or factors of creation, there is no doubt in respect to their future as spiritual beings, as citizens of God's great household, the universe. Whether it be true or not, I do not propose now to argue, although it seems to me that an argument might be constructed on this point; but no man, supporting it to be true, will wish to resist its truth.

It seems to me that the most transcendent vision any one can look upon is that vision which is opened up in Christ Jesus of the condition and destiny of the human race in the ages which are yet to come, when they shall have been clothed in the virtues of the Lord Jesus Christ, and perfected, and brought home to the far-off spheres where perfection shall be consummated, and where we shall know what it is to be the sons of God. "It doth not appear," as the apostle significantly said, "what this means." We are sons of God, but what it is to be sons of God we do not yet know. There is something hidden under that title which man may not know till he attains. For there are no types of experience, and there are no sides of human knowledge which shall throw light on the full meaning of what it is to be a partaker of the divine nature. There are glimpses of what it may be for one to be possessed of perfect intuitional reason. All men, I suppose, sometimes have hours in which they *see*, not *think*. There are those who in certain directions are luminous; and they seem to be universal seers.

The time is to come, I suppose, when all men will dwell in this higher sphere, though probably with conditions and gradations. This dull light which burns as an oil-lamp wick burns, is to glow brighter than the light of the stars or than the sunlight. We are to be partakers of the divine nature.

Among the things which are most developed among men are the social affections. These act with every variation in the household, and with a diminishing ratio as the distance increases from *ego*—from self. But the time is coming when that love which we now see in this world—the noblest love that exists between motherhood or fatherhood and childhood—is to be disclosed in all directions, so that men shall find their whole nature irradiated, ennobled; all their life, so to speak, being filled with golden streams which run through it as a perennial fountain. The time is coming when these dull and obscure affections, which are so often cast aside, or so often used only in single instances, or so often employed as if they were medicines and not food, shall be developed. When every part of men's social nature shall be developed in symmetry and harmony, the soul that loves will be a very different creature from that which we yet have known here—as different as a single bell is from a chime of bells, or as a whistle is from an organ.

We are to be not only sons of God, and partakers of the divine nature, but we are to be *heirs* with Christ to the eternal inheritance which he has with God. And to be a co-heir is to be equal. We are to walk with equal foot-steps, side by side with him. The distance between us and Jesus he is to annihilate by the development and growth which he works in us. And though we are not to partake of the divine nature in the sense of infinity, we are to partake of it in the sense of quality, and with such significant power that we shall be companions with God walking step by step with him.

Henceforth I call you not servants; for the servant knoweth not what his lord doeth: but I have called you friends; for all things that I have heard of my Father, I have made known unto you.

Christ saith to his disciples, "I have made you my con-
fidential friends"; and that which to them was true, is to be
true to all who believe in the Lord Jesus Christ. This work
cannot be consummated in this world. It can only be begun
here. We see the seeds of it. We see its germs and pointings.
The future opens to us as a realm of transmutation, of growth
and development, transcendent above anything that we know
on earth. The apostle; the most inspired of the apostles; the
one most fit to be inspired; the noblest when inspired; in many
respects the greatest nature that ever lived among men—
Paul, with all his visions, with all his experience, with all that
he had of the grace of God wrought out in him—stands looking
into the other life, and says, "We know it only like a speck;
we know it only in spots, here and there." So rich, so radiant,
so glorious is the heavenly sphere, that when the apostle who
had been in the seventh heaven, and seen things which it was
not possible to utter, stood again among men, and looked into
the sphere above, the height, the depth, the length and the
breadth of the glory of God in Jesus Christ, and the power of
his redeeming love, were such that he said, "We know in part.
What we see here compared with what I saw there, is, as
what my childhood was compared with what I am now since
I have become a man."

When I was a child, I spake as a child, I understood as a child,
I thought as a child; but when I became a man, I put away childish
things.

The earth changes. Much that in this world seems to us
radiant and glorious is relative, and passes away. We read that
the things which are transient are to be shaken down, and
that the things which are permanent, which belong to ever-
lastingness, are to remain unshaken. The apostle says that
intellect, great as it is, will be transcended; that knowledge,
much of it as can be accumulated here, and important as it
really is, will be thrown into the shade, by and by; that when

we come to know things as they are, what we think we know now will hardly be as much as a punctuation point in an encyclopedia. Prophecies shall cease, and learning shall cease. All those things shall cease which men think are of so much value. Only three things will remain—hope, love, faith Essential, emotive soul-qualities, which are the marrow and substance of manhood in distinction from animalhood—these things will remain. And about these, as a center, will be gathered all those things which go to constitute the mind of man. These go on in the other life; and there they will far transcend what they are here. So glorious shall we be there that what we are here shall seem as nothing. And as the apostle stood and looked into that future, he said, "I am a child." He, the chiefest of all the apostles, and the noblest of the many inspired men of his time, or of any time, declared that he had but just begun to learn what was in store for him.

If I go to one who is scant of flowers, and carry in from the prairies an armful of blossoming beauty, he looks upon it with rapture, and says, "Where did so many flowers come from?" If I go to a poor garret-born or cellar-bred creature who never has been where flowers are raised, to one who has seen only single flowers, or to one whose nearest idea of vegetation is that of tobacco, and carry a beautiful bouquet to him, he looks upon it, and says, "Oh How wonderful!" But I say to him, "You do not know anything about flowers. Come and ride with me day in and day out, knee deep in them, over the grand prairie, and then tell me if you think this handful amounts to anything."

The man with an experience rich as the apostle's was; the man whose developments, whose traits of character, and whose life were pre-eminent for their likeness to the Spirit of the Lord Jesus Christ, yet said, "It all goes for nothing. We are children. We do not understand what we shall be when that which is perfect is come. That which is relative is to pass away. So great and noble and transcendent and pure and beautiful will be the disclosures of the future, so resplendent will heaven be, when we get there, that all we knew of earthly hope, will, as we look back upon it, scarcely seem to be a germ of that which we shall then realize."

Look at this acorn. How small it is! I can pocket it, and a dozen like it. I can carry it on my little finger. I can snap it. A child might sling it. And when it has grown a year or two it is a mere whip. A boy might uproot it. But let it grow through a hundred years, under the influence both of summer storms and of winter blasts, as well as of the mellow light and warmth of the sun and the sweet and refreshing nourishment of the rains; let it be toughened and made rugged by the changing seasons through a century; it will become an immense outspreading tree: and yet this acre-covering oak which is the product of that acorn is hardly a simile of the products of the world to come compared with the seed-forms of this life. For heaven is wider, infinitely, than the growth of this horizon. They are not to be measured by the growths of this winter sphere.

Now, Christ is not revealed as a heavenly fetich such that if you only believe in him you will by some mysterious arrangement, some superstitious influence, be drawn up and saved at last.

Christ is not revealed, either, as a philosophical problem; but if half the strength which has been exerted to dissect the nature of Christ and fix his place in the divine government, had been expended in discovering the truth of Christ born in you, the hope of glory; if this vast intellectual dialecticism had been inspiration or prophecy drawing the soul toward Christ as a Lover and a sympathizing Friend, how the heavens would by this time have blazed with that name which is above every name! But we turn aside to analyze and reconstruct; and thus the moral and spiritual strength of men, and the church itself, has been thrown away.

Neither is Christ revealed in the New Testament as a mere

ideal of beauty which men may look upon, from the standard of art and poetry. There is that in him which ministers to faith. There is that in him which gives to superstition, even, some degree of warmth. There is that in him which ought to bewilder a poet with joy, and which ought to make prophecy spread its wings as an eagle that is soaring toward the sun.

But it is not this, nor this chiefly, that is disclosed to us. Christ is disclosed to us as the Author and Finisher of our faith. He is so related to the work of developing and glorifying the human race that he is all in all; that he meets every one of those wants in the soul which are necessary for that final disclosure of glory which is to bring us up into the presence of God, and make us what I have been describing as the possibility and reality of the future. He is the Architect, the Engineer, the Leader, the Guide, the Schoolmaster; he is the Friend; he is the Father and Brother; he is the Rescuer and Saviour; he is the great Artisan and Artist of all the things which are required for the education of the race, for the disclosure of the human soul, till it comes to its maximum power and beauty and symmetry and joyfulness in the heavenly land.

Here, then, is the prayer of the apostle. It is a most glowing representation of the dignity and grandeur of the human soul in its future, and also of the glory and sufficiency of the Lord Jesus Christ as the instrument by which its destiny is to be wrought out.

I remark, in the first place, in view of this opening of the text, that we see herein the meagerness of the common ideas of religion. As it is usually regarded, it is a kind of insurance against hell, or a sort of guarantee or indorsement of heaven. I saw it stated, only last week, in a paper, "Mr. Beecher preaches manhood, whereas the Gospel preaches salvation." It is very true that I preach man in Christ Jesus. I am constantly endeavoring to augment a sense of manhood. I seek to inspire a higher ideal of the dignity and worth of men. In one sense it is true that I do not preach salvation, but in another and grander sense I do preach salvation pre-eminently. I say that the road to salvation is *salvableness*. I say that an essential to salvation is that man shall be worth saving. And I preach that Jesus Christ by the divine power fashions men into that which he wants to save, and that we are made salvable by the work which is wrought in us. I, not preach salvation? What is the end and aim of my ministry but to inspire men with a most enthusiastic and ardent longing to be saved? How? As a sneaking thief would be saved who had dodged the sheriff and remained a thief still? As some drunken brute would be saved, wallowing in the stye, but eluding inspection and staggering into the house, and on his bed snoring the fumes of his drunkenness away? No, not unwashed; not ungrown; not unbeautiful. Salvation means to me transformation. It means the fire of the Holy Ghost burning out men's dross. It means inspiration, elevation of soul, God-likeness, Christ-like-ness, heaven in you. Christ *in you*—that is salvation.

Salvation does not mean going where nothing can hurt you. It does not mean poor, beggarly hiding from storms. It is positive, energetic strength. It is manhood in magnitude. It is the power of God in the human soul. It is new life, new being. I, not preach that?

Oh! such a work as this—how different is it from routine experience! A man is convicted that he is a sinner—and that is a good thing. He gets a hope—and that is a good thing. And afterward he says, "I have religion"—and that is a good thing, too. But he goes on for ten years, and is not a bit more generous. He is not a particle more soft or sweet. He is as obstinate as he always was. He is just as irritable and just as unspiritual as ever, understanding nothing that he cannot eat, or that he cannot see and handle; loving money as he always did. If you ask him the reason for the faith that is in him, he informs you that he was convicted once. He tells you what a time he had when he was convicted. And he says that ever since he has had a hope.

Far be it from me to say that these, as stepping stones toward real growth and development, are to be spoken lightly of or to be despised. Yet they are mere transient steps. If a person is brought into manhood sweeter, brighter, nobler and more divine, that is getting religion. It is becoming more and more like God.

There is a great want of litheness and joyfulness and liberty in the experience of average Christians. We are not doing what we were commanded to do. I notice that when men in New York would sell their flowers, they fill their windows full of the most beautiful ones. As I came down Broadway the other evening, and passed the florists' shops, I saw vast bouquets, and vast piles of heliotropes, and rosebuds, and various other tempting flowers lying in the windows; and the sight of them made me wish to jump out, and run in, and get some of them. For they and I are cousins. They know me, and I know them; and I always like to stop and speak to them. I long for their companionship. But what if I had seen in those windows burdock, and bull-thistles, and all manner of ugly and hirsute and stinging nettles, should I have wanted to go near them?

What if some robustious Christians are always thundering out from their conscience censorious remarks about other people; what if other men are narrow and sharp and stringent in their faith; what if other men are oppressive and rigorous; what if other men are lean and gaunt like an empty sack; what if other men are like a plump barrel too much filled; what if there are all manner of characters that lack the Christian graces, does anybody, seeing their good works, want to glorify the Father which is in heaven? Do you suppose that when I see a frozen man I am warmed to glorify God? When I see men who profess to be religious, but whose life is devoid of the spirit of true religion, do not I say, with all my heart, "Deliver me from religion, if that is religion?" But if I see a man who knows how to do good; if I see a man who, doing good, does it from the love of doing it; if I see a man who, when reviled, reviles not again; if I see a man who is full of gentleness, and sweetness, and hope and faith, and who, when other men are alarmed, still goes about good, sweet, true, pure, loving, gentle, faithful to the end, I bow down at his feet, and say, "Where got you that spirit? Your God shall be my God." The gospel that we want to-day is the gospel of sweet manhood. We want a truly transparent gospel. We want a gospel that is translated. We want the gospel in its living forms.

Compare the average Christian life with those transcendent views of the glorification of human nature which are contained in the gospels—especially in those interpretations of the gospels, the epistles. How such a comparison rebukes the way in which we are living as Christian men! How far does it show us to be coming short of the duties which Christianity imposes upon us! But the work of Christianity we cannot see in full. It is a work which is largely in the future, though some of it is here.

Do you recollect going out into Prospect Park in Brooklyn when they were first laying it out? They were going to have a great park; and it *is* a great park. It is one of the most beautiful parks in the world, and you ought to be more proud of it than you are. But how did they go to work to make it? What did they do first? They took off everything that was beautiful from the surface, and heaped it in large stacks. They took off the sod and threw up the sub-soil, and the ground was like a man that had been skinned all over. It was ugly and hideous. By and by, however, there were some little bits improved. They spread out some soil, and put in some shrubs, and some small points here and there were made quite attractive. And they followed up this process little by little. The great bulk of the park, so far as its surface was concerned, was to be created; and here came out a bit, and there a bit, from year to year, and people said, "It is beautiful as far as it goes."

Men grow just so when God takes hold of them, and they begin to be Christians. The old growths are cleaned away, and transformations take place under the divine influence. Oftentimes a man looks less beautiful after the work of grace has first begun in him than he did before; but gradually his nature changes. In some directions it improves. One part after another begins to be wrought out by the divine discipline, and by the concurrent desire of men for education. Little by little the lineaments of the divine character come up. But the whole of it cannot appear until you get into a climate that is without winter. This is such a world that the highest degrees of human excellence cannot be attained until we get out of it. The lower forms, the foundation elements of the great structure, which require a certain physical manipulation, are begun and carried forward here; but as plants that are grown in green-houses are not taken out of doors until winter is gone, and have their glory in summer, so in this green-house of a world, as it were, we are sprouted; and it is not until summer dawns on this sphere, and we are transplanted to a soil where frosts no longer come, that we show all the power and beauty of our character.

So grand a plan demands an Architect and an Artist who is competent to carry it out. When you preach the doctrine of our dependence upon God in a certain way, it discourages men; and yet I think there is a way in which dependence upon God may be preached so as to encourage them. If a man says, "You have no power, and God demands of you things that are impossible to you," and leaves it in that gaunt and dialectic state, my reason is offended. It looks like a charge of injustice against God. I revolt at it.

I proceed, we will suppose, to build me a house on my peaceful hill. *I* proceed to do it. *I*, with my pick-ax, dig the cellar, every bit of it. *I* am able to do it, and wishing to be independent, *I* do it. *I* build the walls of the cellar, and carry the stones, all of them—*I* do it. *I* fix the mortar, and *I* put them in their places. *I* undertake to raise the whole frame. *I* prepare every timber, *I* saw every board, and *I* drive every nail. *I* undertake to build this house. And how long will it take me? There is but just one thing that I shall want when I get through, and that is another house about six feet long and two feet wide. I spend all my life building me a house, and I do it poorer than I could have it done for me. But I can build that house, provided I have an architect to give me a plan, and a contractor who will undertake to execute that plan, and who is competent to do it. And it will be I that build it. The work will be mine. It will be the result of my inspiration. It will be built by me, for my use. But I shall be able to do it because I have such enginery at my command, which works out my will.

I hear the voice of God saying, in the Bible, "Work out your own salvation, with fear and trembling." "Why," I say, "it is too much. I can not do it." "Work out your own salvation," still sounds out to me. But these passions, these irregular appetites, which come and go as ocean tides—how can I control them? How can I stop those storms which rage on the Atlantic? How can I bring down those mountains which are so high, or bring up those valleys which are so low? How can I sweeten those affections which have been created in me? How can I from day to day keep those purposes steadfast which are fugitive as the mercury in the glass? How can I symmetrize every part of myself? In despair I say, "I cannot build that spiritual house." Still the command, is "Work out your own salvation." But, blessed be God, there is something more. "For it is *God which worketh in you* both to will and to do of his good pleasure." There is my hope. I have an Architect. I have a Contractor. I have a mighty Workman. I have all that which is necessary to enable me to accomplish what I undertake. Now I can build my soul-house. Now I can do all that needs to be done, whether it be in time or in the eternal sphere; for it is God that is making out the portraiture and plan, and it is God that has undertaken to carry forward that plan, and it is God that works in me to do what I am doing.

Christ is all in all. In all personal power, he has adaptations to give us what we need. If it be reason that we need, there is the supply in Christ's nature. If it be moral sense or sentiment that we need, Christ stands over against it as bread stands over against the mouth when the body is in need of food. Whatever we need in social affections is provided for by the Spirit of the quickening God. When the will and purpose of men are right, and they attempt to work, everything is prepared for them.

This work is only begun in this world. The best man comes to his death without all this ripeness and glory that is described in the Bible. Men are discouraged, frequently, because they are not as good as persons that they read about in the Bible and in biographies; and one thing is very certain, that when a man is well dead and out of the way, he is a great deal better than he was before. Children that were torments to the whole neighborhood when they were alive—how glorious they are as they appear in Sunday-school books! And after men are once gone, what nobility dawns from them!

Partly this is illusive, and partly it is true. We do not see each other as we are. We do not use our best feelings as instruments by which to see the best things that are in our fellow-men. We use our worst feelings, and interpret the worst sides of those who are around about us. We are guilty of unequable judgments of persons with whom we have to do. And when they are gone, we make a new estimate; we take a new account of stock, and come to the conclusion that they were better men, all things considered, than we supposed they were. This "adulation of death," as it is sometimes called, proceeds from an amiable cause. Nevertheless, men, when they are once gone, are apt to be thought better men than while they yet lingered upon the earth. The best men are imperfect; but as an amusement, I have not the slightest objection to the contemplation of the doctrine of perfection on earth. It is a very pleasing recreation, and I do not know why it may not be indulged in sometimes as well as other recreations. It occupies time that might be worse spent. But the idea of perfection in this world belongs to another system of theology from that in which I believe—an old technical system; a commercial system; a system in which is marked out a line of attainments for men, the reaching of which entitles them to be called perfect. But if you take the spiritual notion of manhood, it is germinent, growing. It is not perfect until Christ is completely ripened in the soul a thing which does not happen in this life. There is no such thing as perfection on earth. There may be approaches in that direction; there may be attainments which point thitherward; but as to perfection, the word does not belong to the Christian scheme in this sphere. We are but begun on earth. In the other world much will be dropped. Much will go with us which belongs to our present state of existence; but much will be left behind.

I do not suppose an old ship-master could see a vessel that has gone over the ocean with him time and again, and that he has had many a good time in, stranded and lying high and dry on the coast, open at every seam, and dropping to pieces, without feelings of sorrow; yet I am not unwilling to drop this old body of mine. It has been a good body to me. It has served me night and day. I have made many pleasant voyages in it. But, after all, it has been a body of death to my soul; and it has hindered me. There has been a sharp contest between the good and the bad. And when I rise to the sphere where there are no such material laws as there are in this world, acting on such material bodies as ours; when to eat and drink and sleep are things of the past, and nothing but a vital soul is left, and I have only a spiritual body, then I shall rejoice. Faithful as this body has been, I shall gladly bid it goodbye. I shall say, without regret, "Farewell, body of death: all hail, body of life!"

We are coming to that land in which we shall lay aside much that belongs to our present state. If you ask me, "What of this enginery is to be left behind?" I reply that I do not know. It is a matter of speculation purely. But whatever is relative will be shaken down before it passes beyond this world, and that which is permanent will remain in the other life. Much will perish, but much will last.

This world is to us as a nest. What is a nest to birds? It is the place where they are born, where they are bred, and where they are fledged. But when once a bird has been born, and has grown strong, and is winged, is the nest a place for him any longer? By as much as it was good for his helplessness, it is worthless for his strength. Now that the bird is developed, and can soar into the hemisphere above, it has no further need of a nest.

This world is good for a nest, but it is bad for a flying-place. It is a good place to be hatched in, but it is a bad place to practice one's wings in. If a man has power to fly, he does not want to be confined to a nest. The glory and power of the eagle is never known while he lives on his cliff—not till he has abandoned that, and sought his new home.

This, to me, casts a cheering light on the matter of dying and death. Death to me is a gate of pearl. It is Milton's "golden gate on golden hinges turning." Dying is more than going home to God. It is more than going home to friends and friendship. It is also going home to find out what we ourselves are. It is going home to find our soul-self. It is going home to our true nature. It is enfranchisement.

There are many a dungeon, to-day, men who have been there, unsunned, for years and years, down deeper than the roots could go. There, in their unventilated prison, vermin-covered, chilled, and almost bereft of reason itself, they drag out a miserable existence. But suppose their prison-doors should be thrown wide open, and they should be called, by some liberating army, as the Italians were, to leave their dungeons, would they think it a misfortune? Would they count liberty to be a burden, and the chance to be free again a thing to be wept about? And we, that are of the earth, earthly; we that are of the flesh, fleshly; we that are infants undeveloped; we that have a thousand germinent points, beginnings, almost none of which are grown; we that are waiting, not for the redemption of the body, but for redemption from the body— for the enfranchisement of the spirit—shall we speak of death gloomily? Shall we count those unfortunate who have gone through the gate of death? All hail! sweet children, who know not the storm nor the winter, but who from out of the warmth of the mother's arms have stepped, at one sweet moment, into the warmth of the Saviour's love. All hail! those who are called in the midst of the battle of life to go to a higher sphere, and to the exaltation of nobler functions. Ye who are from day to day growing weaker, and who seem to go on your way with striving, are still declining in the path, look up and thank God. The night is almost spent to you. Do you see the dawn in the east? and do you know the meaning of that sky? It is heaven. It is immortality.

These views encourage men, instead of discouraging them. I should be discouraged if I felt that all these advantages in life depended on me, or that they were the result of my fidelity in such a sense that every mistake I made would be a mistake whose full weight would rest upon me. But when I think that what I am I am by the grace of God, and that his grace will be ministered to me in the time to come, and that I shall be, not what I am able to attain by my own powers, but what I am able to attain by my strength and wisdom guided by sovereign strength and wisdom, I am encouraged.

More than that, brethren, in these views it seems to me we have that equipoise which we need in the disappointments and afflictions and besetments of life. If a man is going to his treasure, to his life, to his honor and glory, why need he complain of the fare on the way, even though it may be poor?

A man receives a message from Europe, informing him that an uncle of his has died leaving him a hundred and twenty thousand pounds sterling; and he throws off his apron, and says to the old hammer, slinging it in the corner, "Lie there;" and he says to the bellows, "I don't blow you any more;" and he bids farewell to the shop where he has toiled for so many long years, and puts on his best clothes, and starts for New York to take passage for his fatherland. But the weather is dry, and the car is dusty; and suppose the conductor should find him crying because it was so dusty, and because he had nothing to eat, and because, on the whole, the cars jolted so, and because, the train being delayed, he had lost an hour or so? Think of a man whining in that manner on his way to a fortune! It would be impossible. You could not do anything to that man to make him complain. He says to himself, all the time, "I am going to England to get a fortune—half a million." If you listen to his heart, you will find that he is saying. "I am worth half a million, half a million, half a million." Every clock that he sees ticks, "Ducats, ducats, ducats; dollars, dollars, dollars." And what does he care for anything else? If a man insults him he hardly notices it, and says, "That man does not know who I am. He does not know anything about me." Elated and joyous he goes through night and day, and takes everything that comes without a murmur, saying, "Soon I shall be in possession of my fortune; and what do I care for these little things?"

There is no treasure on earth like that which is laid up for us in heaven. There is no honor like that which surrounds that treasure in heaven. No friends on earth stand around the recipient of a great fortune like those friends, pure-handed and pure-hearted, who wait for our coming in heaven. They often come and look through to see how we fare. They stand on the battlements, in sympathy with all God's good universe, and see our warfare and doubts and discouragements, and call out to cheer us by the assurance of the reality of the heavenly life of manhood and joy, and say, "Come! come!" My father calls me to come. Through scores of years I have never ceased to hear the sweet soft voice of my mother saying to me, "Come!" My little children, with hands outstretched, call me, saying, "Come! Come!" and their voices fall as gently on my inward ear as the dew falls upon the flowers. Those that have labored with me, and have gone, say "Come!" The Father, the Spirit, and Jesus, say "Come!" And "let him that heareth say Come! and whosoever will, let him come and take of the water of life freely."

12. CONVERSION

Faith, 1876

BY DWIGHT L. MOODY

Through the winter and early spring of 1876, Moody conducted a series of revival meetings in New York City. As usual, he spoke from notes, and the only real record of his words comes from stenographic reports made by teams of men from the Tribune who struggled to keep up with the torrent of 230 words a minute. If these reporters improved on Moody's often uncertain grammar, their accounts preserve the verbal simplicity, the homely anecdotes and analogy, the unconcern for theological subtlety or moral paradox that contributed to the force of Moody's sermons. Usually more than 12,000 people were packed into the New York Hippodrome to hear him. In his sermon on "Faith," he made crystal-clear just how desperately men needed to be saved, and how simply faith could be achieved.

In beginning his sermon, Mr. Moody called attention to a clause of the 20th verse of the 5th chapter of St. Luke: "When he saw their faith." A little while before this, said he, Christ had been driven out of Nazareth, in his native town, and had come down to Capernaum to live, and He had begun His min-

---

From D. L. Moody, *Glad Tidings* (New York: Daily Tribune, 1876), pp. 21–31.

istry, and some mighty miracles had already been wrought in Capernaum. A little while before this, one of the officers in King Herod's army had a son who had been restored. Peter's wife's mother, that lay sick with the fever, had been healed, and Mark tells us that the whole city was moved, that they had come to the door of the house where He was sitting, the whole city bringing their sick. In fact, there was a great revival in Capernaum. That is what it was, and it is all it was. The news was spreading far and near. Everybody coming out of Capernaum was taking out tidings of what this mighty preacher was doing, and His mighty miracles, and the sayings that were constantly falling from His lips. And we read in a few verses before this 20th verse, that a man full of leprosy had come to Him and said: "Lord, if Thou canst, make me clean," and I want to call your attention to the difference between a man that had the palsy and the man that had the leprosy. The man with the palsy had friends who had faith. The man who had the leprosy had no friends who believed he could be cleansed. There had been no leper cleansed for 800 years, and we read back in the days of Elisha that there was a leper that was cleansed, but none since that time until now. Here is a leper that has faith and goes right straight to the Son of God Himself; and I want to say if there is a poor sinner here to-night that has not got any friends that would pray for him, you can go right straight to Jesus Himself. You don't need any Bishop or priest or potentate to intercede. Right away to Christ came this poor leper. He said: "If Thou will, Thou canst make me clean."

There is faith for you. He did not say, like the man in the 9th chapter of Mark: "If thou canst do anything for us, have compassion." He put the "if" in the wrong place; but this leper said, "If Thou wilt, Thou canst do it." It pleased the Lord, and He said: "I will. Be thou clean," and away went the leprosy. He was made well in a minute, and of course this news had gone out of Capernaum, and not only the city was stirred, but the country also, and now we read that they were coming up from all parts of Judea, from Galilee and all the villages, and even from Jerusalem. The news had reached Jerusalem, and the Pharisees and philosophers and wise men, were coming up to this northern town to see what this great revival meant. They didn't come up to get a blessing. Like a great many who come to these meetings, they came out of curiosity. They came to see how it was that this man was performing such mighty miracles, and they were told that He was in the house. There they were sitting around the Master, and we are told the power of the Lord was present to heal them. But it don't say that they were healed. They didn't think that they were sick and needed a Saviour. Like hundreds now that are drawing around them their filthy rags of self-righteousness, they think they are good enough without salvation, and they just come here to reason out the philosophy of the meeting, and how it is so many people come together night after night to hear this old Gospel, which has been preached 1800 years. "And the power of the Lord was present to heal them." I have thought a number of times what a glorious thing it would have been if they had all been healed. What a glorious thing if those men coming out of Judea had been converted and gone back to publish the glad tidings in their homes and villages. What a revival it would have been. But they didn't come for that purpose, but only to reason out the thing.

But while these things were being done, suddenly a noise was heard overhead. The people heard a noise on the roof and looked up to see what was the matter. Now, there were four men in Capernaum—I have an idea they were young converts—who found a man who had the palsy, and they could not get him to Jesus. Matthew, Mark, and Luke all three give an account, but don't one of them say that the man himself had any faith. I can imagine these four men said to the man with the palsy, "If we can get you to Jesus all He has to do is to speak and the palsy is gone." And I see these four men making arrangements to take this man with the palsy away to Christ. They prepared a couch something like the stretcher we had in the war, and I see these four men each one taking his place to carry that couch through the streets of Capernaum. They go with a firm step and steady tread. They are moving toward that house where Christ is. These men have confidence. They know that the Son of God has power to heal this man, and they say, "If we can only get him to Jesus, the work will be done;" and while these philosophers and scribes and wise men were there, trying to reason out the philosophy of the thing, these men arrived at the door, and for the crowd could not get in. They undoubtedly asked some of the men to come out and let this man with the palsy in; but they could not get them out, and there they are. But faith looks over obstacles. Faith is not going to surrender. Now these men felt they must get in in some way, and I can imagine they went to one of the neighbors and asked them, "Just allow us to use your stair-way. Here is a man that has the leprosy and we want to get him in," and I see the men taking this man up, and at last they got him upon the roof of the house where Christ is preaching; and now you can hear them ripping up the roof, and every-body looks up to see what the noise is; and at last they see that while Christ is preaching these four men are making a hole large enough to let a man down through.

He must have been a good man, or he would have com-plained to see his roof torn up in that way. But these men wanted to get the leper cleansed. That was worth more than the roof. They wanted to get the man blessed. They let the man right down into the presence of these Pharisees and Scribes. It would have been like letting him down into an ice-house if Christ had not been there. Those Scribes and Phari-sees—they didn't have any compassion; they didn't have any sympathy for the fallen; they didn't have any sympathy for the erring. There was One who had sympathy for the man who was suffering. They laid him right down at the feet of Jesus.

My friends, you can't take palsied souls to a better place than
to the feet of Jesus. They called upon the crowd to stand aside
and make room, and they just placed him at the feet of Jesus.
Christ looks up, and when He saw their faith—not the man's
faith; it don't say that he had any—He saw their faith—that's
the point. I believe that that whole miracle is to teach us that
that whole lesson is to teach us Christians that God will honor
our faith. I see the Son of God looking up at those four men
who laid this leper down. He looked up yonder and saw their
faith. There is nothing on this earth that pleases Him so much
as faith. Wherever He finds faith it pleases Him. Twice Christ
marvelled. I believe Christ marvelled only twice. Once He
marvelled at the faith of the Centurion, and He marvelled at
the unbelief of the Jews.

When He saw their faith, He said to the man looking down
at Him, "Be of good cheer; thy sins are forgiven." Why, he
didn't come for that; he only expected to get rid of his palsy;
he didn't expect to have his sins forgiven. These men begun
to look around with amazement. "That is a very grievous
charge; He forgives sin. What right has He to do that? It is
God and God alone who does that." I tell you the Jews to a
man didn't believe in the divinity of Jesus Christ. They began
to reason among themselves, but Christ knew what they were
thinking about. He could read their thoughts. Christ said to
them, "Is it easier for me to say to the man, 'His sins be forgiven,' or for me to say, 'Rise up and walk?' Now that you may
know that the Son of Man hath power to forgive sins, I say,
'Rise up and walk.'" Now the man was a leper. He hadn't the
power to rise, but he leaps up in a minute. He packs up that
old bed that he had lain on for years, and away he goes. The
man walks out with his bed on his back, and away he goes
home. The men began to look at one another with amazement,
and one and another said, "We have seen strange things to-
day." How long did it take the Lord Jesus Christ to heal that

man? Some men say, "Oh, we don't believe in instantaneous conversions." How long did it take the Lord to heal the man of the leprosy? One word, and away went the leprosy. One word, and the man stood up, and he rolled his bed up, and away he went on his way home. I should like to have seen his wife. I can imagine she was about as surprised as any woman you ever saw.

But now the word I want to call your attention to is this: "When He saw their faith." Now, there are a great many men in New York that don't have any faith in the Gospel at all. They don't believe in that Bible. There are a great many men in New York who are infidels. There are a great many skeptics. There is one thing that encourages me very much. The Lord can honor our faith, and raise those men. "When He saw their faith." Suppose a man should go to the house of his neighbor, and say, "Come, let us take neighbor Levi to neighbor Peter's house; Christ is there, and we can get him healed," and the two found they weren't able to carry the man, so they got three, and the three weren't able, so they got the fourth. Now I don't know of anything that would make a man get up quicker than to have four people combining to try to bring him to Christ. Suppose one man calls upon him after breakfast; he doesn't think much about it; he has had some one invite him to Christ before. Suppose before dinner the second man comes, and says, "I want to lead you to Christ. I want to introduce you to the Son of God." The man has got quite aroused now; perhaps he has never had the subject presented to him by two different men in one day. But the third man has come, and the man has got thoroughly aroused by this time, and he says to himself, "Why, I never thought so much about my soul as I have to-day." But before the man gets to bed at night the fourth man has come, and I will guarantee that he won't sleep much that night—four men trying to bring him to Christ. If we can't bring our friends to Christ, let us get others to help us. If four men won't do it, let us add the fifth, and the Lord will see our faith, and the Lord will honor our faith, and we will see them brought to the Son of God.

When I was at Nashville during our late war, I was closing the noon prayer meeting one day and a great strong man came up to me, trembling from head to foot. He took a letter out of his pocket and wanted to have me read it. It was a letter from his sister. The sister stated in that letter that every night as the sun went down she went down on her knees to pray for him. The sister was six hundred miles away, and said the soldier, "I never thought of my soul until last night. I have stood before the cannon's mouth and it never made me tremble, but, Sir, I haven't slept a wink since I got that letter." I think there is many a Christian here who understands what that letter meant. The Lord had seen her faith. It was God honoring faith, and it was God answering prayer. And so, my friends, if God sees our faith, these friends that we are anxious for will be brought to Christ. When we were in Edinburgh a man came to me and said, "Over yonder is one of our most prominent infidels in Edinburgh. I wish you would go over and see him." I took my seat beside him, and I asked him if he was a Christian. He laughed at me and said he didn't believe in the Bible. "Well," said I, after talking for some time, "will you let me pray with you? Will you let me pray for you?" "Yes," said he, "just pray and see if God will answer your prayer. Now let the question be decided." "Will you kneel?" "No, I won't kneel. Who am I going to kneel before?" He said it with considerable sarcasm. I got down and prayed beside the infidel. He sat very straight, so that the people should understand that he was not in sympathy at all with my prayer. After I got through I said, "Well, my friend, I believe that God will answer my prayer, and I want you to let me know when you are saved." "Yes, I will let you know when I am saved," all with considerable sarcasm. At last up at Wick, at a meeting in the open air, one night on the outskirts of the crowd I saw the Edinburgh infidel. He said, "Didn't I tell you God wouldn't answer your prayer?" I said, "The Lord will answer my prayer yet." I had a few minutes conversation with him and left him, and just a year ago this month, when we were preaching in Liverpool, I got a letter from one of the leading pastors of Edinburgh stating that the Edinburgh infidel had found his way to Christ and found the Lord. He wrote an interesting letter, saying how God had saved him. And there may be many in the City of New York who will laugh at this idea, and they will cavil, and perhaps they will say to-night that God don't answer prayer; but He does, if Christians will only have faith. God can save the greatest infidel, the greatest skeptic, the greatest drunkard. What we want is to have faith. Oh, let that word sink down deep into the heart of every Christian here to-night, and let us show our faith by our works.

Let us go out and bring all our friends here, and if there is poor preaching, we can bring down from Heaven the necessary blessings without good preaching. In Philadelphia a skeptic came in just out of curiosity. He wanted to see the crowd, and he hadn't more than crossed the threshold of the door before the Spirit of God met him, and I asked him if there was anything in the sermon that influenced him, in hopes that I was going to get something to encourage me; but he could not tell what the text was. I asked him if it was the singing, but he didn't know what Mr. Sankey had sung. It was the power of God alone that converted him, and that is what we want in these meetings. If we have this power, when we invite our friends here the Lord will meet them and will answer prayer and save them. Let us go and bring our unconverted friends here. All through the services let us be lifting up our hearts in prayer. God save our friend! O God, convert him! And in answer to our prayer the Lord will save them.

While in London there was a man away off in India—a godly father—who had a son in London, and he got a furlough and came clear from India to London to see after his boy's spiritual welfare. Do you think God let that man come thus far without honoring that faith? No. He converted that son, and that is the kind we want—where faith and works go together; and if we have faith God will honor it and answer our prayer. Only a few years ago in the City of Philadelphia there was a mother that had two sons. They were just going as fast as they could to ruin. They were breaking her heart, and she went into a little prayer-meeting and got up and presented them for prayer. They had been on a drunken spree or had just got started in that way, and she knew that their end would be a drunkard's grave, and she went among these Christians and said, "Wont you just cry to God for my two boys?" The next morning those two boys had made an appointment to meet each other on the corner of Market and Thirteenth sts.—though not that they knew anything about our meeting— and while one of them was there at the corner, waiting for his brother to come, he followed the people who were flooding into the depot building, and the spirit of the Lord met him, and he was wounded and found his way to Christ. After his brother came he found the place too crowded to enter, so he too went curiously into another meeting and found Christ, and went home happy; and when he got home he told his mother what the Lord had done for him, and the second son came with the same tidings. I heard one get up afterward to tell his experience in the young convert's meeting, and he had no sooner told the story than the other got up and said: "I am that brother, and there is not a happier home in Philadelphia than we have got;" and they went out, bringing their friends to Christ.

Let us now show our faith by our works. Let us away to our friends, to our neighbors, and to those we have an influence over, and let us talk about Christ and let us plead with God that they may be converted, and instead of there being a few thousands converted in New York, tens of thousands can be converted; and let our prayers go up to God in our homes and around our family altars. Let the prayers go up, "O God, save my unconverted husband." "O God, save my unconverted wife." "O God, save my unconverted children," and God will hear that cry. As I was coming out of a daily prayer-meeting in one of our Western cities, a mother came up to me and said, "I want to have you see my husband and ask him to come to Christ." I took out my memorandum book, and I put down his name. She says, "I want to have you go and see him." I knew the name and that it was a learned judge, and so said to her, "I can't agree with him. He is a good deal older than I am, and it would be out of place. Then I am not much for infidel argument." "Well, Mr. Moody," she says, "that ain't what he wants. He's got enough of that. Just ask him to come to the Saviour." She urged me so hard and so strong, that I consented to go. I went up to the office where the Judge was doing business, and told him what I had come for. He laughed at me. "You are very foolish," he said, and began to argue with me. I said, "I don't think it will be profitable for me to hold an argument with you. I have just one favor I want to ask of you, and that is that when you are converted you will let me know." "Yes," said he, "I will do that. When I am converted I will let you know"—with a good deal of sarcasm. I thought the prayers of that wife would be answered if mine was not. A year and a half after I was in that city, and a servant came to my door and said: "There is a man in the drawing-room." I found the Judge there. He said: "I promised I would let you know when I was converted." I had heard it from other lips, but I wanted to hear it from his own. He said his wife had gone out to a meeting one night and he was home alone, and while he was sitting there by the fire he thought, "Supposing my wife is right, and my children are right: suppose there is a heaven and hell, and I shall be separated from them." His first thought was, "I don't believe a word of it." The second thought came, "You believe in the God that created you, and that the God that created you is able to teach you. You believe that God can give you life." "Yes, the God that created me can give me life. I was too proud to get down on my knees by the fire, and I said, 'O God, teach me.' And as I prayed, I don't understand it, but it began to get very dark, and my heart got very heavy. I was afraid to tell my wife, and I pretended to be asleep. She kneeled down beside that bed, and I knew she was praying for me. I kept crying, 'O God, teach me.' I had to change my prayer, 'O God, save me; O God, take away this burden.' But it grew darker and darker, and the load grew heavier and heavier. All the way to my office I kept crying, 'O God, take away this load.' I gave my clerks a holiday, and just closed my office and locked the door. I fell down on my face; I cried in agony to my Lord, 'O Lord, for Christ's sake, take away this guilt.' I don't know how it was, but it began to grow very light. I said, I wonder if this isn't what they call conversion. I think I will go and ask the minister if I am not converted." The old Judge said to me: "Mr. Moody, I have enjoyed life in the last three months more than all put together." The judge did not believe, the wife did, and God honored her faith and saved that man. And he went up to Springfield, Ill., and the old Judge stood up there and told those politicians what God, for Christ's sake, had done for him. And now let this text sink down deep into your hearts: "When He saw their faith." Let us lift up our hearts to God in prayer that He may give us faith.

13. THE RESPONSIBILITIES OF

THE CONVERTED

Address to Young Converts, 1876

BY DWIGHT L. MOODY

----

*According to his regular practice, Moody devoted the last
meeting of the revival to an address to "young converts." His
words of advice neatly sum up his vision of Christian life, un-
complicated by intellectual challenges, social problems, or
economic dilemmas. After conversion as before, man stood
alone with his God.*

My text this evening is in the 14th chapter of Romans, 4th
verse, "God is able to make him stand." There are a great many
luke-warm Christians that are themselves saved, and yet who
really believe in their hearts that these young converts won't
stand long. Some people will give them six weeks, and some
six months, and then all will be over. That has been the cry
ever since I can remember, ever since I have been a Christian.
I suppose we will hear it to the end of time. Well, there are
some who do not hold out, but think of the thousands and
thousands that do. "He is able to make us stand;" and if you
young converts in the morning of your Christian experience,

From D. L. Moody, *Glad Tidings* (New York: Daily Tribune, 1876),
pp. 446–460.

learn this one lesson, it will save you from many a painful hour. Yes, it is God that will make you stand. You cannot stand yourself.

I hear a young convert get up and say, "I am going to hold out." That is not the way to put it. You will not unless God lets you. He is able to make you stand. He was able to make Joseph stand there in Egypt; He was able to make Elijah stand before Ahab; He was able to make Daniel stand in Babylon. So my friend, you need the same grace and the same power that all these did. They have gone on before you. Your strength lies in God, and not in yourself. The moment you lean on yourself, down you go. The moment we get self-contented and think we are able to stand and overcome, we are on dangerous territory; we are standing upon the edge of a precipice. When I first became a Christian I thought I would be glad when I got farther on, and got established. I thought I would be so strong and there would not be any danger; but the longer I live, the more danger I see there is. The only hope of any Christian in this house is to keep hold of Christ. We may fall after we have been Christians for twenty years; a good many fall at a very old age.

But though we fall, we are not therefore lost. A man may fall and not be lost. Perhaps the old Adam comes uppermost and they commit some sin and then get discouraged. It is no sign that a person is not a Christian because he falls into sin. He is as much a Christian as ever if he repents and hates his sin. If he loves his sin and lives in it, he has never been truly converted. If he hates the sin and turns away from it, and mourns over it, it is a sign that he has been converted. If you fall into sin, do not get discouraged. Take it to God and confess it; tell Him all about it. He will forgive.

I want to guard you against self-confidence; there is the danger. You must keep your eyes open, and not be self-confident. Your strength lies in Another, and not in yourself. Take Christ as your model, not any other man on the face of the earth; because then, if you do sometimes make mistakes, if you do sometimes fall into sin, He will restore you. Just keep your eye fixed upon Him and remember all the while that He is able to make you stand. When we get into temptation, He is able to make a way for your escape, and to deliver you from every temptation. He won't suffer you to be tempted more than you can bear. In the second chapter of Hebrews and the 18th verse, we read "For in that he himself hath suffered, being tempted, he is able to succor them that are tempted."

It is encouraging to think He has been in this dark world and knows all about its trials and temptations. "He is able to succor those that are tempted." When temptation comes, it won't crush you; it won't bear you down. Perhaps the old nature will come up in you, but you must look to Him for strength. You know it is an old maxim "Don't give up to your impulse." That is not the advice I give. I say live right up to your impulse; live up to all the impulse that God gives you. Don't be afraid you are not going to have grace enough in the future. That is a mistake. Use all the grace that God gives you; He has plenty; the more you use, the more you'll get; He is able to succor them that are tempted.

About getting discouraged—when you sin, you know they say short accounts make long friends. Keep short accounts with God. You should see the face of God every morning before you see the face of any human being. If you come to the cross every morning, you never will get but one day's journey from the cross. You must say to yourself, "I want to feed my soul as well as my body a breakfast every morning. I want to see the face of God before I see the face of any earthly man." Just keep close to the cross, and close to Him, and if anything has gone wrong during the day or evening, do not sleep until that account has been settled. Take it to Christ and tell it right out to Him; tell Him how you are sorry, and ask Him to forgive you. He delights to forgive. That is what I mean by keeping a short account with God. You know when you go to a grocery store and get a little sugar, for instance, every few days, in a short time you will soon find that the grocer has a bill against you for ten pounds. You are surprised, and you likely say you never had it. You forget how much you did get. Perhaps then you quarrel with the grocer, and you have a great deal of trouble from it. Perhaps if you kept short accounts you would remember what you owed. Keep short accounts, or else you wont prosper. If you sin, bear in mind that you have an Advocate in Jesus Christ. We read in 2d Timothy, 1st chapter, 12th verse, "Nevertheless I am not ashamed, for I know whom I have believed and I know that He is able to keep that which I have committed unto him against that day." A man was asked what his persuasion was. He said it was the same as Paul's. I don't know what Paul's persuasion was. All persuasions claim him. Sankey says he is a Methodist. "Verily I am not ashamed, for I know whom I believe, and am persuaded that he is able to keep that which I have committed to him." That is Paul's persuasion. You may call it what you have a mind to, it is a good persuasion. If you have really been converted you have committed your soul, your body, your reputation, your life, your money, everything you have, to the Lord. Stick to this text: "He is able to keep that which I have committed to him." If the devil comes and tries to make you everything else but a Christian, don't listen to him, but just refer him right over to Christ. Tell him you have committed your case to Christ. He will take care of your cause; He is able to keep that which you have committed to Him.

A little boy was going home from school one day and met a big fellow who wanted to fight with him. He said "Well, wait till I go and fetch my big brother," and he ran off after his big brother and away ran the boy. So you tell Satan when he threatens to convince you, that you will go after Christ, and let Him settle it for you. You are no match for Satan. He is stronger than you are; but Satan flies when you bring Christ.

Then you are saved, and that is your only refuge. Jesus will be to you an Elder Brother.

A man with whom I was acquainted bought out a certain store. Everybody predicted that he would fail. Two or three men had failed one after another in the store, with more capital than that man had. Well, he went on, and on, and did not fail, and every one wondered why he got along so well. By and by it leaked out that he had a rich brother who kept furnishing money, and he kept close to him. So if you will only keep close to your elder Brother, He has all the treasures of heaven to place at your disposal; He will keep you. There is no trouble about your going back to the world if you keep close to Him.

Men go and put their money in the Bank of England, thinking it the safest Bank in the world. But why is it safe? Because every night when it grows dark you will see a whole band of soldiers going to that Bank. And they stand around it and guard it all night. So are the sentinels of Heaven camped around God's own children to guard them. God has legions of angels that He can send down to protect us when we call upon Him. Our help is in God alone.

O my friends, when Satan comes to you and tries to lure you away, bear in mind that Christ is your keeper, and you are not able to keep yourself. We want these young converts to go to work in God's service. "God is able to make you stand," God has grace enough. He wants you to come up to His throne and get all the grace you need to enable you to do the work. Now every single convert ought to be good for at least a dozen more, and be able to win at least twelve other souls to Christ. A convert lately gave me a list of names of those whom he had been trying to lead to Christ since he was converted. He was converted the 3rd of February, and he brought me a list of fifty-nine names of persons whom he had tried to lead to Christ during that time. Every young convert ought to be good for a dozen at least. If you are rescued you ought to try to rescue others. Every man, woman and child who is a Christian should go to work in this service. He says, "My grace shall abound that I shall be ready for every good work." One day I saw a steel engraving that I liked very much. I thought it was the finest thing I ever had seen, at the time, and I bought it. It was a picture of a woman coming out of the water, and clinging with both arms to the cross. There she came out of the drowning waves with both arms around the cross perfectly safe. Afterwards, I saw another picture that spoiled this one for me entirely, it was so much more lovely. It was a picture of a person coming out of the dark waters, with one arm clinging to the cross and with the other she was lifting some one else out of the waves. That is what I like. Keep a firm hold upon the cross, but always try to rescue another from the drowning. If you are rescued, haste to the rescue of some one else. Then you become stronger and stronger. Everything you do for Christ makes you grow in grace. "He that waters, shall himself be watered." The souls of these people that never do anything for Christ, become all dried up. It is hard to find any chords running from their souls to Him, or to others, because they never try to do anything for anybody.

When I was at Mr. Spurgeon's house, he showed me some pictures of his twin boys. He had had them taken every year since they were born and they were then seventeen. You look at the pictures from year to year, and there is not much difference between them; but in the seventeen years there is a great difference. So with you young converts;—there is not much difference in you from year to year; but as you grow in grace, in the course of seventeen years there will be a very great change. You want to grow from week to week, from month to month, and from year to year steadily, so you will become stronger in the service of God. "God is able to make all grace abound toward you."

You should try to learn from those who have been long in

the Church. If you take my advice you will select your friends from experienced Christians. You must keep in the company of people who know more than yourself. That's the way I do. Of course I get the best of the bargain that way, but that is what you want; you can learn something of them and will not be mingling with the ungodly and the unconverted. You need not become like ungodly people when you happen to be thrown with them; you can be in the world and not of it. Not only that, but what you want is to get in love with this blessed Bible; and the moment you get full of Bible truths, the world has lost its power. Then you wont be saying: "Have I got to give up this? Have I got to give up that?" You never hear Bible Christians talk in that way. There are some things I used to like to do before I was converted that I don't do now; but thank God; I don't want to do them. God has turned my appetite against such things. I have been fed upon this blessed Bible, until I have no longer any taste for the literature I used to like.

There are people who talk about killing and say they like to read novels to kill time. But a good Christian does not need to do that; he never has time enough. Why, if there were forty-eight hours instead of twenty-four, in a day and night, we would still want more time to work for the Lord. It is only a little while, a few days and hours, that we stay here and we have to do all that is given us to do in that short time. No child of God ought to talk of killing time.

I have one rule about books. I do not read any book, unless it will help me to understand *the* book. I want to tell you right here, that this is not anything that I have to give up. It is a great pleasure to get a book that helps unfold the blessed Bible. It is manna to my soul. If you young converts get in love with the Bible it will help you wonderfully. I advise you to go into a good Bible-class, and so get experienced Christians to help you. Go there and learn, and then go out and help teach others, and thus you will grow in grace. I want to have you understand one thing: that I am in favor of all men and women that love Jesus Christ, uniting with some church. And let me say, if the man who is your minister preaches the gospel, you stand by him; pray for him. What a help it is for a man that is preaching to have a lot of people in the pews praying for him. Don't go to church just to criticize. Any one can do that. If you feel inclined to criticize, just stop and ask yourself whether you could do it any better. Some men only make one mistake, that of finding imperfections in everybody and everything. I have got done looking for perfection in this world. If the minister does not preach the gospel, go out of his church and get into some church where the gospel is preached. I don't care what church it is; but if a man does not preach the gospel don't go to his church. And do not be running from one church to another. Go to one church and stand by your minister. If he holds up Christ, preaches the glorious gospel of Jesus Christ, stand by him. In Romans, 4th chapter and 20th verse, it says, "He staggered not at the promise of God through unbelief, but was strong in faith, giving glory to God. And being fully persuaded that what He had promised He was able also to perform."

Now, my friends, bear in mind that God's word is true, and it will help you wonderfully when you take up that word of God, to realize that every word of it is true. Infidels and sceptics will try to make you think it is not true. When they come to me and say that, I tell them "Well, if they can get me a better Bible, I will give this up, but not until then." But when there is no book that will bear any comparison with it or touch it, why should we give it up? What has infidelity to give us in the place of it? Bear in mind that these promises are all true. "He staggered not at the promises of God." Abraham was fully persuaded that God was able to do what he had promised to do.

An old man told me that he had marked at all the promises of God the letters "P. T."—which stood for "Proved" and

"Tried." None of the promises of God ever will or can fail. If you feed upon these promises you will become rich in grace. There is no discount on any word God has ever said. You know when Christ was born, it says that Cæsar sent out a proclamation that the whole world should be taxed, and so Mary was brought to Bethlehem. God had said that the child should be born at Nazareth, and it could not by any possibility have been born at Jerusalem. That tax was not collected for nine years after. The virgin was brought to Bethlehem just at that time, that the word of God might be fulfilled. "Abraham staggered not at the promises of God." Some times when our duty seems to promise some very difficult and almost impossible thing, people say, "But how is He going to do it?" I don't know how, but that is none of your business. A colored woman had it about right when she said that if God should tell her to jump through a stone wall, she would jump right through— that getting through would be God's work and not hers; He would see to it if she did what she was told. Take His Word as "a lamp to your feet and a light to your path" to guide you through this dark world.

In the 24th verse of Jude it says, "Now unto Him that is able to keep you from falling and to present you faultless before the presence of His glory with exceeding joy." That is one of the sweetest verses in the whole Word of God; not the sweetest—it is hard to tell which is the sweetest verse in the Bible. It is like a man that has ten children; he cannot tell which he likes best. How precious, how sweet these promises! Some converts have an idea that sometimes they have to fall. Some people think they have to get lukewarm sometimes, and wander off into the world. You do not get that idea from the Bible. An old man said to me once, "I am an old man now, but I never have lost sight of Christ since I first became converted." You have not got to fall; do not believe it for a moment. "Unto Him that is able to keep you from falling, and to present you faultless before the throne of God with exceeding great joy." May all in this assembly from this night be so kept from falling, and so presented before the throne. There is an institution in London where they take the poor little street Arabs in. They take him in and the first thing they do is to have his picture taken, just as he looks when they find him, in his rags and dirt. Then, after he has grown up there, and has had all the benefit of the institution, before he goes they have his photograph taken again; and they give him the two photographs. One is to show him how he looked when he came to them, and the other, that he may compare them. It would be a good thing if we could remember ourselves distinctly as we were when the Lord first found us, and compare it with ourselves when He leaves us on the hill-tops of glory.

It says in Deuteronomy: "He found him, He kept him, He led him about in the wilderness, and kept him as the apple of His eye." The Lord does it all. He found you; you did not find Him. People say they are seeking the Lord. The Lord seeks you. It is a double seeking. Christ seeks the sinner and the sinner seeks Him. It does not take long for an anxious Saviour and an anxious sinner to meet. The moment you are ready and willing to belong to Christ, He is ready and willing to save you.

Some people ask me questions about their daily walk and conduct. They say, "I would like to know whether it is right for me to go to the theatre?" "I would like to know whether it is right for me to smoke?" or, "to drink moderately?" I cannot carry your consciences; Christ does not lay down rules; He lays down principles. One rule I have had is this: If there is anything I am troubled about in my conscience, and am uncertain whether it is right or not, I give Christ the benefit of the doubt. It is better to be a little too strict than too liberal. And let me say to you young converts and you Christians here, the eyes of the world are upon you; they are watching.

For myself, I could not go to the theatre; I would not like to have my children go. I do not do anything myself that I would not like to have them do. I could not smoke, because

I would not want my boy to smoke. I could not read those flashy novels. I have no taste for them, no desire to read them; but if I did I would not do it. But, if you live to please Him, you will not have any trouble in these things. He says, "If any man lack wisdom, let him call on God"; He will give liberally to all.

Another rule is: Don't do anything you cannot feel like praying over. Once I received an invitation to be at the opening of a large billiard hall. I suppose they thought it was a good joke to invite me. I went before the time came and asked the man if he meant it. He said yes. I asked him if I might bring a friend along. He said I might. I said, "If you say or do any thing that will grieve my friend I may speak to him during your exercises." They didn't know what I meant, and knitted their brows and look puzzled. At last he asked, "You are not going to pray, are you? We never want any praying here." "Well," I said, "I never go where I cannot pray; but I'll come round." "No," said he, "we don't want you." "Well, I'll come, anyway, since you invited me," said I. But he rather insisted that I shouldn't, and finally I told him: "We'll compromise the matter. I won't come if you will let me pray with you now." So he agreed to that, and I got down with one rum-seller on each side of me, and prayed that they might fail in their business, and never have any more success in it from that day. Well, they went on for about two months, and then, sure enough, they failed. God answered prayer that time.

In Europe in a place where there was a good deal of whiskey distilled, one of the men in the business was a church member, and got a little anxious in his conscience about his business. He came and asked me if I thought that a man could not be an honest distiller. I said, you should do, whatever you do, for the glory of God. If you can get down and pray about a barrel of whiskey, and say for instance, when you sell it, "O Lord God, let this whiskey be blessed to the world," it is probably honest.

Do not live to please yourself. Live to please Christ. If you

cannot do a thing honestly, give it up let the consequences
be what they may. If you take my advice you will never touch
strong drink as long as you live. Nearly all the young converts
that have fallen in Europe have been led into it by that cursed
cup. Yes, but you say, some of the church-members, some of
the Christians that stand high, drink moderately. Well, don't
you touch it if they do. Some men have strong wills and can
tell where to stop; but bear in mind that ninety-nine out of a
hundred have not strong wills, and your son may be the very
next one to go too far. If it is not an injury to yourselves,
give it up for Christ's sake, and for the sake of others. And you
that have once been slaves to it, come out and try to rescue
others who are still slaves to it. As Dr. Bonner of Philadelphia
said. "Be sure you do not tarnish the old family name. You
have been born into the family of God, and you must sustain
its high credit." Some of these old families of New York think
a good deal of their names; and that is right. A good name is
worth more than riches. Now that you have become the sons
and daughters of God, do not disgrace the old family name.
The eyes of the world are upon you, walk as a son of a king,
as a daughter of heaven, a child of God, the world will become better for you, and by your walk and conversation you
will light others to Christ.

Turn to the 20th chapter of Acts, 32d verse. "And now
brethren, I commend you to God, and to the word of his grace,
which is able to build up and to give an inheritance among
all them which are sanctified." That was Paul's farewell to the
Ephesians. O, how sweet it is! "He is able to lift you up."
Some of the young converts have got their Bibles out, I see.
That is right. I marked that a good many years ago. It has
been a great help to me. Paul had been three years among
them, and had prayed and wept over them. If you learn your
Bible well you are certain to be good Christians. If the word
of God is not hid in our hearts, how can the Holy Ghost
work through us.

But let me give you a caution. You must not think that you may stop right here and spend the rest of your days giving your experience. I want to warn you against becoming self-satisfied. The moment that young converts come to be wise and to win some souls to Christ, Satan comes up and says, "You are getting along very well," and "Yes, that is a good act; an admirable work you are doing;" and then they get so puffed up with spiritual pride that God cannot use them.

The next danger is that they may be so afraid they will get puffed up, that they don't do anything. We have nothing to be proud of, really. Talk about the great work we are doing here. We haven't done anything. We ought to hang our heads to-night and be ashamed of ourselves,—not ashamed of Christ, but of ourselves,—there is a good deal of difference between those two things. We have not done anything worth speaking of; there is no chance of boasting. Why, if the Christians of New York really did come forward and exert themselves, what a time there would be! Be sure you do not get lifted up with spiritual pride. God will punish that; he hates spiritual pride. Satan knows that if he can get us puffed up with spiritual pride, it is all he wants; so he comes up and says, "What a glorious light he is. He is one of the brightest lights of the church." Look out for spiritual pride, as for one of your greatest enemies.

You have got nothing to be proud of. If you are ever used at all, bear in mind that it is God speaking in you, and not you yourself.

We do not say that gaspipe gives the light; it only conveys it. If we have any light in us, it is Christ's light. Let us be careful that we do not fall into that sin of being proud and lifted up.

That little word "able"—may it sink down deep into your hearts to-night. He is able to do all for you that you need to have done; and if you but make up your minds to rely on Him you will have strength as you need it.

It seems as if during the past ten weeks the Lord has wonderfully answered prayers, and the tide has risen here until it seems very high. Once I was told of a little child who lay dying. As its breath grew feeble, she said, "Lift me, papa." And he put his hand under the child and lifted her a little; and then she whispered "higher," and he raised her higher, and she still said "higher," and again "higher, higher," until he lifted her just as high as his arms could reach, until at last her Heavenly Father lifted her into his Eternal Kingdom.

So our prayer ought to be "Higher, higher, nearer my God to Christ." Every day we ought to make a day's march toward Heaven, and nearer and nearer to Him.

I do not like these farewell meetings. I want from the depth of my heart to bless you all for all your kindness to us here. I am glad so many have been blessed in their souls. Bear in mind that we shall pray for you, and if we do not see you again we shall look for you on the morning of the Resurrection. I don't like to say good-bye. But I can say, as I once heard Lucius Hart say: "I'll bid you all good-night, and I'll meet you in the morning." May God bless you all!

14. GOD'S PLAN OF THE AGES

The Day of Jehovah, 1906

BY CHARLES TAZE RUSSELL

*Many Americans in the late nineteenth century were dubious
about the steady progress of mankind onward and upward.
Leading intellectuals like Henry Adams flirted with the notion
of some impending cataclysm. The recourse for men who
shared this sense but also retained a religious outlook was not
to ideas of entropy or the passing of Anglo-Saxon power but
to pre-millennialism—the belief that the Second Coming of
Christ promised in the Bible had not happened long ago, as
some exegetists believed; and would not come in some almost
imperceptible spiritualization of society, as some liberals hoped
for; but could be expected as an imminent intervention, as
Christ came to rule, to judge, and to punish. Dwight L. Moody
and many other Protestant revivalists preached pre-millennialism, and there was a sharp controversy in the* CATHOLIC WORLD
*stirred by the surge of such cataclysmic thought among Roman
Catholics.*

*Jehovah's Witnesses translated those Biblical passages on
which all "adventists" relied into a peculiarly simple and
straight-forward gospel. Charles Taze Russell (1852–1916), the*

From Charles Taze Russell, *Studies in the Scriptures* (Allegheny,
Pa.: Watch Tower Bible and Tract Society, 1906), pp. 307–342.

real founder of the movement, very early drew a map which showed God's "plan of the ages." By 1906, the Witnesses claimed to have distributed this map, along with Russell's explanatory notes, to more than 3,000,000 Christians. Though all denominations and all social classes were approached, the Witnesses obviously had greatest hopes of reaching those individuals least committed to contemporary society. In one of the last chapters of his commentary, Russell adjured those who now understood man's situation to avoid all entanglements with a culture that God was already beginning to destroy. They should remember, he wrote, "that this is the Lord's battle, and that so far as politics or social questions are concerned, they have no real solution other than that predicted in the Word of God. The duty of the consecrated, therefore, is first of all to see that they are not in the way of Jehovah's chariot, and then to 'stand still and see the salvation of God,' in the sense of realizing that it is no part of their work to share in the struggle, but that it is the Lord's doing, through other agencies."

The "Day of Jehovah" is the name of that period of time in which God's kingdom, under Christ, is to be gradually "set up" in the earth, while the kingdoms of this world are passing away and Satan's power and influence over men are being bound. It is everywhere described as a dark day of intense trouble and distress and perplexity upon mankind. And what wonder that a revolution of such proportions, and necessitating such great changes, should cause trouble. Some revolutions have caused trouble in every age; and this, so much greater than any previous revolution, is to be a time of trouble such as never was since there was a nation—no, nor ever shall be. —Dan. 12:1; Matt. 24:21, 22.

It is called the "Day of Jehovah" because, though Christ, with royal title and power, will be present as Jehovah's representative, taking charge of all the affair during this day of trouble, it is more as the General of Jehovah, subduing all things, than as the Prince of Peace, blessing all. Meantime, as false and imperfect views and systems fall, the standard of the new King will rise, and eventually he shall be recognized and owned by all as King of kings. Thus it is presented by the prophets as Jehovah's work to *set up* Christ's dominion: "*I will give* thee the Gentiles for thine inheritance, and the uttermost parts of the earth for thy possession." (Psa. 2:8.) "In the days of these kings shall the God of heaven set up a kingdom." (Dan. 2:44.) The Ancient of days did sit, and there was brought before him one like unto a son of man, and there *was given him* a dominion, that all kingdoms should serve and obey him. (Dan. 7:9, 13, 14, 22, 27.) Added to these is Paul's statement that, when Christ shall accomplish the object of his reign, "then shall the Son also himself be subject unto him [the Father] that PUT ALL THINGS UNDER HIM."—I Cor. 15:28.

This period is called the "Day of Vengeance of our God," and a "Day of Wrath." (Isa. 61:2; 63:1-4; Psa. 110:5.) And yet the mind that grasps only the idea of anger, or supposes divine malice, seriously errs. God has established certain laws, in harmony with which he operates, and those who from any cause come into conflict with these reap the penalty or wrath of their own course. God's counsel to mankind has been continually rejected, except by the few; and, as we have shown, he permitted them to have their own way and to drop him and his counsels from their hearts. (Rom. 1:28.) He then confined his special care to Abraham and his seed, who professed to desire his way and his service. Their hardness of heart as a people, and the insincerity of their hearts toward God, not only naturally prevented them from receiving Messiah, but just as naturally prepared them for and led them into the trouble which terminated their national existence.

And so the light borne in the world during the Gospel age by the true Church of Christ (the class whose names are written in heaven) has borne witness to the civilized world of the difference between right and wrong, good and evil, and of a coming time in which the one will be rewarded and the other punished. (John 16:8–11; Acts 24:25.) This would have had a wide influence upon men had they heeded the Lord's instruction, but, wilful as ever, they have profited little by the advice of the Scriptures, and the trouble of the Day of the Lord will come as a consequence of the neglect. Again, it may be said to be the wrath of God inasmuch as it comes through disregard of his counsels, and as a reward of unrighteousness. Nevertheless, viewed in another light, the trouble coming upon the world is the natural or legitimate result of sin, which God foresaw, and against which his counsels would have protected them, had they been followed.

While God's message to the Church has been, "Present your bodies a living sacrifice" (Rom. 12:1), his message to the world has been, "Keep thy tongue from evil, and thy lips from speaking guile; depart from evil and do good; seek peace and pursue it." (Psa. 34:13, 14.) Few have heeded either message. Only a little flock sacrificed; and as for the world, though it nailed up the motto, "Honesty is the best policy," it has neglected in general to practice it. It heeded rather the voice of avarice—Get all you can of riches and honor and power in this world, no matter what the method by which you obtain it, and no matter who loses by your gain. In a word, the trouble of this Day of the Lord would not come, could not come, if the principles of God's law were observed to any considerable extent. That law briefly summed up is—Thou shalt love the Lord thy God with all thy heart, and thy neighbor as thyself. (Matt. 22:37–39.) It is because the depraved or carnal mind is opposed to this law of God, and is not subject to it, that, as a natural consequence, the trouble will come, as reaping after sowing.

The carnal or depraved mind, so far from loving its neighbor as itself, has always been selfish and grasping—often leading even to violence and murder to get for self the things possessed by others. However exercised, the selfish principle is always the same, except as governed by circumstances of birth, education and surroundings. It has been the same in every age of the world, and will be, until, by the *force* of the iron rule of Messiah, not might nor greed, but love, will decide what is RIGHT, and *enforce* it, until all may have opportunity to learn the superior benefits of the rule of righteousness and love as compared with that of selfishness and might; until, under the influence of the sunlight of truth and righteousness, the selfish, stony heart of man will become once more as when God pronounced it "very good"—a heart of flesh.—Ezek. 36:26.

Looking back, we can see without difficulty how the change from Godlike love and kindness to hard selfishness came about. The circumstances tending to promote selfishness were encountered as soon as man, through disobedience, lost the divine favor and was exiled from his Eden home, where his every want had been bountifully supplied. As our condemned parents went forth and began the battle of life, seeking to prolong existence to its farthest limit, they were met at once with thorns and briers and thistles and sterile ground; and the contending with these produced weariness and the sweat of face which the Lord had declared. Gradually the mental and moral qualities began to dwarf from lack of exercise, while the lower qualities retained fuller scope from constant exercise. Sustenance became the principal aim and interest of life; and its cost in labor became the standard by which all other interests were estimated, and Mammon became master of men. Can we wonder that under such circumstances mankind became selfish, greedy and grasping, each striving for most— first of the necessities, and secondly of the honors and luxuries bestowed by Mammon? It is but the natural tendency of which Satan has taken great advantage.

During past ages, under various influences (among others, ignorance, race prejudices, and national pride), the great wealth of the world has generally been in the hands of the few—the rulers—to whom the masses rendered slavish obedience as to their national representatives, in whose wealth they felt a pride and an interest as their own representatively. But as the time drew near in which Jehovah designed to bless the world through a Restitution at the hands of Messiah, he began to lift up the veil of ignorance and superstition, through modern facilities and inventions; and with these came the general elevation of the people and the decreasing power of earthly rulers. No longer is the wealth of the world in the hands of its kings, but chiefly among the people.

Though wealth brings many evils, it also brings some blessings: the wealthy obtain better educations—but thus they are lifted intellectually above the poorer people and become more or less associated with royalty. Hence an aristocracy exists which has both money and education to back it, and to assist in its avaricious struggle to get all it can and to keep self in the front rank at any cost.

But, as intelligence spreads, as the people take advantage of educational facilities, now so abundant, they begin to *think* for themselves; and with the self-esteem and selfishness in them led on by *a little* learning—sometimes a dangerous thing —they fancy that they see ways and means by which the interests and circumstances of all men, and especially their own, can be promoted at the cost of the fewer numbers in whose hands the wealth now lies. Many of these, doubtless, honestly believe that the conflicting interests of Mammon's worshipers (themselves on one side, and the wealthy on the other) could be easily and fairly adjusted; and no doubt they feel that were they wealthy they would be very benevolent, and quite willing to love their neighbors as themselves. But they evidently deceive themselves; for in their present condition very few indeed manifest such a spirit, and he that would not be faithful in the use of a little of this world's goods would not be faithful if he had greater riches. In fact, circumstances prove this; for some of the hardest hearted and most selfish among the wealthy are those who have risen suddenly from the humble walks of life.

On the contrary, while by no means excusing but reproving covetousness and grasping selfishness on the part of all classes, it is but proper to notice that the provision made for the sick and helpless and poor, in the way of asylums, hospitals, poor-houses, public libraries, schools and various other enterprises for the good and comfort of the masses, rather than of the wealthy, is maintained mainly by taxes and donations from the rich. These institutions almost always owe their existence to the kind-hearted and benevolent among the rich, and are matters which the poorer classes have neither the time, nor generally the necessary education or interest, to bring into successful operation.

Nevertheless, to-day sees a growing opposition between the wealthy and laboring classes—a growing bitterness on the part of labor, and a growing feeling among the wealthy that nothing but the strong arm of the law will protect what they believe to be *their rights*. Hence, the wealthy are drawn closer to the governments; and the wage-working masses, beginning to think that laws and governments were designed to aid the wealthy and to restrain the poor, are drawn toward Communism and Anarchy, thinking that their interests would best be served thereby, and not realizing that the worst government, and the most expensive, is vastly better than no government at all.

Many scriptures clearly show that this will be the character of the trouble under which present civil, social and religious systems will pass away; that this is the way in which increase of knowledge and liberty will result, because of man's imperfection, mental, moral and physical. These scriptures will be referred to in due course; but here we can only call attention to a few of the many, advising our readers meanwhile that in many of the prophecies of the Old Testament in which Egypt,

Babylon and Israel figure so largely, not only was there a literal fulfilment intended, but also a secondary and larger one. Thus, for instance, the predictions regarding the fall of Babylon, etc., must be considered extravagant beyond measure, did we not recognize a symbolic and antitypical as well as a literal Babylon. The book of Revelation contains predictions recorded long after literal Babylon was in ruins, and hence evidently applicable only to symbolic Babylon; yet the close resemblance of the words of the prophets, apparently directly addressed to literal Babylon, are thus shown to belong in an especial sense to symbolic Babylon. In this larger fulfilment, Egypt represents the world; Babylon represents the nominal Church, called Christendom; while, as already shown, Israel often represents the whole world in its *justified* condition, as it will be—its glorious Royal Priesthood, its holy Levites and its believing and worshiping people, justified by the sacrifice of the Atonement, and brought into a condition of reconciliation with God. To Israel the blessings are promised, to Egypt the plagues, and to strong Babylon a wonderful, complete and everlasting overthrow, "as a great millstone cast into the sea" (Rev. 18:21), never to be recovered, but to be held in everlasting odium.

The Apostle James points out this day of trouble, and tells of its being the result of differences between capital and labor. He says: "Come now, ye wealthy! wail ye, howling at your hardships that are coming upon you. Your wealth has rotted [lost its value], and your garments have become moth-eaten: your gold and silver have become rusted out, and their rust for a witness to you shall be, and shall eat your flesh as fire. Ye treasured it up in the last days. Behold! the wages of the workers who cut down your fields—that which has been kept back by reason of you [of your hoarding] is crying out; and the outcries of those who reaped, into the ears of the Lord of the whole people have entered." (Jas. 5:1-4.) He adds that the class coming into trouble has been used to luxury, obtained largely at the cost of others, among whom were some of the righteous, and out of them, because they resisted not, the very life had been crushed. The Apostle urges the "brethren" to bear patiently whatever their part may be, looking beyond, and expecting deliverance through the Lord. This very condition of things can now be seen approaching; and in the world, among those who are awake, "men's hearts are failing them for looking after the things that are coming on the earth." All know that the constant tendency of our times is toward lower wages for labor, unless where the prices are artificially sustained or advanced by labor combinations, strikes, etc.; and with the present sentiment of the masses, all can see that it is but a question of time when the lowest point of endurance will be reached, and a revolt will surely result. This will alarm capital, which will be withdrawn from business and manufacturing channels and hoarded in vaults and treasuries, to eat itself up with charges for its protection in idleness, to the great annoyance of its owners. This in turn will certainly produce bankruptcy, financial panic and business prostration, because all business of magnitude is now conducted largely on credit. The natural result of all this will be to throw out of employment tens of thousands who are dependent on their wages for daily bread, and to fill the world with tramps and persons whose necessities will defy all law. Then it will be as described by the prophet (Ezek. 7:10–19), when the buyer need not rejoice, nor the seller mourn; for trouble will be upon the entire multitude and there will be no security of property. Then all hands will be feeble and helpless to turn aside the trouble. They will cast their silver in the streets, and their gold will be removed. Their silver and their gold will not be able to deliver them in the day of the Lord's wrath.

It should not be forgotten that though the last forty years of the existence of Israel as a nation was a day of trouble, a "day of vengeance" upon that people, ending in the complete overthrow of their nation, yet their day of wrath was but a shadow or type of a still greater and more extensive trouble upon nominal Christendom, even as their past history as a people during their age of favor was typical of the Gospel age, as will be conclusively shown hereafter. All then will see why these prophecies concerning the Day of the Lord should be, and are, addressed to Israel and Jerusalem more or less directly, though the connections show clearly that all mankind is included in the complete fulfilments.

Take another prophetic testimony (Zeph. 1:7-9, 14-18). "The Lord hath prepared a slaughter, he hath bid his guests. [Compare Rev. 19:17.] And it shall come to pass in the day of the Lord's slaughter that I will punish the princes and the king's children, and all such as are clothed in imported clothing. And I will inflict punishment [also] on all those [marauders] who leap over the threshold on that day, who fill their masters' houses with violence and deceit. [This shows not only that there will be a great overthrow of wealth and power in this time of trouble, but that those who will for the time be the instruments of heaven in breaking down present systems will also be punished for their equally unjust and unrighteous course; for the coming trouble will involve all classes, and bring distress upon all the multitude.]

"Night is the great Day of the Lord: it is nigh. Nearer and louder comes the uproar of the Day of the Lord. There the mighty shall shriek bitterly! That day is a day of wrath, a day of distress and anxiety, a day of wasting and desolation, a day of darkness and obscurity [uncertainty and foreboding, as well as present distress], a day of clouds [trouble] and tempestuous gloom, a day of the trumpet [the seventh *symbolic* trumpet, which sounds throughout this day of trouble—also called the trump of God, because connected with the *events* of this Day of the Lord] and shouting against the fenced cities and the high battlements [clamorous and conflicting denunciations of strong and well-intrenched governments]. And I will bring distress upon men, and they shall walk about as blind men [groping in uncertainty, not knowing what course to pursue], because they have sinned against Jehovah. Their blood shall be poured out as the dust, and their flesh shall be as dung. Neither their silver nor their gold shall be able to deliver them in the day of the Lord's wrath [though previously wealth could furnish ease and every luxury], but the whole land shall be devoured by the FIRE of his *zeal;* for destruction, yea, quite sudden, will he prepare for all them [the wealthy] that dwell in the land." This destruction will destroy many of the wealthy in the sense that they will cease to be wealthy, though doubtless it will also involve the loss of many lives of all classes.

We shall not attempt to follow the prophets in their details, from various standpoints, of the trouble of that day, but shall follow briefly the thought last suggested by the prophet above, namely, the *devouring* of the whole earth with the FIRE of God's zeal. This prophet refers to the same fire, etc., again (Zeph. 3:8, 9), saying: "Wait ye upon me, saith Jehovah, until the day that I rise up to the prey; for my decision is to gather the nations [peoples], to draw together the kingdoms, to pour upon them [the kingdoms] my indignation, even all my fierce anger. [The gathering of the peoples of all nations in common interest in opposition to present governments is growing; and the result will be a uniting of the kingdoms for common safety, so that the trouble will be upon all kingdoms, and all will fall.] For all the earth shall be devoured with the *fire* of my zeal. Yea [*then,* after this destruction of kingdoms, after this destruction of the present social order in the fire of trouble], then will I turn unto the people a pure language [the pure Word—uncontaminated by human tradition], that they may call upon the name of the Lord, to serve him with one accord."

This fire of God's zeal is a symbol, and a forcible one, representing the intensity of the trouble and the destruction which will envelop the whole earth. That it is not a literal fire, as some suppose, is evident from the fact that *the people* remain after it, and are blessed. That the people who remain are not saints, as some would suggest, is evident from the fact that they are then *turned* to serve the Lord, whereas the saints are turned (converted) already.

Throughout the Scriptures, *earth,* when used symbolically, represents society; *mountains* represent kingdoms; *heavens,* the powers of spiritual control, *seas,* the restless, turbulent, dissatisfied masses of the world. *Fire* represents the destruction of whatever is burned—tares, dross, earth (social organization), or whatever it may be. And when *brimstone* is added to *fire* in the symbol, it intensifies the thought of destruction; for nothing is more deadly to all forms of life than the fumes of sulphur.

With this thought in mind, if we turn to Peter's symbolic prophecy of the Day of Wrath, we find it in perfect accord with the above testimony of the prophets. He says: "The world that was, being overflowed with water, perished. [Not the literal earth and literal heavens ceased there, but that dispensation or arrangement of things, existing before the flood, passed away.] But the heavens and the earth which are now [the present dispensation] by the same word [of divine authority] are kept in store, reserved unto fire." The fact that the water was literal leads some to believe that the fire also must be literal, but this by no means follows. The temple of God once was of literal stones, but that does not set aside the fact that the Church, which is the true temple, is built up a spiritual building, a holy temple, not of earthly material. Noah's ark was literal, too, but it typified Christ and the power in him which will replenish and reorganize society.

"The Day of the Lord will come as a thief in the night [unobservedly], in the which the heavens [present powers of the air, of which Satan is the chief or prince] shall pass away with a great [hissing] noise, and the elements shall melt with fervent heat; the earth [social organization] also, and the works that are therein [pride, rank, aristocracy, royalty], shall be burned up. The heavens being on fire shall be dissolved and the elements shall melt with fervent heat. Nevertheless we, according to his promise, look for new heavens [the new spiritual power—Christ's kingdom] and a new earth" [earthly society organized on a new basis—on the basis of love and justice, rather than of might and oppression].—2 Peter 3:6, 7, 10–13.

It should be remembered that some of the apostles were prophets as well—notably Peter, John and Paul. And while as apostles they were God's mouthpieces to expound the utterances of preceding prophets for the benefit of the Church, they were also used of God as prophets to predict things to come, which, as they become due to be fulfilled, become meat in due season for the household of faith, to dispense which, God in his own time raises up suitable servants or expounders. (See our Lord's statement of this fact—Matt. 24:45, 46). The apostles as prophets were moved upon to write things which, not being *due* in their day, they could but imperfectly appreciate, even as it was with the Old Testament prophets (1 Pet. 1:12, 13), though, like them, their words were specially guided and directed so that they have a depth of meaning of which they were not aware when using them. Thus emphatically the Church is ever guided and fed by God himself, whoever may be his mouthpieces or channels of communication. A realization of this must lead to greater confidence and trust in God's Word, notwithstanding the imperfections of some of his mouthpieces.

The Prophet Malachi (4:1) tells of this Day of the Lord under the same symbol. He says: "The day cometh that shall burn as an oven; and all the *proud*, yea, and all that do wickedly, shall be stubble; and the day that cometh shall burn them up . . . that it shall leave them neither root nor branch." Pride, and every other cause from which haughtiness and oppression could again spring forth, will be entirely consumed by the great trouble of the Day of the Lord and by the after disciplines of the Millennial age,—the last of which is described in Rev. 20:9.

But, while pride (in all its forms sinful and detestable) is to be utterly rooted out, and all the proud and wicked are to be utterly destroyed, it does not follow that there is no hope for a reformation in this class. No, thank God: while this fire of God's just indignation will be burning, the Judge will grant opportunity for *pulling some out of the consuming fire* (Jude 23); and those only who refuse the aid will perish with their pride; because they have made it part of their character, and refuse to reform.

The same prophet gives another description of this day (Mal. 3:1-3), in which again, under the figure of fire, he shows how *the Lord's children* will be purified and blessed and brought nigh to him by having the dross of error *destroyed*: —"The Messenger of the Covenant, whom ye delight in: behold, he shall come, saith the Lord of hosts. But who may abide the day of his coming? and who shall *stand* [the test] when he appeareth? for he is as a refiner's fire: . . . and he shall sit as a refiner and purifier of silver: and he shall purify the sons of Levi [typical of believers, of whom the chief are the Royal Priesthood] and purge them as gold and silver, that they may offer unto the Lord an offering in righteousness."

Paul refers to this same fire, and this refining process affecting believers in the Day of the Lord (1 Cor. 3:12-15), and in such a manner as to leave it beyond all question that the symbolic fire will *destroy* every error, and thus effect purification of faith. After declaring that he refers only to those building their faith upon the only recognized foundation, Christ Jesus' finished work of redemption, he says: "Now if any man build [character] upon *this* foundation, gold, silver, precious stones [divine truths and corresponding character, or] wood, hay, stubble [traditional errors and corresponding unstable characters], every man's work shall be made manifest; for THE DAY shall declare it, because it shall be revealed by FIRE; and so every one's work [2 Pet. 1:5-11], whatever it is, the same fire will prove." Surely even the most prejudiced will concede that the fire which tries a spiritual work is not literal fire; fire is an appropriate symbol to represent the utter destruction of conditions represented here by wood, hay and stubble. This fire will be powerless to destroy the faith-and-character structure built with the gold, silver and precious stones of divine truth, and founded upon the rock of Christ's ransom-sacrifice.

The Apostle shows this, saying: "If any man's work abide which he hath built thereupon [upon Christ] he shall receive a *reward.* [His reward will be in proportion to his faithfulness in building, making use of the truth in the development of true character—putting on the whole armor of God.] If any man's work shall be consumed, he shall suffer loss [loss of the reward, because of unfaithfulness], but he himself shall be preserved so as through a fire"—singed, scorched and alarmed. All who build on the rock foundation of Christ's ransom are sure: none that trust in his righteousness as their covering will ever be utterly confounded. But those who *wilfully* reject him and his work, after coming to a clear, full knowledge thereof, are in danger of the second death.—Heb. 6:4-8; 10:26-31.

In yet another way is this trouble of the Day of the Lord symbolically described. The Apostle shows (Heb. 12:26-29) that the inauguration of the Law Covenant at Sinai was typical of the introduction of the New Covenant to the world at the opening of the Millennial age, or reign of Christ's kingdom. He says that in the type God's voice shook the literal earth, but now he hath promised, saying, "Yet once for all [finally], I will shake not only the earth, but the heaven also." Concerning this the Apostle explains, saying, "Now this [statement], Yet once for all, denotes the removal of the things shaken, because they are fabricated [false, made up, not the true], so that the unshaken things [true, righteous things, only] may remain. Wherefore, seeing that we are to receive a kingdom which cannot be shaken, let us hold fast the favor through which we may serve God acceptably with reverence and piety; for [as it is written], Our God is a consuming fire." Thus we see this apostle uses a storm to symbolize the trouble of this Day of the Lord, which he and others elsewhere refer to under the symbol of fire. The same events are here noted that are described under the fire symbol, namely, the sweeping away of all falsities, both from believers and from the world—errors regarding God's plan and character and Word, and also errors as to social and evil affairs in the world. It will be good indeed for all to be rid of these fabrications, which came to man largely through his own depraved desires, as well as by the cunning craftiness of Satan, the wily foe of righteousness; but it will be at great cost to all concerned that they will be swept away. It will be a terribly hot fire, a fearful storm, a dark night of trouble, which will precede the glorious brightness of that Kingdom of Righteousness which can never be shaken, that Millennial day in which the Sun of Righteousness will shine forth in splendor and power, blessing and healing the sick and dying but redeemed world.—Compare Mal. 4:2 and Matt. 13:43.

David, the prophet through whose Psalms God was pleased to foretell so much concerning our Lord at his first advent, gives some vivid descriptions of this Day of Trouble by which his glorious reign will be introduced; and he uses these various symbols—fire, storm and darkness—alternately and interchangeably, in his descriptions. Thus, for instance, he says (Psa. 50:3): "Our God shall come, and shall not keep silence: a fire shall devour before him, and it shall be very tempestuous round about him." In Psa. 97:2–6: "Clouds and darkness are round about him: righteousness and justice are the support of his throne. A fire goeth before him and burneth up his enemies round about. His lightnings give light to the world; the earth seeth it and trembleth. The mountains melt away like wax at the presence of the Lord, at the presence of the Lord of the whole earth. The [new] heavens [then] tell of his righteousness, and all the people see his glory." Psa. 46:6: "The peoples raged, the kingdoms were moved: he uttered his voice, the earth melted." Again (Psa. 110:2–6), "Rule thou in the midst of thine enemies. . . . The Lord at thy right hand shall crush kings in the day of his wrath. He will judge among the nations —there shall be a fullness of corpses. He crusheth the heads [rulers] over many countries." Again (46:1–5), "God is *our* protection; . . . therefore *we* will not fear when the earth [society] is transformed, and when the mountains [kingdoms] are swept into the midst of the sea [swallowed up by the turbulent masses], when the waters thereof roar and are troubled [infuriated], when the mountains shake with the swellings thereof. . . . God will help her [the Bride, the faithful, "little flock"] at the dawning of the morning." And in the same Psalm, verses 6–10, the same story is re-stated in other symbols:—"The peoples rage, kingdoms are displaced: he letteth his voice be heard, the earth [society] melteth. Jehovah of hosts is with *us*, a Tower for us is the God of Jacob." Then, viewing the results of that time of trouble from beyond it, he adds: "Come ye, behold the deeds of the Lord—what desolations he hath made in the earth. . . . Desist [from your former ways, O people] and know [come to the knowledge] that I am God. I will be exalted among the peoples, I will be exalted in the earth." The "new earth" or new order and arrangement of society will exalt God and his law, as over and controlling all.

Another testimony in proof of the fact that the Day of the Lord will be a great day of trouble and of destruction to every form of evil (yet *not* a time of literal burning of the earth) is furnished in the last symbolic prophecy of the Bible. Referring to this time when the Lord will take his great power to reign, the *storm* and *fire* are thus described—"And the nations were enraged and thy wrath came." (Rev. 11:17, 18.) And again, "And out of his mouth proceeded a two-edged broadsword, that with it he should smite the nations: and he shall rule them with a rod of iron: and he treadeth the winepress of the fierceness of the wrath of Almighty God. . . . And I saw the beast [symbolic], and the kings of the earth and their armies, gathered together to make war against him that sat on the horse, and against his army. And the beast was taken, and with him the false prophet. . . . These were cast alive into a lake of fire burning with brimstone."—Rev. 19:15, 19.

We cannot here digress to examine these symbols—"beast," "false prophet," "image," "lake of fire," "horse," etc., etc. For this the reader is referred to a succeeding volume. Now we would have you notice that the great symbolic BATTLE, and the harvesting of the vine of the earth here described as closing the present age and opening up the Millennial age (Rev. 20:1–3), are but other symbols covering the same great and troublous events elsewhere symbolically called fire, storm, shaking, etc. In connection with the battle and winepress figures of Revelation, note the striking harmony of Joel 2:9–16 and Isa. 13:1–11, in describing the same events by similar figures. The variety of symbolic figures used helps us to appreciate more fully all the features of that great and notable Day of the Lord.

THE PRESENT SITUATION

We here leave the prophetic statements regarding that day, to mark more particularly the present aspect of affairs in the world, as we now see them shaping themselves for the rapidly approaching conflict—a conflict which, when its terrible climax is reached, must necessarily be a short one, else the race would be exterminated. The two rival parties to this battle are already visible. Wealth, arrogance and pride are on one side, and widely-prevailing poverty, ignorance, bigotry and a keen sense of injustice are on the other. Both, impelled by selfish motives, are now organizing their forces all over the civilized world. With our eyes anointed with truth, wherever we look we can see that the sea and the waves are already roaring and lashing and foaming out against the mountains, as represented in the threats and attempts of anarchists and discontents whose numbers are constantly increasing. We can see, too, that the *friction* between the various factions or elements of society is rapidly getting to the point described by the prophets, when the earth (society) will be on fire, and the elements will melt and disintegrate with the mutually generated heat.

It is of course difficult for people, on whichever side of this controversy they may be, to see contrary to their own interests, habits and education. The wealthy feel that they have a right to more than their proportional share of this world's goods; a right to purchase labor and every commodity as low as they can; a right to the fruit of their efforts; and a right to use their intelligence so to run their business as to make profit for themselves and to increase their hoarded wealth, no matter who else may be compelled by force of circumstances to drag through life with few of its comforts, even if with all of its necessities. They reason thus: It is the inevitable; the law of supply and demand must govern; rich and poor have always been in the world; and if the wealth were evenly divided in the morning, some would, through dissipation or improvidence, be poor before night, while others, more careful and prudent, would be rich. Besides, they will argue with effect, can it be expected that men of greater brain power will undertake vast enterprises, employing thousands of men, with the risks of large losses, unless there be hopes of gain and some advantage?

The artisan and the laborer, on the contrary, will say: We see that while labor enjoys many advantages to-day above any other day, while it is better paid, and can therefore procure greater comforts, yet it is in this enjoying only its right, from which it has long been debarred to some extent; and it is thus properly deriving a share of the advantages of the inventions, discoveries, increasing knowledge, etc., of our time. We recognize labor as honorable, and that, when accompanied with good sense, education, honesty and principle, it is as honorable, and has as many rights, as any profession. And, on the contrary, we esteem idleness a discredit and disgrace to all men, whatever their talent or occupation in life. All, to be valued and appreciated, should be useful to others in some respect. But though realizing our present improvement and advancement, intellectually, socially and financially, we realize this to be more the result of circumstances than of human design on the part of either ourselves or our employers. We see our improved condition, and that of all men, to be the result of the great increase of intelligence, invention, etc., of the past fifty years particularly. These came up so rapidly that labor as well as capital got a lift from the tidal wave, and was carried to a higher level; and if we could see a prospect that the flood tide would continue to rise, and to benefit all, we would feel satisfied; but we are anxious and restless now because we see that this is not the case. We see that the flood tide is beginning to turn, and that whereas many have been lifted high in wealth by it, and are firmly and securely fixed upon the shore of ease, luxury and opulence, yet the masses are not thus settled and secured, but are in danger of being carried as low as ever, or lower, by the under current of the now ebbing tide. Hence it is that we are disposed to grasp hold of something to insure our present state and our further advancement before it is too late.

To state the matter in other words, we (artisans and laborers) see that while all mankind has largely shared the blessings of the day, yet those who by reason of greater talent for business, or by inheritance, or by fraud and dishonesty, have become possessors of tens of thousands and millions of dollars, have not only *this* advantage over all others, but, aided by the mechanical inventions, etc., they are in a position to continue the ratio of their increase in wealth, in proportion to the decrease in the wage-workers' salaries. We see that unless we take some steps toward the protection of the increasing number of artisans against the increasing power of monopoly, combined with labor-saving machinery, etc., the cold-blooded law of supply and demand will swallow us up completely. It is against this impending disaster, rather than against *present conditions,* that we organize and seek protective arrangements. Each day adds largely to our numbers by natural increase and by immigration; and each day adds to the labor-saving machinery. Each day, therefore, increases the number seeking employment and decreases the demand for their service. The natural law of supply and demand, therefore, if permitted to go on uninterruptedly, will soon bring labor back where it was a century ago, and leave all the advantages of our day in the hands of capital. It is *this* that we seek to avert.

This ultimate tendency of many real blessings to work injury, unless restrained by wise and equitable laws, was long since seen; but the *rapidity* with which one invention has followed another, and the consequent increased demand for labor in providing this labor-saving machinery, has been so great that the ultimate result has been delayed, and instead, the world has had a "boom"—an inflation of values, wages, wealth, credits (debts) and ideas—from which the reaction is now commencing gradually to take place.

In the last few years there have been produced in vast quantities agricultural implements of every description which enable one man to accomplish as much as five could formerly. This has a two-fold effect: first, three times as many acres are worked, giving employment to three out of the five laborers, thus setting two adrift to compete for other labor; secondly, the three who remain can, by the use of the machinery, produce as great a crop as fifteen would have done without it. The same or greater changes are wrought in other departments by similar agencies; for instance, in iron and steel making. Its growth has been so enormous that the number of employes has greatly increased, notwithstanding the fact that machinery has enabled one man at present to accomplish about as much as twelve did formerly. One of the results will be that very shortly the capacity of these extensive works will more than meet the present enormous demands, and the demands, instead of continuing to increase, will probably decrease; for the world is fast being supplied with railroads beyond present needs, and the yearly repairs on these could probably be supplied by less than one-half the present number of establishments.

Thus we are brought in contact with the peculiar condition in which there is an over-production, causing idleness occasionally to both capital and labor, while at the same time some lack the employment which would enable them to procure necessities and luxuries and thus in a measure cure the over-production. And the tendency toward both over-production and lack of employment is on the increase, and calls for a remedy of some kind which society's physicians are seeking, but of which the patient will not make use.

While, therefore (continues the wage-worker), we realize that as the supply begins to exceed the demand, competition is greatly reducing the profits of capital and machinery, and throughout the world is distressing the rich by curtailing their profits, and in some cases causing them actual loss instead of profit, yet we believe that the class which benefited most by the "boom" and inflation *should* suffer most in the reaction, rather than that the masses should suffer from it. To this end, and for these reasons, wage-workers are moving to obtain the following results—by legislation if possible, or by force and lawlessness in countries where, for any cause, the voice of the masses is not heard, and the interests of the masses are not conserved:—

It is proposed that the hours of labor be shortened in proportion to the skill or severity of the labor, without a reduction of wages, in order thus to employ a greater number of persons without increasing the products, and thus to equalize the coming over-production by providing a larger number with the means of purchasing. It is proposed to fix and limit the rate of interest on money at much less than the present rates, and thus compel a *leniency* of the leaders toward the borrowers or poorer class, or else an idleness or rusting of their capital. It is proposed that railroads shall either be the property of the people, operated by their servants, government officials, or that legislation shall restrict their liberties, charges, etc., and compel their operation in such a manner as to serve the public better. As it is, railroads built a period of inflated values, instead of curtailing their capital to conform to the general shrinkage of values experienced in every other department of trade, have multiplied their originally large capital stocks two or three times (commonly called *watering* their stocks), without real value being added. Thus it comes that great railroad systems are endeavoring to pay interest and dividends upon stocks and bonded debts which on an average are four times as great as these railroads would actually cost to-day *new*. As a consequence the public suffers. Farmers are charged heavily for freights, and sometimes find it profitable to burn their grain for fuel; and thus the cost of food to the people is greater without being to the farmer's advantage. It is proposed to remedy this matter, so that railroads shall pay to their stockholders about four per cent. on their present actual value, and not four to eight per cent. on three or four times their present value, as many of them now do, by preventing competition through pooling arrangements.

We well know, says the artisan, that in the eyes of those who hold watered railroad stocks, and other stocks, this reduction of profits on their invested capital will seem terrible, and will come like drawing teeth, and that they will feel that their *rights* (?) to use their franchises granted by the people, to squeeze from them immense profits, based upon fictitious valuations, are being grievously outraged, and that they will resist it all they know how. But we feel that they should be thankful that the public is so lenient, and that they are not required to make restitution of millions of dollars already thus obtained. We feel that the time has come for the masses of the people to share more evenly the blessings of this day of blessings, and to do this it is necessary so to legislate that all greedy corporations, fat with money and power derived from the public, shall be restrained, and *compelled* by law to serve the public at reasonable rates. In no other way can these blessings of Providence be secured to the masses. Hence, while great corporations, representing capital, are to a large extent a blessing and a benefit, we are seeing daily that they have passed the point of benefit and are becoming masters of the people, and if unchecked will soon reduce wage-workers to penury and slavery. Corporations, composed of numbers of people all more or less wealthy, are rapidly coming to occupy the same relation to the general public of America that the Lords of Great Britain and all Europe occupy toward the masses there, only that the corporations are more powerful.

To accomplish our ends, continue the wage-workers, we need organization. We must have the co-operation of the masses or we can never accomplish anything against such immense power and influence. And though we are organized into unions, etc., it must not be understood that our aim is anarchy or injustice toward any class. We, the masses of the people, simply desire to protect our own rights, and those of our children, by putting reasonable bounds upon those whose wealth and power might otherwise crush us—which wealth and power, properly used and limited, may be a more general blessing to all. In a word, they conclude, we would *enforce* the golden rule—"Do unto others as you would that they should do to you."

Happy would it be for all concerned if such moderate and reasonable means would succeed; if the rich would rest with

their present acquirements and co-operate with the great mass
of the people in the general and permanent improvement of the
condition of all classes; if the wage-workers would content
themselves with reasonable demands; if the golden rule of love
and justice could thus be put in practice. But men in their
present condition will not observe this rule without compulsion. Though there be some among the artisans of the world
who would be thus moderate and just in their ideas, the majority are not so, but will be extreme, unjust and arrogant in their
ideas and demands, beyond all reason. Each concession on the
part of capitalists will but add to such demands and ideas; and
all having experience know that the arrogance and rule of
the ignorant poor are doubly severe. And so among those of
wealth—some are fully in sympathy with the laboring classes,
and would be glad to act out their sympathy by making such
arrangements as would gradually effect the needed reforms;
but they are greatly in the minority and wholly powerless in
the operating of corporations and to a great extent in their
private business. If they be merchants or manufacturers, they
cannot shorten the hours of labor or increase the wages of their
employes; for competitors would then undersell them, and financial disaster to themselves, their creditors and their employes would follow.

Thus we see the natural cause of the great trouble of this
"Day of Jehovah." Selfishness, and blindness to all except their
own interests, will control the majority on both sides of the
question. Wage-workers will organize and unify their interests,
but selfishness will destroy the union; and each, being actuated
mainly by that principle, will scheme and conspire in that direction. The majority, ignorant and arrogant, will gain control,
and the better class will be powerless to hold in check that
which their intelligence organized. Capitalists will become convinced that the more they yield the more will be demanded,
and will soon determine to resist all demands. Insurrection
will result; and in the general alarm and distrust capital will

be withdrawn from public and private enterprises, and business depression and financial panic will follow. Thousands of men thrown out of employment in this way will finally become desperate. Then law and order will be swept away—the mountains will be swallowed up in that stormy sea. Thus the social earth will melt, and the governmental heavens (church and state) will pass away; and all the proud, and all who do wickedly, will be as stubble. Then the mighty men will weep bitterly, the rich will howl, and fear and distress will be upon all the multitude. Even now, wise, far-seeing men find their hearts failing them as they look forward to those things coming upon the world, even as our Lord predicted. (Luke 21:26.) The Scriptures show us that in this general rupture the nominal church (including all denominations) will be gradually drawn more and more to the side of the governments and the wealthy, will lose much of its influence over the people, and will finally fall with the governments. Thus the heavens [ecclesiastical rule], being on fire, will pass away with a great hissing.

All this trouble will but prepare the world to realize that though men may plan and arrange ever so well and wisely, all their plans will prove futile as long as ignorance and selfishness are in the majority and have the control. It will convince all that the only feasible way of correcting the difficulty is by the setting up of a strong and righteous government, which will subdue all classes, and enforce principles of righteousness, until gradually the stony-heartedness of men will, under favorable influences, give place to the original image of God. And this is just what God has promised to accomplish for all, by and through the Millennial Reign of Christ, which Jehovah introduces by the chastisements and lessons of this day of trouble.—Ezek. 11:19; 36:25, 36; Jer. 31:29-34; Zeph. 3:9; Psa. 46:8–10.

Though this day of trouble comes as a natural and unavoidable result of man's fallen, selfish condition, and was fully foreseen and declared by the Lord, who foresaw that his laws and instructions would be disregarded by all but the few until experience and compulsion force obedience, yet all who realize the state of things coming should set themselves and their affairs in order accordingly. Thus we say to all the *meek*—the humble of the world, as well as the body of Christ: Seek ye the Lord, ye meek of the earth which have wrought his judgment [his will]; seek righteousness; seek meekness, that ye may be partially hidden in the day of the Lord's anger. (Zeph. 2:3.) None will entirely escape the trouble, but those seeking righteousness and rejoicing in meekness will have many advantages over others. Their manner of life, their habits of thought and action, as well as their sympathies for the right, which will enable them to grasp the situation of affairs, and also to appreciate the Bible account of this trouble and its outcome, will all conspire to make them suffer less than others—especially from harassing fears and forebodings.

The trend of events in this Day of the Lord will be very deceptive to those not Scripturally informed. It will come suddenly, as fire consuming chaff (Zeph. 2:2), in comparison to the long ages past and their slow operation; but not suddenly as a flash of lightning from a clear sky, as some erroneously expect who anticipate that all things written concerning the Day of the Lord will be fulfilled in a twenty-four hour day. It will come as "a thief in the night," in the sense that its approach will be stealthy and unobserved by the world in general. The trouble of this day will be in spasms. It will be a series of convulsions more frequent and severe as the day draws on, until the final one. The Apostle so indicates when he says—"*as travail* upon a woman." (1 Thes. 5:2, 3.) The relief will come only with the birth of the NEW ORDER of things—a new heavens [the spiritual control of Christ] and a new earth [re organized society] wherein dwelleth righteousness (2 Pet. 3:10, 13)—in which justice and love, instead of power and selfishness, will be the law.

Each time these labor pangs of the new era come upon the

present body politic, her strength and courage will be found less, and the pains severer. All that society's physicians (political economists) can do for her relief will be to help, and wisely direct the course of the inevitable birth—to prepare gradually the way for the event. They cannot avert it if they would; for God has decreed that it shall come to pass. Many of society's physicians will, however, be totally ignorant of the real ailment and of the necessities and urgency of the case. These will undertake repressive measures; and as each paroxysm of trouble passes away, they will take advantage of it to fortify the resistive appliances, and will thereby increase the anguish; and while they will not long delay the birth, their malpractice will hasten the death of their patient; for the old order of things will die in the labor of bringing forth the new.

To lay aside the forcible figure suggested by the Apostle, and speak plainly:—The efforts of the masses for deliverance from the grasp of Capital and machinery will be *immature:* plans and arrangements will be incomplete and insufficient, as time after time they attempt to force their way and burst the bands and limits of "supply and demand" which are growing too small for them. Each unsuccessful attempt will increase the confidence of Capital in its ability to keep the new order of things within its present limits, until at length the present restraining power of organizations and governments will reach its extreme limit, the cord of social organism will snap asunder, law and order will be gone, and wide-spread anarchy will bring *all* that the prophets have foretold of the trouble "such as was not since there was a nation"—and, thank God for the assurance added—"nor ever shall be" afterward.

The deliverance of Israel from Egypt and from the plagues which came upon the Egyptians seems to illustrate the coming emancipation of the world, at the hands of the greater than Moses, whom he typified. It will be a deliverance from Satan and every agency he has devised for man's bondage to sin and error. And as the plagues upon Egypt had a hardening effect as soon as removed, so the temporary relief from the pains of this Day of the Lord will tend to harden some, and they will say to the poor, as did the Egyptians to Israel, "Ye are idle," and therefore dissatisfied! and will probably, like them, attempt to increase the burden. (Exod. 5:4-23.) But in the end such will wish, as did Pharaoh in the midnight of his last plague, that they had dealt more leniently and wisely long ago. (Exod. 12:30-33.) To mark further the similarity, call to mind that the troubles of this Day of the Lord are called "seven vials of wrath," or "seven last plagues," and that it is not until the last of these that the *great earthquake* [revolution] occurs, in which every mountain [kingdom] will disappear.—Rev. 16: 17-20.

Another thought with reference to this Day of Trouble is that it has come just in *due* time—God's due time. In the next volume of this work, evidence will be adduced from the testimony of the Law and the Prophets of the Old Testament, as well as from Jesus and the apostolic prophets of the New Testament, which shows clearly and unmistakably that this Day of Trouble is located chronologically in the beginning of the glorious Millennial reign of Messiah. It is this necessary preparation for the coming work of restitution in the Millennial age that precipitates the trouble.

During the six thousand years interim of evil, and until the appointed time for the establishment of the righteous and powerful government of Christ, it would have been a positive injury to fallen men had they been afforded much idle time, through an earlier development of present labor-saving machinery, or otherwise. Experience has given rise to the proverb that "Idleness is the mother of vice," thus approving the wisdom of God's decree, "In the sweat of thy face shalt thou eat bread till thou return unto the dust." Like all God's arrangements, this is benevolent and wise, and for the ultimate good of his creatures. The trouble of the Day of the Lord, which we already see gathering, confirms the wisdom of God's arrangement; for, as we have seen, it comes about as the result of over-production by labor-saving machinery, and an inability on the part of the various elements of society to adjust themselves to the new circumstances, because of selfishness on the part of each.

An unanswerable argument, proving that this is God's due time for the introduction of the new order of things, is that he is lifting the veil of ignorance and gradually letting in the light of intelligence and invention upon mankind, just as foretold, when foretold, and with the results predicted. (Dan. 12:4, 1.) Had the knowledge come sooner, the trouble would have come sooner; and though society might have re-organized after its storm and melting, it would have been *not* a new earth [social arrangement] wherein righteousness would prevail and dwell, but a new earth or arrangement in which sin and vice would have much more abounded than now. The equitable division of the benefits of labor-saving machinery would in time have brought shorter and shorter hours of labor; and thus, released from the original safeguard, fallen man, with his perverted tastes, would not have used his liberty and time for mental, moral and physical improvement, but, as the history of the past proves, the tendency would have been toward licentiousness and vice.

The partial lifting of the veil *now* prepares thousands of conveniences for mankind, and thus furnishes, from the out-start of the age of restitution, time for education and moral and physical development, as well as for preparation for the feeding and clothing of the companies who will from time to time be awakened from the tomb. And furthermore, it locates the time of trouble just where it will be of benefit to mankind, in that it will give them the lesson of their own inability to govern themselves, just at the Millennial dawn, when, by the Lord's appointment, he who redeemed all is to begin to bless them with the strong rule of the iron rod, and with full knowledge and assistance whereby they may be restored to original perfection and everlasting life.

DUTY AND PRIVILEGE OF THE SAINTS

An important question arises regarding the duty of the saints during this trouble, and their proper attitude toward the two opposing classes now coming into prominence. That some of the saints will still be in the flesh during at least a part of this burning time seems possible. Their position in it, however, will differ from that of others, not so much in that they will be miraculously preserved (though it is distinctly promised that their bread and water shall be sure), but in the fact that, being instructed from God's Word, they will not feel the same anxiety and hopeless dread that will overspread the world. They will recognize the trouble as the preparation, according to God's plan, for blessing the whole world, and they will be cheered and comforted through it all. This is forcibly stated in Psa. 91; Isa. 33:2–14, 15–24.

Thus comforted and blessed by the divine assurance, the first duty of the saints is to let the world see that in the midst of all the prevailing trouble and discontent, and even while they share the trouble and suffer under it, they are hopeful, cheerful and always rejoicing in view of the glorious outcome foretold in God's Word.

The Apostle has written that "Godliness with *contentment* is great gain;" and though this has always been true, it will have double force in this Day of the Lord, when discontent is the chief ailment among all worldly classes. To these the saints should be a notable exception. There never was a time when dissatisfaction was so wide-spread; and yet there never was a time when men enjoyed so many favors and blessings. Wherever we look, whether into the palaces of the rich, replete with conveniences and splendors of which Solomon in all his glory knew almost nothing, or whether we look into the comfortable home of the thrifty and temperate wage-worker, with its evidences of taste, comfort, art and luxury, we see that in every way the present exceeds in bountiful supply every other period since the creation, many-fold; and yet the people are *unhappy* and discontented. The fact is that the desires of a selfish, depraved heart know no bounds. Selfishness has so taken possession of all, that, as we look out, we see the whole world madly pushing and driving and clutching after wealth. A few only being successful, the remainder are envious and soured because they are not the fortunate ones, and all are discontented and miserable—more so than in any former time.

But the saint should take no part in that struggle. His consecration vow was that he would strive and grasp and run for a higher, a heavenly prize, and hence he is weaned from earthly ambitions, and labors not for earthly things, except to provide things *decent* and *needful;* for he is giving heed to the course and example of the Master and the apostles.

Therefore they have *contentment* with their godliness, not because they have no ambition, but because their ambition is turned heavenward and absorbed in the effort to lay up treasure in heaven and to be rich toward God; in view of which, and of their knowledge of God's plans revealed in his Word, they are content with whatever of an earthly sort God may provide. These can joyfully sing:—

> Content, whatever lot I see,
> Since 'tis God's hand that leadeth me.

But alas! not all of God's children occupy this position. Many have fallen into the discontent prevalent in the world, and are robbing themselves of the enjoyments of life because they have left the Lord's footsteps and are casting their lot and taking their portion with the world—*seeking* earthly things whether attaining them or not, sharing the world's discontent, and failing to realize the contentment and peace which the world can neither give nor take away.

We urge the saints, therefore, to abandon the strife of greed and vainglory and its discontent, and to strive for the higher riches and the peace they do afford. We would remind them of the Apostle's words:—

"Godliness with contentment is great gain; for we brought nothing into this world, and it is certain we can carry nothing out. And having [*needful*] food and raiment, let us therewith be content. But they that will [to] be rich [whether they succeed or not] fall into temptation and a snare, and into many foolish and hurtful lusts which *drown* [sink] men in ruin and destruction. For a root of all vices is the love of money [whether in rich or poor], which some being *eager for* were led away from the faith and pierced themselves through with many pangs. But thou, O man of God, flee from these, and be pursuing righteousness, godliness, faith, love, endurance, meekness; be contesting in the *noble contest* of the faith, lay hold on everlasting life, unto which thou wast called and didst make a noble covenant."—1 Tim. 6:6–12.

If the example of the saints is thus one of contentment and joyful anticipation, and a cheerful submission to present trials in sure hope of the good time coming, such living examples alone are valuable lessons for the world. And in addition to the example, the counsel of the saints to those about them should be in harmony with their faith. It should be of the nature of ointment and healing balm. Advantage should be taken of circumstances to point the world to the good time coming, to preach to them the coming Kingdom of God, and to show the real cause of present troubles, and the only remedy.— Luke 3:14; Heb. 13:5; Phil. 4:11.

The poor world groans, not only under its real, but also under its fancied ills, and especially under the discontent of selfishness, pride and ambitions which fret and worry men because they cannot fully satisfy them. Hence, while we can see both sides of the question, let us counsel those willing to hear to contentment with what they have, and to patient waiting until

God in his due time and way brings to them the many blessings which his love and wisdom have provided.

By probing and inflaming either real or fancied wounds and wrongs, we would do injury to those we should be helping and blessing, thus spreading their discontent, and hence their trouble. But by fulfilling our mission, preaching the good tidings of the *ransom* given for ALL, and the consequent *blessings* to come to ALL, we shall be true heralds of the kingdom—its ambassadors of peace. Thus it is written, "How beautiful upon the mountains [kingdoms] are the feet of him [the last member of the body of Christ] that bringeth good tidings, that publisheth peace, that bringeth good tidings of good."—Isa. 52:7.

The troubles of this "Day of Jehovah" will give opportunity for preaching the good tidings of coming good, such as is seldom afforded, and blessed are they who will follow the footsteps of the Master, and be the good Samaritans binding up the wounds and pouring in the oil and wine of comfort and cheer. The assurance given such is that their labor is not in vain; for when the judgments of the Lord are in the earth, the inhabitants of the world *will learn* righteousness—Isa. 26:9.

The sympathy of the Lord's children, like that of their heavenly Father, must be largely in harmony with the groaning creation, striving for any deliverance from bondage; although they should, like him, remember and sympathize with those of the opposing classes whose desires are to be just and generous, but whose efforts are beset and hindered, not only by the weaknesses of their fallen nature, but also by their surroundings in life, and their association with and dependence upon others. But the Lord's children should have no sympathy with the arrogant, insatiate desires and endeavors of any class. Their utterances should be calm and moderate, and always for peace where principle is not at stake. They should remember that this is the Lord's battle, and that so far as politics or social questions are concerned, they have no real solution other than that predicted in the Word of God. The duty of the consecrated, therefore, is first of all to see that they are not in the way of Jehovah's chariot, and then to "stand still and see the salvation of God," in the sense of realizing that it is no part of their work to share in the struggle, but that it is the Lord's doing, through other agencies. Regardless of all such things, they should press along the line of their own mission, proclaiming the heavenly kingdom at hand as the only remedy for all classes, and their only hope.

15. TESTIMONIES OF THE
GIFTS OF PENTECOST

The Gift of Tongues and Related Phenomena
at the Present Day, 1909

BY FREDERICK G. HENKE

The blessings of Pentecost were by no means confined to city people. Baptism "of fire" and the possession of "tongues" occurred in Australia, Wales, India, Norway, and Korea about the turn of the twentieth century, and reports of these dramatic experiences no doubt helped kindle outbreaks in other areas, including the cities of the United States. Just as the sermon was the characteristic mode of discussion and definition in established Protestant churches, so the testimony served the Pentecostals. Frederick Henke, a student of comparative religions at the University of Chicago, wrote an article summarizing some of these testimonies, and presenting an eye-witness account of Pentecostal meetings in Chicago. Detached and critical as he was, he was greatly struck by the absolute conviction of the people; he quoted the English Methodist min-

---

From Frederick G. Henke, "The Gift of Tongues and Related Phenomena at the Present Day," *American Journal of Theology*, XIII (1909), 196–198, 200–201.

ister T. B. Barratt as insisting that he "would sooner die than give way to a humbug. I know that what the Pentecost God in His mercy gave me is the same kind of blessing as that received by the disciples at Pentecost in Jerusalem, and that the gift of tongues given to me is as pure as the gift spoken by Paul to the Corinthians. And I know that numbers are now rejoicing in this blessing. . . ."

In concluding the historical sketch of this revival movement, I shall take the liberty of presenting some typical facts gathered from meetings which I have attended in five different places in Chicago.

The meeting is opened by a short song service, toward the close of which the leader comes to the front. He has been praying for the meeting; for he must be positive that the Spirit has taken entire possession of him before he takes part. His evidence of the presence of the Spirit appears to be the violent jerking of his head. One Sunday morning, for example, a man from the congregation had begun to expound a chapter, when the leader, who was standing four or five feet behind him, apparently working up automatic action of his head and shoulders, suddenly stepped forward, seized him by the shoulder, and in a mandatory tone gave him to understand that he himself would now take charge of the service.

Early in the meeting, an opportunity is given for requests for prayer. The following are some examples: "For a man who don't believe anyone. His wife says there is no hope for him;" "for a woman who has been sick for nine months;" "for a woman possessed with a devil;" "for wickedness in my family." By this time, automatic movements of the head usually appear in various parts of the house, the tendency being for others to imitate the leader or those who are most pronounced in their demonstrations. The congregation kneels for prayer, and several lead. Speaking in tongues is sometimes introduced

into one or the other of these prayers. The people having risen
from their knees, an opportunity is given for testimonies. A
colored man rises and gives a rousing testimony, "I feel a burning inside in the inner man like a coal of fire. Glory to God!"
At once there is a response from all over the house (about three
hundred are present), some shouting, some manifesting violent
jerks, some screaming, and some laughing aloud. A woman
next follows with her testimony. "Six years ago," she says, "I
was partly healed in Zion [Dowie's church], but now I am
fully restored. During the past week, I picked out the cancer
entirely and put it into a dish." She now is thoroughly under
the influence of her emotions. She begins to speak in tongues.
From this she passes into singing in tongues. Her countenance
is lighted up with ecstatic joy and serenity as she passes from
one key to another, improvising her own tunes. When she had
finished, the leader immediately arises to interpret the message
spoken in an unknown tongue: "The Lord is the strength of
my life; of whom shall I be fearful? The Lord is my light and
my salvation; whom shall I fear?" Emotion and suggestibility
now reign in the meeting. Arms move frantically, heads jerk
so violently that some of the women are unable to keep their
hats on, and speaking in tongues is heard in nearly every testimony that follows. This speaking in tongues varies from a
mere rapid repetition of a few syllables to a complex combination of euphonious sounds. For instance, a girl in the meeting
so loses her inhibitions that she jerks all over. Suddenly she
begins to speak in tongues, "Yah-yah-yeh-yeh-yeh-yeh-yah-
yah." In contrast to this, another individual speaks somewhat
after the following manner, "Kah-tah-lan-see-ah, oh-nee-han-
see-ah, oh-nee-see-nee-nah," etc. Of the two, the former is a
novice, the latter an expert.

After fifteen or twenty testimonies, the leader preaches. His
theme is, "Coworkers with God." He dwells for some time on
the baptism in the Spirit. "The head, the understanding," he
says, "cannot perceive the Holy Ghost. He must enter the

heart, the fleshly valvular heart. The Holy Spirit came in through my legs, November 20, 1906." The sermon is followed by invitations. Those who are seeking the baptism of the Spirit are asked to gather in a back room for prayer, and those who desire conversion or healing are requested to kneel at the altar in the assembly-room. Then follows a scene of storm and stress in the main room. A woman at the altar throws herself upon the floor and writhes as though in the most excruciating pain. The elders pray over her a few moments. Soon she rises and goes away apparently at rest. . . .

[TESTIMONY OF REVEREND A. E. STREET (1907)]

Some twelve years ago [he writes,] I began to long for Pentecost as described in the Bible and all these years have been praying for that baptism. . . . About a year ago the burden of prayer became greater and greater, increasing until in February, night after night, I was waiting on the Lord until 5 o'clock in the morning. These were not hours of agonizing prayer, but rather a determined struggle to get quiet before him and to stop all my own thoughts and desires. . . . It required months to reach the lower parts of the valley of humiliation and be empty in thought. Finally I went to the mission at 328 W. Sixty-third St., Chicago, asking only one question, "Why do I not receive the baptism?" . . . The good friends prayed with me and said that nothing was wrong, I only needed to wait. . . . They were right, for the first time that I knelt at the altar on Sunday afternoon, March 17, the power began to seize me and I laughed all through the following communion service. In the evening, at about 11 P. M., I knelt with a few of the friends praying for me. (Elder Sinclair placed his hands on my head for a short time several times during the afternoon and evening.) After some little waiting I began to laugh or rather my body was used to laugh with increasing power until I was flat on my back laughing at the top of my voice for over half an hour. On rising I found that I was drunk on the "New Wine," acting just like a drunken man in many ways and full of joy. On kneeling to meet the Lord again I was suddenly seized with irresistible power of beseeching with groanings. The power of this praying was too great for me to endure and suddenly my eyes opened to see Elder Sinclair, who was standing a few feet distant, fall as though he had been struck. I was relieved and in a few seconds was straight up in the air shouting "Glory" at the top of my voice. Again kneeling my eyes grew dark and I was rolled over onto the floor, lying there some time unconscious. Then coming to and kneeling I felt my jaws and mouth being worked by a strange force. In a few seconds some baby gibberish was uttered, then a few words in Chinese that I understood, and then several sentences in a strange tongue. This turned into singing and I did not speak again in tongues until Wednesday. . . . On Wednesday morning. . . . I began to sing the heavenly music at the top of my voice and during the entire half-hour, even while I was in the water in the bath tub, that great volume of song was pouring out of my throat! . . .

On Thursday night I was awakened out of my sleep and began to pray for the gift of interpretation. After a few words the prayer was taken out of my control and the same mighty force that had prayed for me to come all the way uttered a few sentences asking for the gift. That seemed to be sufficient and all was quiet. Then for an hour I received a lesson in interpreting. A word was given in a strange tongue. This was followed by its English meaning and the two were repeated until it was plain that they meant the same. Then a short sentence was interpreted in the same way and finally a hymn. From that hour whenever anyone speaks in tongues the interpretation comes if I ask it.

16. RELIGION AS HEALING

Precept and Practice, 1902

BY MARY BAKER EDDY

Through most of her early years, Mrs. Eddy (1820–1910) suffered a variety of illnesses. "I sought knowledge from the different schools," she later remarked, "—allopathy, homeopathy, hydropathy, electricity, and from various humbugs—but without receiving satisfaction." Shortly after she encountered Phineas Quimby, a healer who is now regarded as the father of New Thought, she was cured. Her ability to recover from a subsequent serious fall confirmed her sense of mastery over illness, and she began a career of healing through mental illumination. SCIENCE AND HEALTH, which incorporated her doctrines, first appeared in 1875, and though the volume was slow to attract an audience, it did get through sixteen editions by 1885, when Mrs. Eddy revised it. Thereafter it remained virtually intact. Regarded by loyal Christian Scientists as a new gospel which improved on but did not controvert the Bible, SCIENCE AND HEALTH explained the early career of the prophet, her notions of disease, and the general principles of Christian Science healing.

From Mary Baker Eddy, *Science and Health, with Key to The Scriptures* (Boston: Christian Science Publishing House, 1902), pp. vii–xii, 165–177, 368–377.

PREFACE

To those leaning on the sustaining Infinite, to-day is big with blessings. The wakeful shepherd beholds the first faint morning beams, ere cometh the full radiance of a risen day. So shone the pale star to the prophet-shepherds; yet it traversed the night, and came where, in cradled obscurity, lay the young child who should redeem mortals, and make plain to human understanding the way of salvation. Now across a night of error dawn the morning beams, and shines the guiding star of Truth. The Wisemen are led to behold and follow the daystar of divine Science, lighting the way to eternal harmony.

The time for thinkers has come. Truth, independent of doctrines and time-honored systems, knocks at the portal of humanity. Contentment with the past and the cold conventionality of materialism are crumbling away. Ignorance of God is no longer the stepping-stone to faith. The only guarantee of obedience is a right apprehension of Him whom to know aright is Life eternal. Though empires fall, "He whose right it is shall reign."

A book introduces new thoughts, but cannot make them speedily understood. It is the task of the sturdy pioneer to hew the tall oak, and to cut the rough granite. Future ages must declare what the pioneer has accomplished.

Since the author's discovery of the adaptation of Truth to the treatment of disease as well as of sin, her system has been fully tested, and has not been found wanting; but to reach the heights of Christian Science man must live in obedience to its divine Principle. To develop the full might of this Science, the discords of corporeal sense must yield to the harmony of spiritual sense; even as the science of sound corrects false tones caught by the ear, and gives sweet concord to music.

Theology and physics teach that both Spirit and matter are real and good; whereas the fact is that one is good and real, and the other is its opposite. The question, What is Truth? is answered by demonstration,—by healing both disease and sin; and this shows that Christian healing confers the most health and makes the best men. On this basis Christian Science will have a fair fight. Sickness has been fought for centuries by doctors using material remedies; but the question arises, Is there less sickness because of these practitioners? A vigorous 'No' is the response deducible from two connate facts—the reputed longevity of the Antediluvians, and the rapid multiplication and increased violence of diseases since the Flood.

In the author's work, *Retrospection and Introspection,* may be found a biographical sketch, narrating experiences which led her, in the year 1866, to the discovery of the system which she denominated Christian Science. As early as 1862 she began to write down and give to friends the results of her Scriptural study, for the Bible was her sole teacher; but these compositions were crude,—the first steps of a child in the newly discovered world of Spirit.

She also began to jot down her thoughts on the main subject; but these jottings were only infantile lispings of Truth. A child drinks in the outward world through the eyes, and rejoices in the draught. He is as sure of the world's existence as of his own; yet he cannot describe it. He finds a few words, and with these he stammeringly attempts the conveyance of his feeling. Later, the tongue voices the more definite thought, though still imperfectly.

So was it with the author. As a certain poet says of himself, she "lisped in numbers, for the numbers came." Certain essays written at that early date, are still in circulation among her first pupils; but they are feeble attempts to state the Principle and practice of Christian healing, and are not complete nor satisfactory expositions of Truth. To-day, though rejoicing in some progress, she finds herself still a willing disciple at the heavenly gate, waiting for the Mind of Christ.

Her first pamphlet on Christian Science was copyrighted in 1870; but it did not appear in print until 1876, as she had learned that this Science must be demonstrated by healing, before a work on the subject could be profitably studied. From 1867 until 1875 copies were, however, in friendly circulation.

Before writing this work, *Science and Health,* she made copious notes of Scriptural exposition, which have never been published. This was between the years 1867 and 1868. These efforts show her ignorance of the great subject up to that time, and the degrees by which she came at length to the solution of the stupendous Life-problem; but she values them as a parent may treasure the memorials of a child's growth, and would not have them changed.

The first edition of *Science and Health* was published in 1875. Various books on mental healing have since been issued, most of which are incorrect in theory and filled with plagiarisms from *Science and Health.* They regard the human mind as a healing agent; whereas this mind is not a factor in the Principle of Christian Science. A few books, however, which are based on this book, are useful.

The author has not compromised conscience to suit the general drift of thought, but bluntly and honestly given the text of Truth. There has been no effort on her part to embellish, elaborate, or treat in full detail so infinite a theme. By thousands of well-authenticated cases of healing, many of her students have proven the worth of her teachings. These for the most part have been cases abandoned as hopeless by regular medical attendants. Few invalids will turn to God till all physical supports have failed, because there is so little faith in His disposition and power to heal.

The Principle of her system is demonstrable in the personal experience of any sincere seeker of Truth. Its purpose is good, and its practice is more safe and potent than that of any other sanitary method. The unbiased Christian thought is soonest touched by Truth, and convinced of it. Those only quarrel with her method who have not understood her meaning, or discerning the Truth, come not to the light lest their works should be reproved. No intellectual proficiency is requisite in the learner, but sound morals are most desirable.

Many imagine that the phenomena of physical healing in Christian Science present only a phase of the action of the human mind, which in some unexplained way results in the cure of sickness. On the contrary, Christian Science rationally explains that all other pathological methods are the fruits of human faith in matter,—in the workings, not of Spirit, but of the fleshly mind, which must yield to Science.

The physical healing of Christian Science results now, as in Jesus' time, from the operation of divine Principle, before which sin and disease lose their reality in human consciousness, and so disappear as naturally and as necessarily as darkness gives place to light, and sin to reformation. Now, as then, they are not supernatural, but supremely natural. They are those "mighty works," which were the sign of Immanuel, or "God with us,"—an influence ever present in human consciousness, and coming now again, as was promised aforetime.

> To preach deliverance to the captives [of sense],
> And recovering of sight to the blind,
> To set at liberty them that are bruised.

When God called her to proclaim His Gospel to this age, there came also the charge to plant and water His vineyard.

The first school of Christian Science Mind-healing was begun by the author in Lynn, Massachusetts, about the year 1867, with only one student. In 1881, she opened the Massachusetts Metaphysical College, in Boston, under the seal of the Commonwealth,—a law relative to colleges having been passed, which enabled her to get this institution chartered for medical purposes. No charters were granted to Christian Scientists for such institutions after 1883; and up to that date, hers was the only college of this character which had ever been established in the United States, where Christian Science was first introduced.

During seven years over four thousand students were taught by the author in this college. Meanwhile she was pastor of the first established Church of Christ, Scientist; president of the first Christian Scientist Association, convening monthly; publisher of her own works; and (for a portion of this time) sole editor and publisher of the Christian Science Journal, the first periodical issued by Christian Scientists. She closed her college, October 29, 1889, in the height of its prosperity, with a deep-lying conviction that the next two years of her life should be given to the preparation of the revision, in 1891, of *Science and Health.*

In the spirit of Christ's charity,—as one who "hopeth all things, endureth all things," and is joyful to bear consolation to the sorrowing, and healing to the sick,—she commits these pages to honest seekers for Truth. . . .

PHYSIOLOGY

Physiology is one of the apples from "the tree of knowledge." Evil declared that eating this fruit would open man's eyes, and make him as a god. Instead of so doing, it closed mortal eyes to man's God-given dominion over the earth.

To measure intellectual capacity by the size of the brain, and strength by the exercise of muscle, is to subjugate intelligence, to make mind mortal, and to place this so-called mind at the mercy of material organization and non-intelligent matter.

Obedience to the so-called physical laws of health has not checked sickness. Diseases have multiplied, since man-made material theories have taken the place of spiritual truth.

You say that indigestion, fatigue, sleeplessness, cause distressed stomachs and aching heads. Then you consult your brain, in order to remember what has hurt you, when your remedy lies in forgetting the whole thing; for matter has no sensation of its own, and the human mind is all that can produce pain.

As a man thinketh, so is he. Mind is all that feels, acts, or impedes action. Ignorant of this, or shrinking from its implied responsibility, the healing effort is made on the wrong side, and thus the conscious control over the body is lost.

The Mohammedan believes in a pilgrimage to Mecca for the salvation of his soul. The popular doctor believes in his recipe, and the druggist believes in the power of his prescription to save a man's life. The first is a religious delusion; the second is a medical delusion.

The erring human mind is inharmonious in itself. From this arises the inharmonious body. To ignore God as of little use in sickness is a mistake. Instead of thrusting Him aside in times of bodily trouble, and waiting for the hour of strength in which to acknowledge Him, we should learn that He can do everything for us in sickness as in health.

Failing to recover health through adherence to physiology and hygiene, the despairing invalid often drops them, and turns in his extremity, and only as a last resort, to God. His faith in the divine Mind is less than it was in drugs, air, and exercise, or he would have resorted to Mind first. The balance of power is conceded to be with matter, by most of the medical systems; but when Spirit at last asserts its mastery, then, and not before, is man found to be harmonious and immortal.

Should we implore a corporeal God to heal the sick out of His personal volition? or should we understand the infinitely divine Principle which heals? If we rise no higher than blind faith, the Science of healing is not attained, and Soul-existence, in the place of sense-existence, is not comprehended. We apprehend life in divine Science, only as we live above corporeal sense, and correct it. Our proportionate admission of the claims of Good or of evil determines the harmony of our existence,— our health, our longevity, and our Christianity.

We cannot serve two masters, nor perceive divine Science through the material sense. Drugs and hygiene cannot successfully usurp the place and power of the divine Source of all health and perfection. If God constituted man both good and evil, man must remain thus. What can improve His work? Again, an error in the premise must appear in the conclusion. To have one God and avail yourself of the power of Spirit, you must renounce matter.

The "flesh lusteth against the Spirit." They can no more unite in action, than good can coincide with evil. It is not wise to take a halting and half-way position, or to expect to work equally with Spirit and matter, Truth and error. There is but one way—namely, God and His idea—which leads to spiritual life. The scientific government of the body must be attained through the divine Mind. It is impossible to gain control over it in any other way. On this fundamental point timid conservatism is absolutely inadmissible. Only through radical reliance on Truth can scientific healing power be realized.

Substituting good words for a good life, fair seeming for straightforward character, is a poor shift for the weak and worldly, who think the standard of Christian Science too high for them.

If the scales are evenly adjusted, the removal of a single weight from either scale gives preponderance to the opposite. Whatever influence you cast on the side of matter you take away from Mind, which would otherwise outweigh all else. Your belief militates against your health, when it ought to be enlisted on the side of health. When sick (according to belief) you rush after drugs, search out the so-called laws of health, and depend upon them to heal you, though you have already brought yourself into the slough of disease through just this false dependence.

Because man-made systems insist that man becomes sick and useless, suffers and dies, all in consonance with the laws of God, are we to believe it? Are we to believe an authority which denies God's spiritual command relating to perfection,— an authority which Jesus has proved to be false? He did the will of the Father. He healed sickness, in defiance of what is called material law, but in accordance with God's law, the law of Mind.

I have discerned disease in the human mind, and recognized the patient's fear of it, months before the so-called disease made its appearance in the body. Disease being a belief,—a latent illusion of mortal mind, the sensation would not appear if this error were met and destroyed by Truth.

Here let a word be introduced which may be frequently used hereafter,—*chemicalization.* By chemicalization I mean the process which mortal mind and body undergo in the change of belief from a material to a spiritual basis.

Whenever an aggravation of symptoms has occurred, through mental chemicalization, I have seen the mental signs, assuring me that danger was over, before the patient felt the change; and I have said to the patient, "You are healed,"—sometimes to his discomposure, when he was incredulous; but it always came about as I had foretold.

I name these facts to show that disease has a mental, mortal origin,—that faith in rules of health or in drugs begets and fosters disease, by attracting the mind to the subject of sickness, by exciting fear of it, and by dosing the body in order to avoid it. The faith reposed in these things should find stronger supports and a higher home. Understanding the control of Mind over body, we should put no faith in material means.

Science not only reveals the origin of all disease as wholly mental, but it also declares that all disease is cured by divine Mind. There can be no healing except by this Mind, however much we trust a drug, or any other means toward which human faith, or endeavor, is directed. It is mortal mind, not matter, which brings to the sick whatever good they may seem to receive from drugs. But the sick are never really healed, except by means of the Divine power. It is only the action of Truth, Life, and Love, that can give harmony.

Whatever teaches man to have other laws, and acknowledge other power than the divine Mind, is anti-Christian. The good that a poisonous drug seems to do is evil, for it robs man of reliance upon God, omnipotent Mind, and according to belief poisons the human system. Truth is not the basis of theogony. Modes of matter form neither a moral nor a spiritual system. The discord which calls for them is the result of the exercise of faith in matter instead of Spirit.

Did Jesus understand the economy of man less than Graham or Cutter? Christian ideas certainly embrace—what human theories exclude—the Principle of man's harmony. The text, "Whosoever liveth and believeth in me shall never die," not only contradicts human systems, but points to the self-sustaining and eternal Truth.

The demands of Truth are spiritual, and reach the body through Mind. The best interpreter of man's needs said: "Take no thought for your life, what ye shall eat, or what ye shall drink."

If there are material laws which prevent disease, what then causes it? No divine law, for Christ healed the sick and cast out error, always in opposition, never in obedience, to physics.

Spiritual causation is the one question to be considered, for more than all others it relates to human progress. The age seems ready to approach this subject, to ponder somewhat the supremacy of Spirit, and at least touch the hem of its garment.

The description of man as purely physical, or as both material and spiritual,—but in either case dependent on his physical organization,—is the Pandora box, from which many evils have gone forth, especially despair. Matter, which takes divine power into its own hands, and claims to be a creator, is a fiction, in which paganism is so sanctioned by society that mankind has caught its moral contagion.

Through discernment of the spiritual opposite of materiality, even the way through Christ, Truth, man will reopen, with the key of divine Science, the gates of Paradise which human beliefs have closed, and will find himself unfallen, upright, pure, and free, not needing to consult almanacs for the probabilities of life, or to study brainology in order to learn how much of a man he is.

Mind's control over the universe, including man, is no longer an open question, but is demonstrable Science. Jesus illustrated the divine Principle, and the practice of immortal Mind, by healing sickness and sin, and destroying the foundations of death.

Mistaking his origin and nature, man believes himself to be combined matter and Spirit,—that Spirit is sifted through matter, carried on a nerve, exposed to ejection by the operation of matter. Think of it! The intellectual, the moral, the spiritual,—yea, infinite Mind,—subjected to non-intelligence!

No more sympathy exists between the flesh and Spirit than between Belial and Christ.

The so-called laws of matter are nothing but false beliefs in the presence of intelligence and life where Mind is not. This is the procuring cause of all sin and disease. The opposite truth—that intelligence and life are spiritual, never material—destroys sin, sickness, and death.

The fundamental error lies in the supposition that man is a material outgrowth, and that the cognizance of good or evil, which he has through the bodily senses, constitutes his happiness or misery.

Theorizing about man's development from mushrooms to monkeys, and from monkeys into men, amounts to nothing in the right direction and very much in the wrong.

Materialism grades the human species as rising from the dust upward; how then is the material species maintained when man passes through what we call death,—and imagine to be the Rubicon of spirituality? Spirit can form no real link in this supposed chain of material being, but reveals the eternal chain as uninterrupted and wholly spiritual; yet this can be realized only as the discordant sense of being disappears.

If a man was first a material being, he must have passed through all the forms of matter, in order to become man. If the material body is man, he is mere matter, or dust. On the contrary, man is the image and likeness of Spirit; and the belief that there is Soul in sense, or Life in matter, belongs to mortal mind, to which the Apostle refers, when he says we must "put off the old man."

What is man? Brain, heart, blood, the material structure? If the real man is in the material body, you take away a portion of the man when you amputate a limb; the surgeon destroys manhood, and worms annihilate it. But the loss of a limb, or injury to a tissue, is sometimes the quickener of manliness; and the unfortunate cripple may present more nobility than the statuesque athlete,—teaching us by his very deprivations, that "a man's a man, for a' that."

When we admit that matter (heart, blood, brain, acting through the five physical senses) constitutes man, we fail to see how anatomy can distinguish between humanity and the brute, or determine when man is really *man*, and has progressed farther than his animal progenitors.

The theory that Spirit is distinct from matter, but must pass through it, or into it, to be individualized, reduces Truth to the dependency of error, and requires the sensible to be made manifest through the insensible.

What is termed matter manifests nothing but a material mentality. Not a glimpse or manifestation of Spirit is obtainable through matter. Spirit is positive. Matter is its supposed opposite, the absence of Spirit. For positive Spirit to pass through a negative condition would be its destruction.

Anatomy declares man to be structural. Physiology continues this explanation, measuring human strength by bones and sinews, and human life by material law. Man is spiritual, individual, and eternal; material structure is mortal.

Phrenology makes man knavish or honest, according to the development of the cranium; but anatomy, physiology, phrenology, do not define the image of God, the real immortal man.

Human reason and religion come slowly to the recognition

of spiritual facts, and so continue to call upon matter to remove the error which the human mind alone has created.

The idols of civilization are far more fatal to health and longevity than the idols of barbarism. They call into action less faith than Buddhism, in a supreme governing Intelligence. The Esquimaux restore health by incantations, as effectually as civilized practitioners by their more studied methods.

Is civilization only a higher form of idolatry, that man should bow down to a flesh-brush, to flannels, to baths, diet, exercise, and air? Nothing save Divine power is capable of doing as much for man as he can do for himself.

The footsteps of thought, as they pass higher from material standpoints, are slow, and portend a long night to the traveller; but the angels of His presence—the spiritual intuitions that tell us when "the night is far spent, the day is at hand"—are our guardians in the gloom. Whosoever opens the way in Christian Science is a pilgrim and stranger marking out the path for generations yet unborn.

The voices of Sinai, and the Sermon on the Mount, are pursuing and will overtake the ages, rebuking in their course all error, and proclaiming the kingdom of heaven on earth. Truth is revealed. It only needs to be practised.

Belief is all that ever enables a drug to cure mortal ailments. Anatomy admits that mind is somewhere in man, though out of sight. Then, if one is sick, why treat the body alone, while we administer a dose of despair to the mind? Why declare that the body is diseased, and picture this disease to the mind, rolling it under the tongue as a sweet morsel, and holding it before the thought of both physician and patient? We should understand that the cause of disease rests in the mortal human mind, and its cure with the immortal divine Mind. We should prevent the images of disease from taking form in thought, and we should efface the outlines of disease already formulated in mortal mind.

When there are fewer doctors, and less thought is given to

sanitary subjects, there will be better constitutions and less disease. In old times who ever heard of dyspepsia, cerebrospinal meningitis, hay-fever and rose-cold?

What an abuse of natural beauty to say that a rose, the smile of God, can produce suffering! The joy of its presence, its beauty, and purity should uplift the thought, and destroy any possible fear of fever. It is profane to fancy that the sweetness of clover and the breath of new-mown hay may cause glandular inflammation, sneezing, and nasal pangs.

If a random thought, calling itself dyspepsia, had tried to tyrannize over our forefathers, it would have been routed by their independence and industry. Then the people had less time for selfishness, coddling, and sickly after-dinner talk. The exact amount of food the stomach could digest was not discussed according to Cutter, nor referred to sanitary laws. A man's belief in those days was not so severe upon the gastric juices. Beaumont's "Medical Experiments" did not govern the digestion.

Damp atmosphere and freezing snow empurpled the plump cheeks of our ancestors; but they never indulged in the refinement of inflamed bronchial tubes, because they were as ignorant as Adam before he ate the fruit of false knowledge, of the existence of such things as tubes and troches, lungs and lozenges.

"Where ignorance is bliss, 'tis folly to be wise," says the English poet; and there is truth in his sentiment. The action of mortal mind on the body was not so injurious before inquisitive modern Eves took up the study of medical works, and unmanly Adams attributed their own downfall, and the fate of their offspring, to the weakness of their wives.

The primitive custom of taking no thought about food, left the stomach and bowels free to act in obedience to nature, and gave the gospel a chance to be seen in its glorious effects upon the body. A ghastly array of diseases was not paraded before the imagination. There were fewer books on digestion, and more "sermons in stones, and good in everything." When the mechanism of the human mind gives place to the divine Mind, selfishness and sin, disease and death, will lose their foothold.

Human fear of miasma would load with disease the air of Eden, and weigh down mankind with superimposed and conjectural evils. Mortal mind is the worst foe of the body, while divine Mind is its best friend.

Should all cases of organic disease be treated by a regular practitioner, and the Christian Scientist try his hand only on cases of hysteria, hypochondria, and hallucination? One disease is no more real than another. All disease is the result of education, and can carry its ill-effects no farther than mortal mind maps out the way. Christian Science heals organic disease as well as functional. It finds that decided types of acute disease are quite as ready to yield to Truth as the less distinct type and chronic form of disease. It handles the most malignant contagion with perfect assurance.

Human mind produces what is termed organic disease as certainly as it produces hysteria, and it must relinquish all its errors, sicknesses, and sins. I have demonstrated this beyond all cavil. The evidence of divine Mind's healing power and absolute control is to me as certain as the evidence of my own existence. . . .

CHRISTIAN SCIENCE PRACTICE

Against the fatal belief that error is as real as Truth,—that evil is equal in power to Good, if not superior, and that discord is as normal as harmony,—even the hope of freedom from the bondage of sickness and sin has little inspiration to nerve endeavor. When we come to have more faith in the Truth of being than we have in error, more faith in Spirit than in matter, more faith in living than in dying, more faith in God than in man, then no material conditions can prevent us from healing the sick and destroying error through Truth.

That Life is not contingent on bodily conditions is proven, when we see that life and man survive this body. Neither evil, disease, nor death can be discerned spiritually, and the mortal sense of them disappears in the ratio of our spiritual growth. Because matter has no consciousness, or Ego, it cannot act; its conditions are unreal, and these false conditions are the source of all seeming sickness. Admit the existence of matter, and we admit that mortality (and therefore disease) has a foundation in fact. Deny the existence of matter, and we can destroy the belief in these conditions, and with it disappears the foundation of disease. Once let the mental physician believe in the reality of matter, and he must admit also the reality of all its discordant conditions, and this prevents his destroying them. Then he is even less fitted for the treatment of disease than the ordinary medical practitioner.

In proportion as matter, to human sense, loses all entity as substance, in that proportion does man become its master. He enters into a diviner sense of the facts, and comprehends the theology of Jesus, as demonstrated in healing the sick, raising the dead, and walking over the wave. All these deeds manifested Christ's control over the belief that matter is substance, that it can be the arbiter of life, or the constructor of any form of existence.

We never read that Jesus made a diagnosis of a disease, in order to discover some means of healing it. He never asked if it were acute or chronic. He never recommended attention to laws of health, never gave drugs, never prayed to know if God were willing a man should live. He understood man to be immortal, whose Life is God,—and not that man has two lives, one to be destroyed, and the other to be made indestructible.

The prophylactic and therapeutic (that is, the preventive and curative) arts belong emphatically to Christian Science; as would be readily seen, if psychology, or the Science of Soul, were understood. Material medicine is finding its proper level. Limited to matter, by its own law, it has none of the advantages of Mind and immortality.

No man is physically healed in sin, or by it, any more than he is morally saved in or by sin. To be every whit whole, he must be better spiritually, as well as physically. To be made whole, we must forsake the mortal sense of things, turn from the lie of false belief to Truth, and gather the facts of being from the immortal divine Mind. The body improves under the same regimen which improves the thought; and if this is not made manifest, it proves that it is not Truth which is influencing us. This is the law of cause and effect, or like producing like.

Homœopathy furnishes this evidence to the senses, namely, that the symptoms produced by a certain drug, it removes by using the same drug which might cause them. This confirms my theory that faith in the drug is the sole factor in the cure. The effect that mortal mind produces through a certain belief, it removes through an opposite belief; but it uses the same drug in both cases.

The moral and spiritual facts of health, whispered into thought, produce very direct and marked effects on the body. A physical diagnosis of disease—since mortal mind must be its cause, if it exists—generally has a tendency to induce disease.

According both to medical testimony and individual experience, a drug eventually loses its supposed power, and can do no more for the patient. Hygienic treatment also loses its efficacy. Quackery likewise fails at length to inspire the credulity of the sick, and then they cease to improve. These lessons are useful. They should naturally and gently change our basis from sensation to Christian Science, from error to Truth, from matter to Spirit.

Physicians examine the pulse, tongue, lungs, to discover the condition of matter; when in fact all is Mind, and the body is the substratum of mortal mind, to whose higher mandate it must respond.

Disquisitions on disease have a mental effect similar to that produced by telling ghost-stories in the dark. By those un-instructed in Christian Science, nothing is really understood of material existence. Mortals are believed to be here without their consent, and to be removed as involuntarily, not knowing why or when. As children look everywhere for the imaginary ghost, so sick humanity sees danger in every direction, and looks for relief in all ways except the right one. Darkness in-duces fear. The adult, in bondage to his beliefs, no more com-prehends his real Being than does the child; and he must be taken out of his darkness, before he can get rid of the illusive sufferings which throng the gloaming. The way in divine Sci-ence is the only way out of this condition.

I would not transform the infant at once into a man, nor would I keep the suckling a lifelong babe. No impossible thing do I ask when urging the claims of Christian Science; but be-cause this teaching is in advance of the age, we should not deny the need of spiritual understanding. Mankind will im-prove through Science and Christianity. The necessity for up-lifting the race is father to the fact that Mind can do it; for Mind can impart purity instead of impurity, beauty instead of deformity, and health instead of sickness. Truth is an alter-native in the entire system, and can make it "every whit whole."

Remember, brain is not mind. Matter cannot be sick, and Mind is immortal. Your mortal body is only a mortal belief of mind in matter. What you call matter was originally error in solution, elementary mortal mind,—likened, by Milton, to "chaos and old night." One theory about this mortal mind is, that its sensations form blood, flesh, and bones. The Science of Being, wherein all is divine Mind, or God and His thought, would be clearer in this age, but for the belief that matter can produce mind, or that mind can enter its own embodied thought, bind itself with its own beliefs, and then call its bonds material and name them divine law.

If man is absolutely governed by God, or Spirit, then man

is not subject to matter, "neither indeed can be;" and therefore man cannot suffer, neither can he infringe his Maker's spiritual law. Christian Science and Christianity are one. How then in Christian Science, any more than in Christianity, can we believe in the reality and power of both Truth and error, and hope to succeed with either? Error is not self-sustaining. Its false supports fail, one after another. It succeeds for a period, only by parading in the stolen vestments of Truth.

"Whosoever shall deny me before men, him will I also deny before my Father which is in heaven." A denial of Truth is fatal to Christian Science. A just acknowledgment of Truth, and what it has done for us, is an effectual help. If pride, superstition, or any error, prevents the honest recognition of benefits received, this will be a hindrance to the recovery of the sick and the success of the student.

If we are Christians on all moral questions, but are in darkness as to the physical exemption which Christianity includes, then we must have more faith in God on this subject, and be more alive to His promises. It is easier to cure the most malignant disease than it is to cure sin. The author has raised up the dying, partly because they were willing to be restored; while she has struggled long, and perhaps in vain to lift a student out of a chronic sin. Under all modes of pathological treatment, the sick recover more rapidly from disease than the sinner from his sin. Healing is easier than teaching, if the teaching is faithfully done.

The fear of disease and the love of sin are the springs of man's enslavement. "The fear of the Lord is the beginning of wisdom!" but the Scriptures also declare, through the exalted thought of John, that "perfect Love casteth out fear."

The fear occasioned by ignorance can be cured; but you cannot remove the effects of fear produced by sin, so long as the sin remains. Disease is expressed not so much by the lips, as in the functions of the body. Establish the scientific sense of health, and you relieve the oppressed organ, and the inflammation, decomposition, or deposit will abate; and the disabled organ will resume its healthy functions.

When the blood rushes madly through the veins, or languidly creeps along its frozen channels, we call these conditions disease. This is a misconception. Mortal mind is producing the propulsion or the languor; and we prove this to be so when by mental means the circulation is changed, and returns to that standard which mortal mind has decided upon as essential for health. Anodynes, counter-irritants, and depletion never reduce inflammation scientifically; but the Truth of being, whispered into the ear of mortal mind, will bring relief.

Error, and its effects on the body, are removed by Truth. Because mortal mind seems to be conscious, the sick say: "How can my mind cause a disease I never thought of, and knew nothing about, until it appeared on my body?" The author has answered this question, in her explanation of disease as originating in human belief before it is apparent on the body, which is in fact the objective state of mortal mind, though it is called matter. This mortal blindness, and its sharp consequences, show our need of metaphysics. Through immortal Mind, or Truth, we can destroy all ills which proceed from mortal mind.

Ignorance of the cause or approach of disease is no argument against its mental origin. You confess to ignorance of the future, and incapacity to preserve your own existence; and this belief helps rather than hinders disease. Such a state of mind induces sickness. It is like walking in darkness, on the edge of a precipice. You cannot forget the belief of danger, and your steps are less firm because of your ignorance of mental power.

Heat and cold are products of mind. The body, when bereft of mortal mind, at first cools; and afterwards it is resolved into its primitive mortal elements. Nothing that lives ever dies, and *vice versa*. Mortal mind produces animal heat; and then expels it through the abandonment of a belief, or increases it to the point of self-destruction. Hence it is mortal mind, not matter,

which says, "I die." Heat would pass from the body as pain-
lessly as gas when it evaporates, but for the belief that inflammation and pain must accompany this separation.

Chills and heat are often the form in which fever manifests
itself. Change the mental state, and the chills and fever disappear. The old-school physician proves this when his patient
says, "I am better," but believes that matter, not mind, has
helped him. The Christian Scientist demonstrates that immortal Mind heals the case, while the hypnotist dispossesses
the patient of his mind in order to control him. No person is
benefited by yielding his own mentality to this mental des-
potism. Therefore all unscientific mental practice is dangerous,
and should be understood and so rendered fruitless. The
genuine Christian Scientist is adding to his patient's mental
power, and increasing his spirituality, while he is restoring
him physically.

Palsy is a belief that matter attacks mortals, and paralyzes
the body, making certain portions of it motionless. Destroy
the belief, show mortal mind that muscles have no power to
be lost, for Mind is supreme, and you will cure the palsy.

Consumptive patients always show great hopefulness and
courage, even when supposed to be in hopeless danger. This
state of mind seems anomalous, except to the expert in Christian Science. The mental state is not understood, simply
because it is a stage of fear so excessive that it amounts
to fortitude. The belief in consumption presents to mortal
thought a hopeless state, an image more terrifying than most
other diseases. The patient turns involuntarily from the contemplation of it; but, though unacknowledged, the latent fear,
and despair of recovery, remain in thought.

Just so it is with the greatest sin. It is the most subtle, and
does its work almost unperceived. The diseases deemed dangerous sometimes come from the most hidden, undefined, and
insidious beliefs. The pallid invalid, whom you declare to be
wasting away with consumption of the blood, should be told

that blood never gave life, and can never take it away,—that Life is Spirit, and that there is more Life and immortality in one good motive and act, than in all the blood which ever flowed through mortal veins, simulating a corporeal sense of material life.

If the body is material, it cannot, for that very reason, suffer with a fever. Because the so-called material body is a mental concept, and governed by mortal mind, it manifests only what that mind impresses upon it. Therefore the efficient remedy is to destroy the patient's unfortunate belief, by both silently and audibly arguing the opposite facts in regard to harmonious being,—representing man as healthful instead of diseased, and showing that it is impossible for matter to suffer, to feel pain or heat, to be thirsty or sick. Destroy fear, and you end the fever. Some people, mistaught as to Mind-science, inquire when it will be safe to check a fever. Know that in Science you cannot check a fever after admitting that it must have its course. To fear and admit the power of disease, is to paralyze mental and scientific demonstration.

If your patient believes in taking cold, mentally convince him that matter cannot take cold, and that thought governs this liability. If grief causes suffering, convince the sufferer that sorrow is not the master of joy, and that he should rejoice always in ever-present Love.

Invalids flee to tropical climates, in order to save their lives; but they come back no better than when they went away. Then is the time to cure them through Christian Science, and prove that they can be healthy in all climates, when their fear of climate is driven out.

Through different states of mind, the body becomes suddenly weak or abnormally strong, showing mortal mind to be the producer of strength or weakness. A sudden joy or grief has caused what is termed instantaneous death. Because a belief originates unseen, the mental state should be continually watched, that it produce not blindly its bad effects. The author

never knew a patient who did not recover when the belief of
the disease was gone. Remove the leading error and governing
fear of this lower mind, and you remove the cause of any disease, as well as the morbid and excited action of any organ.
You also remove, in this way, what are termed organic diseases as readily as functional difficulties.

17. CHRISTIAN SCIENCE DEFENDED

Questions and Answers, 1896

BY MARY BAKER EDDY

The CHRISTIAN SCIENCE JOURNAL *was a vehicle for occasional essays or sermons by Mrs. Eddy, for lists of authorized Christian Science practitioners, and for a Questions and Answers column in which Mrs. Eddy could distinguish the precepts and practices of Christian Science from the many competing mind-faiths. In 1896 she published a selection of these "miscellaneous writings" for the purpose, she noted in the preface, of making them "accessible as reference, and reliable as old landmarks."*

Must I have faith in Christian Science in order to be healed by it?

This is a question that is being asked every day. It has not proved impossible to heal those who, when they began treatment, had no faith whatever in the Science,—other than to place themselves under my care, and follow the directions given. Patients naturally gain confidence in Christian Science as they recognize the help they derive therefrom.

What are the advantages of your system of healing, over the ordinary methods of healing disease?

From Mary Baker Eddy, *Miscellaneous Writings, 1883–1896* (Boston: Christian Science Publishing House, 1896), pp. 33–43, 52–55.

Healing by Christian Science has the following advantages:—

First: It does away with all material medicines, and recognizes the fact that, as mortal mind is the cause of all "the ills that flesh is heir to," the antidote for sickness, as well as for sin, may and must be found in mortal mind's opposite,—the divine Mind.

Second: It is more effectual than drugs; curing where these fail, and leaving none of the harmful "after effects" of these in the system; thus proving that metaphysics is above physics.

Third: One who has been healed by Christian Science is not only healed of the disease, but is improved morally. The body is governed by mind; and mortal mind must be improved, before the body is renewed and harmonious—since the physique is simply thought made manifest.

Is spiritualism or mesmerism included in Christian Science?

They are wholly apart from it. Christian Science is based on divine Principle; whereas spiritualism, so far as I understand it, is a mere speculative opinion and human belief. If the departed were to communicate with us, we should see them as they were before death, and have them with us; after death, they can no more come to those they have left, than we, in our present state of existence, can go to the departed or the adult can return to his boyhood. We may pass on to their state of existence, but they cannot return to ours. Man is *im*-mortal, and there is not a moment when he ceases to exist. All that are called "communications from spirits," lie within the realm of mortal thought on this present plane of existence, and are the antipodes of Christian Science; the immortal and mortal are as direct opposites as light and darkness.

Who is the Founder of mental healing?

The author of "Science and Health with Key to the Scriptures," who discovered the Science of healing embodied in her works. Years of practical proof, through homœopathy, revealed to her the fact that Mind, instead of matter, is the Principle of pathology; and subsequently her recovery, through the supremacy of Mind over matter, from a severe casualty pronounced by the physicians incurable, sealed that proof with the signet of Christian Science. In 1883, a million of people acknowledge and attest the blessings of this mental system of treating disease. Perhaps the following words of her husband, the late Dr. Asa G. Eddy, afford the most concise, yet complete summary of the matter:—

"Mrs. Eddy's works are the outgrowths of her life. I never knew so unselfish an individual."

Will the book Science and Health, that you offer for sale at three dollars, teach its readers to heal the sick,—or is one obliged to become a student under your personal instruction? And if one is obliged to study under you, of what benefit is your book?

Why do we read the Bible, and then go to church to hear it expounded? Only because both are important. Why do we read moral science, and then study it at college?

You are benefited by reading Science and Health, but it is greatly to your advantage to be taught its Science by the author of that work, who explains it in detail.

What is immortal Mind?

In reply, we refer you to "Science and Health with Key to the Scriptures," Vol. I. page 14: "That which is erring, sinful, sick, and dying, termed material or mortal man, is neither God's man nor Mind; but to be understood, we shall classify evil and error as mortal mind, in contradistinction to good and Truth, or the Mind which is immortal."

Do animals and beasts have a mind?

Beasts, as well as men, express Mind as their origin; but they manifest less of Mind. The first and only cause is the eternal Mind, which is God, and there is but one God. The ferocious mind seen in the beast is mortal mind, which is harmful and proceeds not from God; for His beast is the lion that lieth down with the lamb. Appetites, passions, anger, revenge, subtlety, are the animal qualities of sinning mortals; and the beasts that have these propensities express the lower qualities of the so-called animal man; in other words, the nature and quality of mortal mind,—not immortal Mind.

What is the distinction between mortal mind and immortal Mind?

Mortal mind includes all evil, disease, and death; also, all beliefs relative to the so-called material laws, and all material objects, and the law of sin and death.

The Scripture says, "The carnal mind [in other words, mortal mind] is enmity against God; for it is not subject to the law of God, neither indeed can be." Mortal mind is an illusion; as much in our waking moments as in the dreams of sleep. The belief that intelligence, Truth, and Love, are in matter and separate from God, is an error; for there is no intelligent evil, and no power besides God, good. God would not be omnipotent if there were in reality another mind creating or governing man or the universe.

Immortal Mind is God; and this Mind is made manifest in all thoughts and desires that draw mankind toward purity, health, holiness, and the spiritual facts of being.

Jesus recognized this relation so clearly that he said, "I and my Father are one." In proportion as we oppose the belief in material sense, in sickness, sin, and death, and recognize ourselves under the control of God, spiritual and immortal Mind, shall we go on to leave the animal for the spiritual, and learn the meaning of those words of Jesus, "Go ye into all the world . . . heal the sick."

Can your Science cure intemperance?

Christian Science lays the axe at the root of the tree. Its antidote for all ills is God, the perfect Mind, which corrects mortal thought, whence cometh all evil. God can and does destroy the thought that leads to moral or physical death. Intemperance, impurity, sin of every sort, is destroyed by Truth. The appetite for alcohol yields to Science as directly and surely as do sickness and sin.

Does Mrs. Eddy take patients?

She now does not. Her time is wholly devoted to instruction, leaving to her students the work of healing; which, at this hour, is in reality the least difficult of the labor that Christian Science demands.

Why do you charge for teaching Christian Science, when all the good we can do must be done freely?

When teaching imparts the ability to gain and maintain health, to heal and elevate man in every line of life,—as this teaching certainly does,—is it unreasonable to expect in return something to support one's self and a Cause? If so, our whole system of education, secular and religious, is at fault, and the instructors and philanthropists in our land should expect no compensation. "If we have sown unto you spiritual things, is it a great thing if we shall reap your carnal things?"

How happened you to establish a college to instruct in metaphysics, when other institutions find little interest in such a dry and abstract subject?

Metaphysics, as taught by me at the Massachusetts Metaphysical College, is far from dry and abstract. It is a Science that has the animus of Truth. Its practical application to benefit the race, heal the sick, enlighten and reform the sinner, makes divine metaphysics needful, indispensable. Teaching metaphysics at other colleges means, mainly, elaborating a man-made theory, or some speculative view too vapory and hypothetical for questions of practical import.

Is it necessary to study your Science in order to be healed by it and keep well?

It is not necessary to make each patient a student in order to cure his present disease, if this is what you mean. Were it so, the Science would be of less practical value. Many who apply for help are not prepared to take a course of instruction in Christian Science.

To avoid being *subject* to disease, would require the understanding of how you are healed. In 1885, this knowledge can be obtained in its genuineness at the Massachusetts Metaphysical College. There are abroad at this early date some grossly incorrect and false teachers of what they term Christian Science; of such beware. They have risen up in a day to make this claim; whereas the Founder of genuine Christian Science has been all her years in giving it birth.

Can you take care of yourself?

God giveth to every one this *puissance;* and I have faith in His promise, "Lo, I am with you alway"—*all the way.* Unlike the M. D.'s, Christian Scientists are not afraid to take their own medicine, for this medicine is divine Mind; and from this saving, exhaustless source they intend to fill the human mind with enough of the leaven of Truth to leaven the whole lump. There may be exceptional cases, where one Christian Scientist who has more to meet than others needs support at times; then, it is right to bear "one another's burdens, and so fulfil the law of Christ."

In what way is a Christian Scientist an instrument by which God reaches others to heal them, and what most obstructs the way?

A Christian, or a Christian Scientist, assumes no more when claiming to work with God in healing the sick, than in converting the sinner. Divine help is as necessary in the one case as in the other. The scientific Principle of healing demands such cooperation; but this unison and its power would be arrested if one were to mix material methods with the spiritual,—were to mingle hygienic rules, drugs, and prayers in the same process,—and thus serve "other gods." Truth is as effectual in destroying sickness as in the destruction of sin.

It is often asked, "If Christian Science is the same method of healing that Jesus and the apostles used, why do not its students perform as instantaneous cures as did those in the first century of the Christian era?"

In some instances the students of Christian Science equal the ancient prophets as healers. All true healing is governed by, and demonstrated on, the same Principle as theirs; namely, the action of the divine Spirit, through the power of Truth to destroy error, discord of whatever sort. The reason that the same results follow not in every case, is that the student does not in every case possess sufficiently the Christ-spirit and its power to cast out the disease. The Founder of Christian Science teaches her students that they must possess the spirit of Truth and Love, must gain the power over sin in themselves, or they cannot be instantaneous healers.

In this Christian warfare the student or practitioner has to master those elements of evil too common to other minds. If it is hate that is holding the purpose to kill his patient by mental means, it requires more divine understanding to conquer this sin than to nullify either the disease itself or the ignorance by which one unintentionally harms himself or another. An element of brute-force that only the cruel and evil can send forth, is given vent in the diabolical practice of one who, having learned the power of liberated thought to do good, perverts it, and uses it to accomplish an evil purpose. This mental malpractice would disgrace Mind-healing, were it not that God overrules it, and causes "the wrath of man" to praise Him. It deprives those who practise it of the power to heal, and destroys their own possibility of progressing.

The honest student of Christian Science is purged through

Christ, Truth, and thus is ready for victory in the ennobling strife. The good fight must be fought by those who keep the faith and finish their course. Mental purgation must go on: it promotes spiritual growth, scales the mountain of human endeavor, and gains the summit in Science that otherwise could not be reached,—where the struggle with sin is forever done.

Can all classes of disease be healed by your method?

We answer, Yes. Mind is the architect that builds its own ideas, and produces all harmony that appears. There is no other healer in the case. If mortal mind, through the action of fear, manifests inflammation and a belief of chronic or acute disease, by removing the cause in that so-called mind the effect or disease will disappear and health will be restored; for health, *alias* harmony, is the normal manifestation of man in Science. The divine Principle which governs the universe, including man, if demonstrated, is sufficient for all emergencies. But the practitioner may not always prove equal to bringing out the result of the Principle that he knows to be true.

After the change called death takes place, do we meet those gone before?—or does life continue in thought only as in a dream?

Man is not annihilated, nor does he lose his identity, by passing through the belief called death. After the momentary belief of dying passes from mortal mind, this mind is still in a conscious state of existence; and the individual has but passed through a moment of extreme mortal fear, to awaken with thoughts, and being, as material as before. Science and Health clearly states that spiritualization of thought is not attained by the death of the body, but by a conscious union with God. When we shall have passed the ordeal called death, or destroyed this last enemy, and shall have come upon the same plane of conscious existence with those gone before, then we shall be able to communicate with and to recognize them.

If, before the change whereby we meet the dear departed, our life-work proves to have been well done, we shall not have to repeat it; but our joys and means of advancing will be proportionately increased.

The difference between a belief of material existence and the spiritual fact of Life is, that the former is a dream and unreal, while the latter is real and eternal. Only as we understand God, and learn that good, not evil, lives and is immortal, that immortality exists only in spiritual perfection, shall we drop our false sense of Life in sin or sense material, and recognize a better state of existence.

Can I be treated without being present during treatment?

Mind is not confined to limits; and nothing but our own false admissions prevent us from demonstrating this great fact. Christian Science, recognizing the capabilities of Mind to act of itself, and independent of matter, enables one to heal cases without even having seen the individual,—or simply after having been made acquainted with the mental condition of the patient.

Do all who at present claim to be teaching Christian Science, teach it correctly?

By no means: Christian Science is not sufficiently understood for that. The student of this Science who understands it best, is the one least likely to pour into other minds a trifling sense of it as being adequate to make safe and successful practitioners. The simple sense one gains of this Science through careful, unbiased, contemplative reading of my books, is far more advantageous to the sick and to the learner than is or can be the spurious teaching of those who are spiritually unqualified. The sad fact at this early writing is, that the letter is gained sooner than the spirit of Christian Science: time is required thoroughly to qualify students for the great ordeal of this century.

If one student tries to undermine another, such sinister rivalry does a vast amount of injury to the Cause. To fill one's pocket at the expense of his conscience, or to build on the downfall of others, incapacitates one to practise or teach Christian Science. The occasional temporary success of such an one is owing, in part, to the impossibility for those unacquainted with the mighty Truth of *Christian* Science to recognize, as such, the barefaced errors that are taught—and the damaging effects these leave on the practice of the learner, on the Cause, and on the health of the community. . . .

What do you think of marriage?

That it is often convenient, sometimes pleasant, and occasionally a love affair. Marriage is susceptible of many definitions. It sometimes presents the most wretched condition of human existence. To be normal, it must be a union of the affections that tends to lift mortals higher.

If this life is a dream not dispelled, but only changed, by death,—if one gets tired of it, why not commit suicide?

Man's existence is a problem to be wrought in divine Science. What progress would a student of science make, if, when tired of mathematics or failing to demonstrate one rule readily, he should attempt to work out a rule farther on and more difficult—and this, because the first rule was not easily demonstrated? In that case he would be obliged to turn back and work out the previous example, before solving the advanced problem. Mortals have the sum of being to work out, and up, to its spiritual standpoint. They must work out of this dream or false claim of sensation and life in matter, and up to the spiritual realities of existence, before this false claim can be wholly dispelled. Committing suicide to dodge the question is not working it out. The error of supposed life and intelligence in matter, is dissolved only as we master error with Truth. Not through sin or suicide, but by *overcoming* temptation and sin, shall we escape the weariness and wickedness of mortal existence, and gain heaven, the harmony of being.

Do you sometimes find it advisable to use medicine to assist in producing a cure, when it is difficult to start the patient's recovery?

You only weaken your power to heal through Mind, by any compromise with matter; which is virtually acknowledging that under difficulties the former is not equal to the latter. He that resorts to physics, seeks what is below instead of above the standard of metaphysics; showing his ignorance of the meaning of the term and of Christian Science.

If Christian Science is the same as Jesus taught, why is it not more simple, so that all can readily understand it?

The teachings of Jesus were simple; and yet he found it difficult to make the rulers understand, because of their great lack of spirituality. Christian Science is simple, and readily understood by the children; only the thought educated away from it finds it abstract or difficult to perceive. Its seeming abstraction is the mystery of godliness; and godliness is simple to the godly; but to the unspiritual, the ungodly, it is dark and difficult. The carnal mind cannot discern spiritual things.

Has Mrs. Eddy lost her power to heal?

Has the sun forgotten to shine, and the planets to revolve around it? Who is it that discovered, demonstrated, and teaches Christian Science? That one, whoever it be, does understand something of what cannot be lost. Thousands in the field of metaphysical healing, whose lives are worthy testimonials, are her students, and they bear witness to this fact. Instead of losing her power to heal, she is demonstrating the power of Christian Science over all obstacles that envy and malice would fling in her path. The reading of her book, "Science and Health with Key to the Scriptures," is curing hundreds at this very time; and the sick, unasked, are testifying thereto.

Must I study your Science in order to keep well all my life?
I was healed of a chronic trouble after one month's treatment
by one of your students.

When once you are healed by Science, there is no reason why you should be liable to a return of the disease that you were healed of. But not to be subject again to any disease whatsoever, would require an understanding of the Science by which you were healed.

Because none of your students have been able to perform
as great miracles in healing as Jesus and his disciples did, does
it not suggest the possibility that they do not heal on the same
basis?

You would not ask the pupil in simple equations to solve a problem involving logarithms; and then, because he failed to get the right answer, condemn the pupil and the science of numbers. The simplest problem in Christian Science is healing the sick, and the least understanding and demonstration thereof prove all its possibilities. The ability to demonstrate to the extent that Jesus did, will come when the student possesses as much of the divine Spirit as he shared, and utilizes its power to overcome sin.

Opposite to good, is the universal claim of evil that seeks the proportions of good. There may be those who, having learned the power of the unspoken thought, use it to harm rather than to heal, and who are using that power against Christian Scientists. This giant sin is the sin against the Holy Ghost spoken of in Matt. xii. 31, 32.

PART FIVE

ATTEMPTS AT REINTEGRATION

18. A NEW TYPE OF PASTORATE

Three Episodes in the Reconstruction of a
Downtown Church, 1922

BY W. S. RAINSFORD

---

*Rainsford (1850–1933) was born in Dublin, and spent his early
years in a largely Roman Catholic neighborhood where his father was an Episcopalian rector. After his own ordination, he
labored as an evangelist in the depressed areas of East London.
When he came to America, therefore, in 1876, he was no novice
to the problems of religion in the cities. Furthermore, he
brought with him the conviction, fostered by his own labors
and by firsthand experience with Moody's revivals, that more
radical measures were needed. Nothing in a brief first visit to
New York or in an extended pastorate in Toronto altered this
belief. When he was invited in 1883 to become rector of St.
George's Episcopal Church in New York City, he accepted only
after receiving assurances that he would be free to innovate
boldly. In his autobiography he recollected three crucial epi-
sodes in the early years of his ministry at St. George's.*

[A FREE CHURCH]

I had two great advantages in coming to St. George's. The
first was the emptiness of the church. There had been an interim of two years, after Doctor Williams resigned, during

From W. S. Rainsford, *The Story of a Varied Life* (Garden City, N.Y.:
Doubleday, 1922), pp. 208–218, 234–243, 277–284.

which the church was without a rector. Several had been
"called," but the rectorate had been declined. I found about
twenty families that were still in partly regular attendance.
Among these I knew full well I would discover some who
were far from approving of a free church. They resented a
policy that called on them to surrender their property rights
in their pews. Some might be prepared within reasonable limits to be hospitable to strangers. Others felt as the Scotsman
did, who complained to his rector that a gentleman not of his
acquaintance had been put into his pew.—"I would not disturb divine service by putting him out, Sir, but I took the
liberty of sitting on his hat." (In those days they wore tall
"chimney pots.") And so I was glad that their number was no
larger. Some of the twenty soon left, and of this I was glad,
for departures were less depressing than funerals, and it had
to be one or the other.

My second advantage was that we began very unostenta-
tiously and put no advertisements in the papers. I insisted on
this, for I wanted to feel my way. I wanted to be sure what I
would do and not do; where I had best leave things alone and
where change them. Crowds of curious "casuals" are an un-
profitable and disturbing element. I wanted first to know pretty
thoroughly what material I had ready to hand in the Sunday
School and the church. Then I had to study "the plant" of St.
George's, making up my mind where I could change, and
where it was necessary to discard or create.

The building itself, while impressive outside, specially so
long as the open stone-work towers were standing, was sadly
ugly and depressing inside; and, in addition to this, was about
as hard a building to hear in as an architect had ever devised.
Its great flat stone wall spaces made the voice of the preacher
rattle from side to side like peas in a shaken bladder. The
effect when a great congregation sang was fine. The resonance
helped the music, but when the preacher spoke from the low
pulpit, near the Holy Table, the echo was baffling. . . .

St. George's stands facing the east, looking over Stuyvesant Square, which is cut in two by Second Avenue. Stuyvesant Square had not so completely fallen from grace as had its neighbor, Tompkins Square, where in those days you took considerable chances if you walked across it at night. But it was a dirty, neglected mockery of what a city park might be. Its fountains were waterless, the basins filled with rubbish from the street. I myself saw dead cats and empty tomato cans piled in them. There was no attempt to plant flowers or renew the long-neglected grass, or to protect the park at all.

One of the first things I did was to visit the families whose names I found remaining on the church roll. Looking over my list, I noticed the name "Croker." I made inquiries, and found that the famous Tammany boss's mother was one of my members, and was then an old woman living on Staten Island. Duty and policy suggested an immediate call. I found a charming old lady, who evidently appreciated my searching her out, and asked me to return and give her the Holy Communion. This I did. Not long after I had a very courteous letter from Mr. Croker, saying that he appreciated my taking the long trip to Staten Island to see his mother, who had not had a clerical call for years, and that he hoped I would remember that at any time he would be glad to pay me any courtesy in his power.

After that, the change in our park, if not immediate, was assured; and in time we had quite beautiful flowers grouped round the fountains, and, what was even more important than a restored beauty, we had the invaluable service and coöperation of an intelligent and sympathetic park policeman, who greatly helped us for many years. Then I had Japanese creeper planted round the brownstone walls of the church, and this added, specially in autumn time, to the quiet beauty of the square.

St. George's, in the '60's, had been successful. Since 1865 it had slowly fallen down. I found it empty, expensive to run, and very costly to heat; ill-adapted in many ways to the work it ought to do.

Evidently the old methods were a total failure. New ones must be invented. When I found my vestry disturbed a little at the radical changes I proposed, I told them a story I had heard by the banks of a Canadian salmon river. The salmon had ceased to visit the stream, and the scattered settlers on its banks, who had depended on their salmon nets, were in a bad way for a living. All but one man. He, cannier than the rest, sold his salmon nets and bought smelt nets. He changed the size of his mesh, and soon was better off than he had been before.

The old methods of all the Protestant churches were adapted to the family. The new must be adapted to the individual. The days of the Individual were upon us, let us deplore it as we might. The essential principle I stood for took shape in what, very inaccurately, came to be called the "institutional Church."

My first move was to make the outside of the church and its setting in its little park more tidy and attractive. The next, to change as much as possible what was amiss in the inside. Here my vestry backed me up with extraordinary unanimity. We not only declared the church free, but we made men and women and children feel that it was free. . . .

On the question of free church I stand to-day where I stood then. There should be one place besides the grave—to which all should have a common right: that place is the Church of God. To my mind, as between free church and pew church, there is no choice at all. The one is right; the other is wrong. You cannot preach one thing from the pulpit and practise another in the pew. I do not care how liberal pew-holders may be, or how hospitable they may show themselves. To own or rent a foot of the floor of the house we claim to be the House of God is to contradict and deny in practice the Gospel of Jesus. In theory at least, in this as in many other matters, the custom of the Roman Catholic Church is better, wiser, more apostolic than is the custom of those churches which have broken away from her.

In the early '8o's the free church ideal was not popular, and many were the arguments I had with clerical brethren on account of it. In the "club," an unusually able body of clergy, to which I had the honour of being elected, I stood alone on that question. I had fallen foul of Phillips Brooks when in Boston, on the question of free church. With him I did not venture an argument. It was not much use arguing with Phillips Brooks. I just held my ground. Years after, when he was Bishop, he visited me, and then said: "We all laughed at your pleas for free church, but you were right, and I was wrong. What influence I have as Bishop of Massachusetts I shall steadily use to make every church in the diocese free." . . .

The next change I strove for was in the church music, and here I first encountered opposition. My plans were revolutionary—nothing less than a new organ, new organist, new choir, and a complete change of the whole plant from the east end of the church to the west end, where stood the Communion Table. I wanted congregational singing. Quartet and double quartet to me were anathema, for with them congregational singing was impossible. I could not pay for good soloists, even if I wanted them. Moreover, I had my own settled idea of what St. George's choir should be. Its front line should be of boys, drawn from its own Sunday School. Back of them must be women, for the quality of an American boy's voice is too thin, too sharp, to serve adequately in soprano parts, and needs the richer support of the female voice tone. I am speaking of course of the material I had, or could hope to have, to my hand. With time and large means the right sort of boys' voices can be found and trained; but I, having neither time nor money, could not hope to have good congregational singing led by male voices alone.

There was another reason, too. I did dearly want to make

the services of the church appeal to *all,* not part of my people. I wanted a chancel choir, but I wanted it of women as well as of boys and men, and this being my aim, *that choir must be a surpliced choir.* There lay the difficulty. My vestry was divided. Surpliced choir in old St. George's! That was too much, even for them. Hence my first opposition. That was forty years ago (though I can scarcely believe it), and it may be hard for a younger generation to enter into their feeling; but the change I advocated could not fail to seem to some of my vestry a deliberate flouting of what the old church had so stoutly stood for in the days of its strength and glory.

Over this controversy one or two of my vestry left me. . . .

The congregations at first were small—some two hundred and fifty. I had the ushers show all who came to seats well up in front. Propinquity counts for something in worship, and I locked the galleries up for several months. I preached poorly, and I knew it. It has always been so with me. I cannot remember ever having made a specially successful start in anything I attempted to do, except in my mission at Toronto.

I noted the faces before me morning by morning. (This was not hard to do, for there was no crowd.) One man particularly I saw, who came regularly. In the plates carried in the central aisle there lay a note of considerable amount whenever he was there. . . . (Remember, these were the days of small things.) Then one Sunday I asked for $500 to start a lending library for the children of the Sunday School. On the plate that day was a cheque for $250, signed "A. C. C——." How well I remember it! It was the very first that had come to me on the church plate. I found Mr. C——'s address and called to thank him for his help, and to explain why I specially wanted that library for my East Side children. There was a little library of sorts—oh, such sorts!—too goody-goody to interest or help any healthy child.

Mr. C—— asked me to dinner, and I saw that he was deeply interested in St. George's. He made me tell him my plans. He evidently was prepared to approve them, and was wholeheart-

edly free church. "Now," said he: "What about your music?
It should be first class." I agreed, naturally, and we fell to
talking about the music. Alas, I quickly realized that here I
had one idea and Mr. C——another. I wanted a choir of my
people, and by my people; and as far as possible a voluntary
body. He had in view the best organist and the best double
quartet that could be had for money. I wanted a choir formed
out of St. George's itself, part of the church's life, an organization so attractive that my prospective East Side boys and girls
(I had not got them yet) should plan and study to win entrance
to it. A choir where brownstone-housed ladies and Wanamaker's "shop ladies" should sit side by side, Mr. C——listened,
interested, but I could see that he was not enthusiastic over
my choir dream.

Mr. C——was one of my audience the very first Sunday I
preached, and he attended regularly for some months. During
that time I saw him several times. We were growing; the
morning and evening congregations increasing. But though we
were out of debt, we were not yet paying the running expenses
of the church—and there were so many things that might be
attempted, if only we had the money! And here was a man who
had the money, and seemed to have a hearty will to help us.

One evening, after dinner at his apartment, Mr. C——
asked me into his study and said: "I am heartily with you.
Tell me frankly your plans for the future. I don't ask out of
curiosity; I want to stand back of you." So I told him what,
till then, I had spoken of to no one. Told of a building I
wanted, large, beautiful, commodious, where rich and poor
should meet; a building that should be a visible evidence of
the church's recognition of the needs and wrongs of the city
toilers and their children. *It should be a teaching house and a
dancing house; a reading house and a playing house; and because it was these, it should be a preaching house, bidding the
neighborhood look for, strive for, and believe in a better manhood and a better day.*

Mr. C—— expressed whole-hearted approval, and said: "Do

you not see that to succeed in these radical changes you must
depute parts of your work to others? You must find those who
agree with you and who trust you; men whom you can trust,
men willing to coöperate fully. Now you can count on me as
such a helper. I am with you heart and soul. I have now to
make to you a proposition. Hand over all the musical matters
of the church to my keeping and control; free your mind of
them altogether. I will give you the best organ, best organist,
and best choir in New York, and will meet all the expenses."

I did not answer at once, though of course I saw that this
tempting scheme would not work. I had not abolished my
musical committee, composed of old members of the vestry, to
hand over the whole conduct of the church's music to one man,
however efficient and generous he might be. Mr. C—— saw
my hesitation. "Wait a moment," he said, "before you reply to
my offer." He rose and went to his desk. "What do you think
your parish building would cost?" "About $200,000." He wrote
a cheque for that amount, and pushing it toward me, said, "I
want to help you; let me."

Here was my dream come true. The old church securing a
clear-headed and most generous helper, and the success of
my pet scheme assured. But it might not be. If I was to surrender control of one department of my difficult work to one
man it could only be a matter of time till other departments
would be surrendered also. I could not hold my vestry together if I permitted any autocracy other than my own. I
never tried harder in my life to make my side of a question
plain than I did for the next few minutes to this good, head-
strong, would-be aid of mine, Mr. A. C. C——. But, though
I did my best, with sinking heart I knew I must fail. He was
a very rich man; he had had his own way; he was wholly bent
on having it now, and sooner or later he and I were bound to
disagree. Then he would leave me. Besides these general considerations, I could not, I would not give up my large chancel
choir idea, its members recruited from the congregation, lead-

ing that congregation in its worship because they wanted to lead it, not because they were paid. *I say I would not give up that ideal for any quartet music, however good.*

Often and often in my Cambridge days I used to sit in the evening gloom of that wonderful Henry VII chapel at King's College, listening as the best choir in the University sang some anthem by the masters of their great art. And music and setting moved me. But when I hear a congregation of all sorts and conditions of men joining with heart and soul in such a hymn as Isaac Watts' "Jesus shall reign where'er the sun," or Lyte's "Abide with me, fast falls the eventide," my whole being, the best that is within me, thrills to what I must believe is the voice of God. Then new hopes are quickened, and old resolutions are reborn. *That is worship.* A man can give to others only what is given to him.

Congregational worship I was going to work for in St. George's. That meant a spontaneous congregational response, inspiring in its unison, whether in prayer or in praise. To me it was too plain that here, at the very outset, Mr. C——'s ideals and mine were wide apart. Mr. C—— had said, "I want to help you; let me." I replied, "God knows no clergyman in New York needs such help as you can give more than I do, but I cannot have you help me in this way. I cannot surrender the direction of St. George's music to you."

"Then I will never put my foot inside your church again."

I said, "You are doing wrong, sir. You should not have offered me that money."

I never saw Mr. A. C. C—— again. He died a few years later.

I was going to Jekyll Island Club, in 1889, for a much-needed rest. I had been very ill. On the little steamer that took passengers from Brunswick to the Island I met Mr. F. B——. He was, I knew, head of the great concern that Mr. A. C. C—— had been president of. When I knew Mr. C——, Mr. B—— was his secretary. At the club I got to know Mr. B—— pretty

well, and he told me that Mr. C—— often spoke kindly of
St. George's progress and of me. He had told him all about our
falling out, and declared frankly that I had been right and
he wrong.

I will depart a little from the order of events in order to
tell the sequel of this story. From earliest days I fell into the
habit of breakfasting once a week with Mr. Morgan.[1] Shortly
after my disaster with Mr. C——, I was at Mr. Morgan's table,
and when breakfast was over, I told him the whole story. He
listened carefully to all I had to say, but, as was his custom,
he said nothing. The parish building scheme he had not heard
of before. Twelve months passed, and of it I said no more to
him, nor had he made any reference to the matter. One morning in early spring, a shabby hired coupé stopped at the door
of the rectory. In it was J. P. Morgan. In those days he never
drove in any other vehicle. He was on his way to the steamer;
he was sailing for Europe that day. "I have come to bid you
good-bye," he said. Then, pulling a letter out of his pocket.
"I think this is what you want, Rector. If I have left anything
out, you can tell me when I come back." And he was off.

On reading the paper, I found that every single detail of
what I had said that morning a year previous had been remembered, and was here specified in this sketch of a deed of gift.
On Mr. Morgan's return he and I went over the matter again
together, and the result was the following:

To the Rector, Church Wardens, and Vestrymen of St. George's
Church, New York City:

GENTLEMEN:

On behalf of the family of the late Senior Warden, Charles Tracy,
I wish to communicate to you officially, their wish to erect to his

---

[1] [J. P. Morgan was Senior Warden of the vestry at St. George's. For
another aspect of Rainsford's relations with Morgan, see the third episode
in this Document. Ed.]

memory a church house to be styled, "The Memorial House of St. George's Church."

My proposition is this: that your corporation shall transfer to me, in fee simple, the plot of ground on East 16th Street.

Upon receiving from you the deed of the property mentioned, I will engage to have erected upon the entire property a church house, which house shall include an adequate chapel and Sunday-school rooms, rooms for the resident clergy, an office for the Corporation, and rooms for the mission work of the parish, these latter to include suitable accommodations for the Boys' and Girls' Clubs, Girls' Friendly Society, Helping Hand, etc., etc. Also bathrooms and a gymnasium.

When completed, the property to be deeded, free of debt, to the Rector, Church Wardens, and Vestrymen of St. George's Church, New York, on condition that they keep the same in good repair, and use the same exclusively for the parish work in perpetuity.

If this proposition meets your approval, I suggest that a committee, consisting of the Rector, the Wardens, Mr. Spencer, Mr. Cutting and Mr. Tracy, be appointed, with full power to assist in carrying out the same.

Yours truly,
J. Pierpont Morgan.

WORK WITH THE POOR

. . . I had a notice board fixed to the stone pillars of the church porch. It read: "Come in, rest and pray." Many such can be seen in New York now. Ours was the first and it did steady work, that notice board! It spoke to the passer-by of what the church stood for. . . .

The church did not stand on a thoroughfare. For what we were attempting it was not well-placed, for it faced a quiet square and no great thoroughfare ran near us. But into the square came some of the drifting element of the East Side, some "bums," some tired and disheartened folk, and they read our sign, and sometimes came in. They soiled a few cushions, they stole a few church books, but they were never shown the door. Of course they did not come to the church services. Such beaten folk had got too far from any church for that. But some of them began to show interest in us—and on a cold day, to a badly clothed man, it was a pleasant place. On Sundays I stood at the church door till a few minutes before the services opened. I also got back to the door as soon after the blessing was given as I could.

In August, 1884, I rented, at $5 a day, a large room back of a saloon at 253 Avenue A, between 15th and 16th streets. I persuaded some of the small local storekeepers to display placards I had printed asking the neighbours to come to a religious service on Sunday afternoon. The only entrance was through the saloon, where, in spite of the Sunday closing law, an active trade in drinks of many sorts, all of them strong, was always going on, and a rough crowd was smoking and playing billiards and cards. A questionable environment it seemed for a "baby mission," but the thing in its favour that decided me was that there was no stand-offishness about it. Here was a meeting place of the people I was after, a meeting place of their own choosing and making, not one that the church made and thrust on them. I had walked many, many miles in those dirty swarming streets (where women and children hung in midsummer out of windows and doors in a way that made you think they were pushed out from inside), looking for a place, before I found what I wanted. No. 253 Avenue A suited me well.

Since that beginning in the little Baptist chapel in Bethnal Green almost twenty years before, I had made a good many experiments in the missionary field, but as I made my way, that hot August afternoon, to the saloon in Avenue A, I felt I was on ground absolutely unknown to me. Of what was going to happen I had no idea whatever. . . .

I found the room almost full of children and rough boys, a few poor women, and no men except those whose heads were occasionally thrust through the door dividing us from the saloon, and who were evidently interested only in what a figure these new adventurers into the tenement region would cut. A babel of voices greeted our entering. The boys were on their feet, rushing after each other all round the place—a regular "follow-my-leader" scramble. The girls were there too for a lark, and took their fair share in raising a row. It was a youthful but an exceedingly tough looking crowd.

I called them to order and tried to speak. This brought things to an immediate crisis. Those boys formed a flying wedge. It was well and promptly done, and I was knocked flat on the floor. It was all play, rough play—no viciousness in it, but play with a definite purpose. They knew the purpose; so did I. It was to decide who was the master in that room, and certainly they won the first round. When I got up from the floor we had a lively time of it, singling out the leaders and getting them outside.

As you can imagine, after this beginning the rest of the proceedings were somewhat disturbed. When we had locked up the room and turned homeward the neighborhood gave us another taste of its quality. I had hardly reached the street when I found that behind me quite a procession of youngsters had formed. They fell into line and where I went they went, joining in a sort of chant as they marched which ran: "Won't he be a comfort to his mummy when he's grown up?"

That first hot afternoon taught me afresh a lesson I was prepared to learn. To the young I must look for my allies. 'Tis they who are ready to follow a leader. St. George's future on the East Side depended on its success or its failure in winning the confidence of its neglected little ones.

Here I had my first real meeting with the living thing Jacob Riis afterward immortalized as "Tony," and I love to remember that Riis first saw Tony pasting the ugly old stained-glass windows of St. George's (the lower ones) with mud. If we had things to teach Tony, Tony certainly had much to teach us. His home a slum tenement, no room or little room for him at school, no understanding of him when he did get a place in school, and when he broke from school's unsympathetic and most unnatural restraint, then a bad law, shamefully administered, which tied his wild, vivid boyhood up with older and vicious criminals, in a prison for truants. No place to play but the street, and no peace in the street for the ubiquitous "cop," his natural enemy. Everything that stood for order and for property, the policeman, the landlord, the church, all were against him. Even in the parks he was faced with "Keep off the grass." So there was nothing left him but the gutter.

Yes, as I got up that afternoon with very considerable difficulty and delay from the accumulated dirt of that squalid room back of the saloon on Avenue A, my heart went out to those romping ragamuffins who had thrown me on the floor. What a dirty and neglected crew they were, and yet what infinite possibilities! What abundant life was packed away under their ragged jackets! I had started out intending to reach their fathers and mothers, and *here the children had pushed in between.* Though they may not have been aware of it, they had a purpose. They wanted to see and know if we had anything to give them worth while; if to their so empty and neglected lives we could bring anything better than they had been accustomed to.

I shook as much of the filth off my clothes as I could and went home with much to think about. . . .

The effect that little school had (we opened it first on Sunday afternoons, then in the mornings as well) on the whole work of the church was profound. It illustrated and explained our purpose as nothing else could. The place came to serve as a common meeting ground, a modest bridge across which East Siders who had given up all church life did seek and find a place in the great congregation composed of all sorts and conditions of men. But to win and hold that meeting ground took intelligent, self-denying, and regular work; and for giving it, a debt is due to that first little band of volunteers who so promptly came to my call.

I will tell another story of those early days. One Sunday afternoon I noticed a big, strong, fine-looking young man come into the room after I had opened the school. He stood at the door looking over the classes. There were a dozen, with about one hundred boys and girls. Presently he picked out a class of elderly boys taught by a good-looking lady and seated himself at the upper end of the form near her. I watched him and presently saw my teacher's face flush as she moved her chair farther away from the man. I suspected what had happened. The man was drunk and was talking smut to the teacher. I walked over and told him to get out. He looked defiance and refused to move. I said, "We are here to help you people, and you know it. This lady only comes here because she wants to help you. She is not paid anything for coming; you know that, too. Now you are enough of a man to respect a lady. Why do you sit here and try by your talk to make it impossible for her to teach her boys or to come here at all? You are drunk or you would not do so unmanly a thing. I don't want to call a policeman. You get up and go out of the room quietly."

I was watching my man carefully, meanwhile. He was just drunk enough to be ugly and there was fight in his eyes. So I edged my foot back a bit till I felt firmly the iron leg of the form that was screwed to the floor and got a good purchase against it. I had spoken quietly, not raising my voice, and as I said "Go out," he swore at me and jumped to his feet. He was almost as tall and quite as heavy as I was, but before he could raise his hands I hit him on the chin with all the power of arm and body I could put into a right-hand jog. He went down in a heap and lay there. When he began to come to I stood over him and said, "Have you had enough?" He said, "Yes." "All right; now get out," and he went.

Some weeks after we got into a slight scrimmage outside the

Sunday-school room with some toughs, one of whom seemed to want a fight. To my horror I saw, elbowing his way through the crowd, this same tall handsome rascal that I had knocked out, and I began to feel that I was in serious trouble. To my amazement and relief he walked up to the ringleader and said, "The Doctor and me can clean out this saloon; you get out." He got out at once.

My story has a tragic ending: I think it must have been a year later when the big fellow came to me at the rectory one night. "Doctor, I do want to go straight. I have been a bartender; I have been a thief." He linked the two professions together. "I can get a good paying job in more than one saloon round here for I know the boys and they come where I am. But whiskey makes me a brute as you know, and as long as I tend bar I can't keep away from it and I can't break with the gang. I want to quit drink, and I want to quit the 'business,' " (of a thief, he meant), "and I have tried and tried, but I can't get another job. The cops know me and are against me. If you will trust me with the money I'll work a push cart, and I think I can make it go."

"How much do you want?"

"Seventy-five dollars."

I gave him the money and said what cheering things I could, for here was Tony grown up and I truly longed for that man. He was so fine and well-built, so handsome and strong; vice had not yet spoiled either his face or figure. A splendid bit of manhood gone wrong—nay, more, pushed wrong. He would have made a first-class soldier.

In a couple of months he paid me back the money. It was some time before I saw him again, but one night he came to my study at 209 East 16th Street.

"It's no good, Doctor. I can't make it. I did well at first, but these damned Jews are crowding me out. I am going back into 'business,' but I won't do it any longer in a small way, and

I'll promise you one thing: I'll never take another man's life."
He had made up his mind and I could not move him.

Not very long after a band of three burglars were cornered
by the police in the act of boring the safe of a large bank, I
think in Jersey City. One of them, at the point of the pistol,
held off the police while his confederates escaped. At last the
police rushed him and beat him down. He had held them up
with an *unloaded* revolver. It was my poor fine "Tony" of Avenue A. I saw him in prison, where very soon he died of gallop-
ing consumption. . . .

We put into that mission all our energy. For the time being
other church work was regarded as of secondary importance.
But its results, so far as I could judge of them, were far from
satisfactory. I felt more convinced than ever that the emphasis was wrong. *A down-and-out man, a bum, a drunkard,
these are the very last who should be pushed to their feet
to tell to the others a religious experience that they have had
or suppose themselves to have had.* To do so is to strike
strings already out of tone, and none I think can attend such
services and listen for long to the experiences they produce
and attach real importance in permanent value to the one
or the other. Dealing with human nature is serious and responsible work, and to suppose that mortal wounds that have
drained the life blood for years can be quickly cured by a
"first aid to the injured" sort of religion is a very dangerous
error. That is my criticism in a nutshell of the Gospel Mission
method of saving a city's "rounders." We have only a short
time to work and very limited means to work with. Our duty
is to employ that time and those means in the most fruitful
way we know.

There are degrees of lostness in men. It is folly to ignore
them. Though we worked long and faithfully at Avenue A, we
succeeded in drawing into healthy church relationships a few,
only a few, of those adults who had lapsed from all church at-

tendance for a long time. We did not, so far as I can remember, get one single genuine "down-and-outer" to join the
church. But we got children for the asking, and during my
twenty-four years' rectorship we received into the church's
membership more than three thousand young people from
the East Side alone.

As I read over what I have written I feel that I may seem
to criticize unfairly the work of some of the very best men I
have known. Such is not my desire. But here again in New
York I could not but see that the same mistake had been
made, and still was being made, that the Evangelical party I
knew so well had made in England long before. The church's
emphasis was wrong. Men outside her fold were crying not
for *rescue* but for *justice*. They called for bread; we gave them
a stone—a religious stone.

The church's policy was a hand-to-mouth policy; for the
contaminating and spreading evil of a bad environment the
church had no policy at all. To comfort and help with doles
an overworked and "sweated" family was not what was wanted
and the sufferers knew it. What was needed was a radical
change in those conditions that made such householding
possible. . . .

There are many who are disheartened as they face the evil
of a great city. If they but knew how great has been the advance since the time I speak of they would not be so despon-
dent. The moral advance in the life of the community has been
a steady advance. But as an agency for effecting God's will,
the churches have lost a great chance. They are not reaching
and there is small prospect that they will reach the labouring
class. They are *not* associated, in the worker's mind, with any
intelligent, persistent effort to gain, for him and his, common
justice. They turned a stupid, deaf, unbrotherly ear to Labour's bitter cry, and Labour has now turned away its ear
from the Church's appeal. Labour told us what it wanted years
ago; common sense should have told us it was only justice **it**

wanted. In the United States as in England Labour wanted a fair show, a fair chance to launch its little boat on life's great sea. In short, sympathetic aid in bettering an unfair, uneconomic, and unjust condition of life. To such a demand "Come to Jesus and be saved" is no answer whatever. . . .

[RELATIONS WITH J. P. MORGAN]

I thought my people and my work would hold together, even during the long absence that followed my collapse in 1889; but what I found when I returned to New York amazed me. I had left my flock scattered in many corners of a wide field. I found it drawn closer together.

In that remarkable band that held things together one man stood forth. Round him, while its membership scarcely knew it, St. George's gathered, and when with absolute regularity, Sunday morning by Sunday morning, half an hour or more before the service began, Mr. Morgan stood at the church door, welcoming those he knew and did not know, church members and strangers alike felt that St. George's, without a rector, was still a going concern. I am not exaggerating the stimulating influence of my senior warden. He had extraordinary powers of inspiration and encouragement about him when he chose to exercise them.

I think I could have made a success of my rectorate in any case. The time was ripe for what I attempted, the fields stood ready to be sown and reaped. But without Pierpont Morgan I certainly could not have made the success I did; and seeing how widely different in many important matters were our views, the mighty help he gave me, the confidence he showed in my judgment, are matters worth dwelling on. It would be impossible indeed to tell my life story and leave them out. The time to write his life has not yet come. Great men (and he must finally be numbered among the great) rouse our passions; and while these boil within us, the time for history writing is not yet. But of some things about him I must write, for, better than most, I knew him, and I loved him, and what is here put down I feel very sure he would confirm and approve.

First I mention a purely personal matter. I do it because it seems to me a plain duty when you know of a kind good thing done to tell of it, to pass it round. If our faulty nature needs criticism, let us give it praise when we can and criticism when we must.

I was never again as strong after 1889 as I had been before. I did not show it. I do not think my friends noticed it, but I knew it. I had lost vitality somehow. Work tired me, and preaching, as they never used to. I could not sleep as well, nor could I walk as far. Mr. Morgan saw most things he wanted to see, and he noticed the change in me. Soon after my return, in his quiet way, he drew me aside one day and, slipping a paper into my hand, said: "Don't work too hard; you ought not to have to worry about money. Don't thank me, and don't speak of it to any one but your wife." He had created a modest trust for me and mine. So he lifted from my shoulders a burden that has crushed the life out of many a good soldier; worn out not so much by the fighting, as by the intolerable weight of the personal pack he had to carry in the long marches between and after his battles.

When again in 1902 I was much run down in health, he said to Mrs. Rainsford: "He cannot do much longer what he has been doing. You have not a home of your own; don't you want one?" She said it was what we both longed for. "Go and build it." That was Pierpont Morgan. When Mrs. Rainsford lay for many long weeks between life and death at Roosevelt Hospital, he, who at that time was carrying a load of responsibility heavier, perhaps, than any other man in the United States carried, except its President, found time again and again to bring roses to her sick room, and would wait outside her door till the nurse permitted him to lay them by her bed. That, too, was Pierpont Morgan.

I have told one side of my warden's character. I will now tell of another. Both went to make the man. I never had but one serious falling out with Mr. Morgan, but that difference strained for a time the relations between us. Of it I will now speak. J. P. Morgan, if a democrat in theory, was sometimes an autocrat in practice. No sane, strong man is always consistent. Consistency is a second-class virtue. He would have been more than human if the power he wielded, and the adulation it brought to him, had not on him their inevitable result. He grew I think to believe that as the rector was autocratic in the pulpit, where it was the warden's duty to support him, in the vestry the senior warden's will should, at least on matters financial, be supreme. There is much to be said for such a theory.

Now my aim had ever been to make St. George's increasingly democratic. Mr. Morgan had pledged himself to aid me and stand back of me in this. He had never forgotten his pledge to me, that memorable first night in his study, when he looked me in the face and said: "Done!" and he had never shirked that promise. But when, in the pursuance of this policy, I began steadily to attempt an alteration in the make-up of my vestry, he balked.

Legislation lately passed at Albany permitted certain very needful elasticities in the organization of vestries in the Protestant Episcopal Church in the state. I wished to take advantage of this to increase my vestry, at this time consisting of the usual eight vestrymen and two wardens. Of these vestrymen I have spoken again and again. They were an unusually capable body of men, but efficient and loyal as they had proved themselves, they in my opinion but very partially represented St. George's extraordinarily heterogeneous congregation. In my weekly talks after breakfast with Mr. Morgan, I had many times brought up this subject, but in vain I tried to get a response from him. He had nothing to say, and that meant, I knew well, that he remained quite unmoved by my arguments. This being the situation, I made up my mind to wait a while. I had never found it necessary, since 1884, to bring up in the vestry a matter in which my warden and I were opposed. I always strove to settle such divergency of views "out of school." In 1884, when I insisted on putting the choir into surplices, he almost had a panic, and for a time opposed the move fiercely. Since then we had been a unit at all vestry meetings, and indeed, I usually got him to propose at vestry meetings such measures as I desired carried.

However, it was not so to be in this matter. The vestry met at 8:30 P. M. in the Corporation room in the Parish House. There, one night, I had the surprise and the fight of my life. I had no hint of what was coming when, ordinary business being over, Mr. Morgan rose and said: "I have a motion to make, Mr. Chairman, and I think that the vestry will agree with me it had better be passed without debate." He then read his motion. It was that the vestry be reduced from eight members and two wardens to six members and two wardens. Having read it, he said: "I think the vestry will agree with me that when I get a seconder it had better be passed without debate."

I was fairly stunned. I am not, I have never been, quick to act on the occasion, but I saw that as chairman I must dominate the situation instantly, or I was undone and my vestry divided. I said: "Mr. Morgan, before I ask for a seconder to your motion, I must say that I think on a matter so important as the alteration of this vestry, you surely should have said something to me of this radical policy you propose before you advanced it here. Since I stood in your study that night when you called me to the church, I think you will bear witness that I have never advocated any important matter in this, our church's counsel, without first discussing it with you. Here now you spring this revolutionary proposition on me, and on the vestry, without any warning whatever; and you ask that we should proceed to pass it without any discussion. This I cannot agree to, and I must ask you, before you get a seconder, to explain to me and to this vestry your reasons for proposing so important a change. We have done good work together, constituted as we are. If a small vestry is for St. George's a better vestry, there must be reasons for it. What are your reasons?"

Very unwillingly Mr. Morgan got on his feet. What he said was what I feared he was going to say. In brief outline, it was this: "Rector, we are all more than satisfied with what you have accomplished. You have done your part well. We are glad and proud to have aided you. But this, your vestry, has its part to do. Yours is a spiritual responsibility. Your part is to teach the Christian religion, and all that implies, to the congregation. The vestry's part is fiduciary. Our obligations are financial. I am its senior warden and responsible officer. I am ageing. I want at times to have these vestry meetings held in my study. This vestry should be composed, in my judgment, of men whom I can invite to my study, and who can help me to carry the heavy financial burden of the church. Surely all will agree that such responsibilities as ours can best be discharged in this way and by such a body of men. The rector wants to democratize the church, and we agree with him and will help him as far as we can. But I do not want the vestry democratized. I want it to remain a body of gentlemen whom I can ask to meet me in my study."

The issue was plain, no evading it. If my senior warden was to have his way, St. George's vestry would pass under his control. It would not, it could not be, in any true sense, representative of the congregation. In the long fight, for fight it was, which began shortly after nine o'clock and did not end till almost midnight, I did all I could do, all that love for my friend and love for my people prompted, to turn him from his purpose, but I failed completely. And as I opposed that purpose unflinchingly, his anger at opposition rose. Seeing I could gain nothing there, I spoke over his head to my vestry: "Yes, your obligation is fiduciary, as my warden says, but I protest with all my soul that the main purpose you have been elected to fill is not fiduciary but spiritual. A few years ago, you thought I would never stand in the pulpit and preach to you again. If that had been so, on whom would have fallen responsibility of choosing someone to teach and help this multitude of young people that, with your aid, has been gathered here? Is there one of you to-night who will say that any question of finance can be as important as that duty? To-night, for the first time since I have been your rector, I find myself in opposition to my senior warden. Mr. Morgan has laid his plan for what this vestry should be before you, and you must vote on it. Before you do so, I will as frankly tell you mine. I do not want a smaller vestry. I want a larger one. For here in our parish council, I want men who are actually representative of St. George's membership, men who know what that great body wants and feels. I will be specific. Our Sunday School of two thousand is a church within a church. One man in that school has done more for its efficiency than any other. For many years he has been practically its head. He knows the hundred and sixty men and women who form a band of teachers the like of which, I make bold to say, cannot be found in any church in our Communion in this land. He has had more to do with choosing them than have I or my clergy. I want that man on my vestry, and I want him because one who has done what he has done, and knows what he knows, should have a voice in deciding the policy of a church into which he has helped, more than any one other man, to bring over fifteen hundred new young members in ten years. But others, too, I want in this vestry, who would represent fittingly the very great number of wage earners that are now regular members of St. George's. These should be represented *by one of their own number and class.*"

I could feel that, as I pleaded with all my soul for a democratic and more representative vestry, I had the support, as yet unspoken, of a majority of those present; but I wanted to win a verdict if possible without a division. I would have done almost anything to save my warden from pushing to certain defeat his motion. "Will you not withdraw your motion?" I said. "Do not let us divide; we never have had a division on any serious question in this vestry since I sat at your head."

Here Seth Low, Mayor of New York, who had for years been the teacher of the senior Men's Bible Class in our Sunday School, appealed to Mr. Morgan in a moving speech to withdraw his motion. Mr. Morgan remained immovable. Then a dramatic thing happened. A member of the vestry, one of his oldest friends, one to whom in these financially troublesome times through which we were then passing Mr. Morgan had been of immense service (I did not know this till later) slowly rose. He was white to the lips, and, turning to Mr. Morgan, he said: "Mr. Morgan, I am compelled to agree with our rector fully in this matter, and I move that this vestry be increased to eleven." Mr. Low seconded the motion at once. Mr. Morgan would not withdraw but could get no seconder. So I put the second motion, which was carried. The vote stood seven to one.

For a moment we all sat in intense silence. What would this man whom we all loved and honoured do? How take this cruel rebuff, so unwillingly given him? Not one in that vestry but felt he had been honoured in sitting in it with him.

He rose and, speaking slowly, said: "Rector, I will never sit in this vestry again." Then, as all still sat in silence, he walked out. I gave the blessing, and everyone went home. It had been a hard night for the vestry, a harder one for me. And hardest of all, I believe, for my warden.

Next day I had Mr. Morgan's written resignation, with a request to submit it to the vestry without delay. I acknowledged his letter, and nothing more, going to breakfast next week at 219 Madison Avenue as usual. As I expected, he was very grumpy, and at the breakfast table conversation was limited to the weather. Next week I went again to breakfast. He had nothing to say to me at the table.

As I asked for a cigar, in his study afterward, he said, "Have you submitted my resignation?"

"I have not, and I will not."

"Why not?"

"Because I will not now or ever put you in the position of going back on your pledge to the rector and the vestry of St. George's Church."

"What do you mean?"

"You know what I mean. When I first came to you I came because you gave me your hand and your promise to stand by me in the hard work that lay ahead. I told you I was a radical. I told you I would do all I could to democratize the church. I am only keeping my word. I certainly shall not now, nor at any time, do anything to help you break yours."

Dead silence. So I lit my cigar and walked away.

I think after that I went to breakfast three times before Mr. Morgan sailed for Europe. He never made another allusion to his resignation, nor did he enter into any private conversation with me. The day he sailed, I did what I had not done before, I went to the dock to bid him good-bye. On this occasion, in the days I am writing of, the late '90's, a rather miscellaneous crowd was wont to gather to bid him good-bye. It had become quite a function, and I did not usually care to take part in it. As I went up the gangplank, I saw Mr. Morgan standing at some distance surrounded by his friends. At the same instant he saw me, and coming out of the group, signed to me to follow him. He made for his cabin, entered quickly, without saying a word, and shut and bolted the door behind us. We never had another falling-out. . . .

19. THE INSTITUTIONAL CHURCH

The Institutional Church, 1907

BY CHARLES STELZLE

In his autobiography, Stelzle (1869–1941) proudly called himself A SON OF THE BOWERY; *he also liked to point out that he had been a skilled laborer before he turned to the Presbyterian ministry. As a result, he brought to the analysis of urban religious problems no fond memories of the natural harmonies of religion and rural culture. Nor was he so overwhelmed by the modern city as to be unable to see that by the turn of the century living conditions had improved greatly. It was because of this capacity for understanding the city that Stelzle was appointed Superintendent of the Department of Church and Labor created by the Presbyterian Church in 1903.*

CHRISTIANITY'S STORM CENTRE, *from which this document is taken, declared that new social organizations were emerging to cope with city men's social and economic needs. Stelzle was delighted with the Kaffee Klatsches for women, labor unions for men, the Salvation Army for down-and-outers, the settlement houses for the immigrants, the YMCA for the young. Still, in 1907, he regarded the institutional church as normative. But he was able to recognize how precarious was the hold of*

From Charles Stelzle, *Christianity's Storm Centre: A Study of the Modern City* (New York: Fleming Revell, 1907), pp. 163–191.

most institutional churches on the masses. A few years later, in his AMERICAN SOCIAL AND RELIGIOUS CONDITIONS *(New York: Fleming Revell, 1912), he would argue that an institutional church could succeed only in conjunction with such unchurchly enterprises as the Labor Temple which he had founded in 1910, where workingmen were invited to voice their darkest suspicions of organized religion. But in 1907 he was already persuaded that there was no single solution to the problem of the churches and the city.*

CHANGING SOCIAL CONDITIONS

The most superficial study of religious work reveals the fact that in almost every large city most of the great church "missions" which were once so successful have either gone out of existence altogether, or else they are being conducted upon a much smaller scale than formerly. There is scarcely a church mission in the United States but what is making a struggle for its existence—at least in comparison with its former glory.

There are several reasons for this decline. While there is still a great deal of poverty in the city, that poverty is not so hopeless as it once was. The actual poverty may be as great, and there may be even more of it, but there has come to the masses a hope for better things, sometimes through the labor and the Socialistic press and their general literature, as well as through the daily papers, which are read by even the poorest. The common people have had a vision of the coming democracy. Any one who has known the East Side of New York for a score of years—and the same thing is true of most other large cities—knows of the change that has come over the people in this respect. There are still dull, plodding, unpenetrating individuals, but no one can question the statement that in recent years there has been a great civic awakening among the common people.

Another reason for the change lies in the fact that the foreigner has come in to displace those who were once sympathetic toward the mission. But, strange to say, it is this very foreigner who has helped so largely to introduce the civic pride which has taken hold of the people. The political campaign clubs organized by the young Russian Jews, for instance, put to shame the indifference of many a citizen who was "freeborn."

It is sometimes said that city mission work has failed because of the introduction of the social settlement, and many city mission workers have become bitter against these institutions because of their apparent rivalry, forgetting that in but few instances have they been guilty of proselyting. Their field of operation has, in most cases, been one which was altogether untouched by the mission. Frequently they have come into fields which had been deserted by the churches, from which the churches were compelled to flee in order to "save" their lives.

Generally, it is intimated that the mission has failed because the people have become indifferent, and that they do not care for the "old Gospel." But what seems to be the cause is simply the effect. To say that many of the people have become indifferent is quite true. But why have they become indifferent? There are, of course, numerous reasons for this indifference, but in most cases it is due not so much to the people as it is to the mission itself. In the causes which have just been given, it will be agreed that every factor, in itself, is an encouraging one. Who does not rejoice that poverty is less distressing, that the immigrant is being aroused to a sense of citizenship, that the settlement wields a helpful influence in forsaken fields? But to what extent has the mission met its obligation in these particulars?

True, it has helped many, individually, to better things. But how often has it inspired the great masses so that they have taken on fresh courage in times of social and economic distress? Why has it left this almost exclusively to the despised agitator? How far has the mission helped the immigrant to understand his true relationship to his adopted country? How far has the average mission gone in actually bringing about changed physical conditions in the community, by going directly to the officials of the municipality in behalf of those who needed a spokesman? Here and there an individual, overworked pastor has attempted it, but in comparison with the work of the social settlement, the mission's influence has been small indeed.

But, somebody will say: "The mission has nothing to do with civic righteousness and the political education of the immigrant." And that is precisely the reason why the people in the community have gone over to these other organizations, because a man's physical wants are always more apparent than his spiritual needs. And this accounts, in a measure, for the failure of the mission. As the social conditions of the people changed, the mission failed to adjust itself to these changing conditions. As new needs arose, the mission went on, blind to its opportunities, with the result that other forces took its place in the hearts of the people. It lost its spiritual grip, because it failed to enlarge its own life and vision, by taking on the life of its constituency. Thus it has happened that some of the very things which should have strengthened religious work in the community have helped to break it down.

Reference has already been made to the growing spirit of democracy among the people. This also accounts for the failure of the mission. The people demand democratic organizations, in which they themselves have a part in the management. What is needed, therefore, is a regularly organized Church, which ministers to all the needs of the people living in the community. Such a Church, properly organized and aggressively conducted, with an evangelistic basis, is sure to win the people.

PRESSING SOCIAL NEEDS

The author of "The Long Day," writing out of an experience among working-women, in relation to proposed remedies for the evils by which they are surrounded, says:

"The . . . need is for a greater interest in the workwoman's welfare on the part of the Church, and an effort by that all-powerful institution to bring about some adjustment of her social and economic difficulties. I am old-fashioned enough to believe in the supreme efficacy of organized religion in relation to womanhood and all that pertains to womanhood. I believe that, in our present state of social development, the Church can do more for the working-girl than any of the proposed measures based upon economic sciences or the purely ethical theory. Working-women, as a class, are certainly not ripe for the trades-union, and the earnest people of the 'settlements' are able to reach but a small part of the great army of women marching hopelessly on, ungeneralled, untrained, and, worst of all, uncaring.

"But a live and progressive church—a church imbued with the Christian spirit in the broadest and most liberal interpretation of the term—can do for us, and do it quickly and at once, more than all the college-settlements and the trades-unions that can be organized within the next ten years could hope to do. And for this reason: The Church has all the machinery ready, set up and waiting only for the proper hand to put it in motion to this great end. The Christian Church has a vast responsibility in the solution of all problems of the social order, and none of those problems is more grave or urgent than the one affecting the economic condition of the wage-earning woman.

"In the days when I could see no silver lining to the clouds, I tried going to a Protestant church, but I recognized very shortly the alienation between it and me. Personally, I do not like to attend Salvation meetings or listen to the mission evangelists. So I ceased any pretension of going to church, thus allying myself with that great aggregation of non-church-going Protestant working-women who have been forced into a resentful attitude against that which we should love and support. It is encouraging, however, to find that the Church itself has, at last, begun to heed our growing disaffection and alienation."

Some excellent people are insisting that the Church has but one mission—to preach the "simple" Gospel, whatever that may mean. They are saying that when a man becomes a Christian, all of these things take care of themselves. Indeed, they say, he will find so much joy in the Christian life that the demands of the social and the physical will no longer have any control over him. Undoubtedly, this is true, in many cases, but we are dealing with the average man, who has not the resources within himself that some other people have. There are pulseless, nerveless, bloodless individuals who simply cannot comprehend the struggles of the man who is like a throbbing human engine, fired with a rush of thought that arouses the deepest passions. There are men and women who, from their earliest childhood, have been raised in an environment from which was shut out everything that was coarse and brutal and vicious, but there are others who knew practically nothing else from the moment that they were cursed into the world. Over these needy ones the Church must ever have watchful care, ministering first of all and principally to their spiritual needs, but never forgetting that they have bodies, which sometimes so strongly assert themselves that spiritual truth makes almost no impression upon them.

It must not be imagined that New York and Chicago have a monopoly of the tenement houses which present conditions that demand the social ministry of the Church. The pastor of a Minneapolis church found within a block of his church a nine-room house with a family in every room. In St. Louis four Syrian workingmen, three of whom were married, and having six children between them, were occupying two rooms. Sometimes the tenements in the smaller cities are in a worse sanitary condition, having no more sunlight and as much filth, as the frequently described tenements in New York City. Recently it was reported that the social conditions in some sections of the city of Washington were worse than they are in New York.

A St. Louis pastor thus describes the community in which his church is situated:

"I have in mind a typical tenement. There are thousands so nearly like it—almost anywhere within two miles north or south of Market Street, and within ten squares from the river—that it is unnecessary to specify the location of this particular house. Four families occupy the front building, and four live in the rear. Thus the children of eight families must use the dirt or brick-paved court between the houses, or go on the streets. There is not much space for them when the coal sheds and other out-buildings are provided. Sometimes a third tenement is crowded to one side of the court, between front and rear buildings.

"The entrance to the court is through a narrow, brick-paved gangway, which, tunnel-like, pierces the walls of the front tenement. All families in the houses use this gangway, as they must enter their homes by the stairways from the yard, or by the doors under these stairways.

"The visitor enters by the kitchen, for this is, necessarily, the front room. It is not much larger than a fair-sized bathroom, being little more than twice the width of its one window. The next room is lighted from the kitchen, and from the single window in the blackness under the stairway. On a light day this room is gloomy, to say the least. Frequently a visitor has difficulty in distinguishing the features of a sick person in this room. The third room is the front room—it fronts on the narrow alley. Another tenement is almost within reach of the windows; or, perhaps, there is a stable across the way. When the rent-collector calls, he secures from eight to eleven or twelve dollars a month for the three rooms.

"The vacation problem is easily solved by the dwellers in the tenements. Few of them have any vacation. 'I have had one day off in five years, and I'd like to go so much,' said one factory-worker, a woman sixty years old. 'But I am not as young as I once was. And I dare not go for even a week. When I come back they'd be sure to have some younger person in my place. Then what would we do at home?'

"One day a visitor to one of the homes was urged by four boys: 'Come and see our clubroom.' Gleefully they took him to a rough shed, thrown together of waste timbers picked up on the street. How proudly they looked at their possessions! A few newspaper pictures on the walls. A game of checkers on a chair. A baseball bat in one corner. But the crowning feature was a placard which one of the boys had laboriously fashioned:

NO SMOKING • NO SWEARING
NO CANNING BEER HERE

" 'We don't want none of that, 'cause we see enough of it, and what it means,' the maker of the notice explained, as he observed the direction of the visitor's gaze."

DEMANDING SOCIAL LEADERS

How shall these conditions be met? And who shall lead in this important work? During recent years we have been hearing much about the "social spirit." But comparatively few in our churches seem to understand the significance of the phrase. It possesses a far wider meaning than most of us think. The Church has been so exclusively engaged in its work for the individual, that it has had little inclination to grapple with the questions that concern the masses of the people aside from their purely so-called religious interests.

The young men in our theological seminaries have been trained to look upon their future work as having to do simply with the preparation of sermons, pastoral calling, and the performance of the functions which thus far have belonged peculiarly to the minister. Their studies, while in the seminary, have been confined almost exclusively to theology, the dead languages, the sacraments, Church history, and homiletics. Practically the only touch with the throbbing life of the world outside the seminary walls has been the teaching of a mission Sunday School class, the leading of a prayer meeting, or the holding of a service in a country schoolhouse.

It is immensely gratifying that a few of our seminaries are realizing the inadequacy of their courses of study to meet present-day social needs, and are introducing features which must result in a type of leaders who shall have more of the social spirit than is often found among the ministers of a past generation.

But the theological seminary is not altogether to blame in this matter. It cannot always secure the kind of men who will naturally become leaders of the type needed. It must do the best it can with the material it has to work with.

Frequently we are told that the country supplies the Church with practically all her ministers. There is no doubt as to the truthfulness of this statement. Among a hundred preachers in a particular conference, most of whom had city charges, it was discovered that only two were born and reared in the city. All praise to the country for its contribution to the religious life of the city. But the fact presented partially accounts for a condition to which the Church is already giving her serious attention, viz., that the average city church falls woefully short in its work among the city's masses.

Most of our city churches, even among the larger ones, are trying to meet town conditions by an elaborated country church programme. Sometimes an enthusiastic minister will try to galvanize his church into an appearance of city efficiency, but the best results do not come that way. They come because of a consistently carried-out programme based upon an intelligent conception of actual conditions. Many fine young ministers who came to our cities finally succeed in a very difficult task, but most of them drift into the ways of their predecessors, ministering to a constituency of long-time church attendants, a large percentage of whom have also come from the country, and to whom the spirit and the method are perfectly acceptable.

Frankly, how can a young man who knows practically nothing of city thought and life—the thought and life of the man outside the Church—because he has been raised in a country atmosphere, take his college and seminary course, where he certainly does not catch the spirit of the city, and then, at twenty-five, make a success of a city church, which is situated in the midst of a people whose mode of life is a deep and profound mystery to the young theologue? Some are doing it, but this success is due to unusual ability, which would manifest itself in any other occupation.

Sometimes it is pathetic to see a highly finished product of the schools almost broken-hearted in a city field, simply because he has failed to get a vision of the real needs of the people for whom he would fain give his very life. One such actually resigned his city mission charge, because he was overwhelmed by the great numbers of people by whom his church was surrounded, and to which his country training had made him peculiarly sensitive. And yet, here was a condition which should have stirred him to his very depths, as he saw the possibilities in that great mass, and sent him out to courageously grapple with the vital problems of his community. But he was absolutely helpless because he could not get the proper conception of his task. People who naturally drift into our city churches need the ministration which the average church can give through its pastor; but here are millions who are being deliberately deserted—simply—and it is said advisedly—because we haven't enough of the right kind of men in the ministry. The city offers the Church a magnificent field for the best talent that any city man ever put into business or philanthropic life. But it will require a city programme, put into operation by a city man, who understands the city *Zeitgeist*. The overheard conversation of business men on the trains indicates it. The sentiments expressed by workingmen in the shop proves it. The attitude of the people in the slums verifies it.

The city has no right to expect country men to solve its church problems—social, philanthropic, religious. The splendid ability found in the city church must be consecrated to the task of working out the salvation of the city's life. This task clearly rests upon the layman.

More and more is this becoming the layman's day. The multiplication of "Brotherhoods" and men's clubs, the fine response by business men to definite service rightly presented, the high ideals which have come from the laymen themselves, and the growing disposition to become jealous of what they consider their rightful place in the administration of the affairs of the Church, all give promise of better things to come.

DEFINING SOCIAL SERVICE

The spirit and the aim of the institutional church is expressed in the platform of the Open and Institutional Church League—"Inasmuch as the Christ came not to be ministered unto, but to minister, the open and institutional church, filled and moved by His spirit of ministering love, seeks to become the centre and source of all beneficent and philanthropic effort, and to take the leading part in every movement which has for its end the alleviation of human suffering, the elevation of man, and the betterment of the world.

"Thus the open and institutional church aims to save all

men and all of the man by all means, abolishing, so far as possible, the distinction between the religious and secular, and sanctifying all days and all means to the great end of saving the world for Christ."

Josiah Strong, in his "Religious Movements for Social Betterment," points out its distinguishing characteristic in these words:

"The Church and the home are the two great saving institutions of society. When the home is what it ought to be, it affords such an environment as makes possible a normal development of body and soul. When it is pretty much all that it ought not to be, and is corrupting to both soul and body, the appeals of the Church to the spiritual life are to little or no purpose. Hence, as the tenement house has been substituted for the comfortable home, the churches working on the old lines have either died or have followed the well-to-do class uptown.

"The institutional church, however, succeeds because it adapts itself to changed conditions. It finds that the people living around it have in their homes no opportunity to take a bath; it therefore furnishes bathing facilities. It sees that the people have little or no healthful social life; it accordingly opens attractive social rooms, and organizes clubs for men, women, boys and girls. The people know little of legitimate amusement; the Church, therefore, provides it. They are ignorant of household economy; the Church establishes its cooking-schools, its sewing-schools, and the like. In their homes the people have few books and papers; in the Church they find a free reading-room and library.

"The homes afford no opportunity for intellectual cultivation; the Church opens evening schools and provides lecture courses. As in the human organism, when one organ fails, its functions are often performed by some other organ; so in the great social organism of the city, when the home fails, the Church sometimes undertakes the functions of the home. Such a church we call 'Institutional.'"

TYPIFYING SOCIAL ACTIVITY

Probably no church in the entire world is doing a greater work on social lines than that being done by St. Bartholomew's Protestant Episcopal Church in New York City. Over two hundred meetings, of various kinds, are held weekly. There are 2,952 communicants in the parish. The Sunday Schools have a membership of 1,610.

If one includes choir members, clerks, porters, cleaners, teachers, engineers, etc., there are 249 salaried workers. Including members of boards, officers of societies, teachers, ushers, physicians, choir members, and those who are working members in clubs and societies, there are 896 volunteer workers.

Sunday services are held in the Parish House for Germans, Armenians, and Chinese, and there are regular services in the Swedish Chapel. Each of these nationalities has a surpliced choir which renders music in its own language. Many of these foreigners have been greatly interested in teaching their fellow-countrymen lessons in American patriotism.

The church supports one of the best equipped dispensaries in the city. Fifty-four physicians volunteer their services. Last year 15,227 new patients were treated, the total number of consultations have been 50,452. The total number of prescriptions written was 23,090, of which 22,527 were paid for. The Loan Association, which is conducted upon a business basis, received during the year $101,517.59, and disbursed $91,345. Loans are made to the poor at a reasonable rate of interest, the department being so managed as to make it self-supporting.

On top of the nine-storied building in which are hived the many enterprises of the parish, is a beautiful roof garden. The children plant flowers in long boxes and tubs, and here the kindergarten holds many of its sessions. In the evening the various societies of the parish have their meetings on the roof, and on Sundays religious services are held.

Club life is prominent. There are clubs for men and women,

boys and girls, with a total membership of 2,796. Membership in the Girls' Evening Club entitles the holder to the use of the clubrooms and library; access to the large hall every evening after nine o'clock, to the physical-culture classes, lectures, talks, entertainments, discussion class, glee club, literature class, English composition class, the Helping Hand Society, Penny Provident and Mutual Benefit Funds; the privilege of joining one class a week in either dressmaking, millinery, embroidery, drawn-work, system sewing or cooking; also, by paying a small fee, the privilege of entering a class in stenography, typewriting, French, or bookkeeping. Corresponding advantages attend membership in the other clubs.

For those seeking work and for those desiring workers, an efficient employment bureau is conducted. During the past year 2,531 situations were filled. The kindergarten enrolled 259 children, the Industrial School, 336. The Fresh Air work of the parish gave outings to thousands of mothers and their children. Garments were provided for the poor, such as were able paying a small amount for them. The Penny Provident Fund received $31,483.29 from 5,196 depositors.

The amount expended by the Church on the Parish House, during the year, was $91,043.99, and the total amount given for home expenditures and for benevolent contributions was $219,641.19. The splendid work of St. Bartholomew's shows what can be done when occurs the rare combination of a big brain, a big heart, and a big treasury.

Few churches that desire to engage in institutional work have so large a fund to draw upon. Fortunately, one may do things without very much money. It is quite possible to conduct an institutional church on one hundred dollars a year aside from the expense of carrying on the work of an ordinary church.

It can be done, because it has been done. After the demonstration had been made in one instance, there was no difficulty in getting the money needed. It is a good policy never to ask a man for money simply on the argument that a certain kind of work could be done with a large amount of money. A better way is to prove with the means at hand that the work can be done, and that you are the man to do it.

Ministering to the needs of the community in which it is situated—that is the principle upon which the institutional church is operated. By this is meant the needs not supplied by some other helpful agency. For instance, a gymnasium conducted by German infidels is not such an agency. A church conducted for the benefit of the well-to-do need not operate a free dispensary, whatever else it may attempt along institutional lines. We are more directly concerned with the church that is trying to reach and help the workingman and his family.

With a building that is lighted and heated—perhaps with only two rooms—one is ready for the work as outlined below. Few things are more popular than an illustrated lecture course. An admission fee of five cents pays all expenses. In most instances one may secure the lecturers in one's high school or college, and sometimes a preacher or business man in the neighborhood has a lecture on his travels, or on some other interesting subject. Always remember that it is the personal element that makes the lecture of interest to the people, so if a man can tell the story of his own experience, even in a very ordinary way, he may hold his audience better than some others who may have had some supposed advantages over him. Most of the lecturers will give their services gratuitously, and will be glad of the opportunity to be used when they can speak to an appreciative audience. If enough volunteers cannot be secured, one may do the lecturing himself. Slides and readings on many subjects may be obtained from supply houses in any large city. One can study the reading so that he need not depend upon it altogether when lecturing.

A song service may be held before each lecture, the hymns being thrown on the canvas. An occasional moving picture entertainment is a good thing when only the best class of pictures are shown. It is best to examine them one's self, because the average operator has not a very keen sense of what is appropriate for a church.

Ushers and other workers should understand fully just what is expected of them. It is always best to fix the responsibility for every detail. This applies not only to the lecture course, but to every other department. Much must be entrusted to others, because it is a physical impossibility to do everything one's self. As soon as a new department is organized get somebody to take hold of it. Do not wait to find the ideal person. Sometimes a very ordinary worker will develop into a magnificent helper, simply because of his faithfulness, and that is the chief talent.

Sometimes when a church is situated in a downtown district, and there are in the neighborhood many foreigners and others not sympathetic toward a Protestant church, it is a difficult matter to reach the children through the Sunday School. A "Children's Hour" on a weekday afternoon is useful. A children's choir, recitations by the children, a solo—anything that children can do—will be appreciated. Have them sing hymns— when you can. In one Children's Hour, the children sang street songs of the best type. They contained sentiment that was helpful, as many popular ballads do, and the children were delighted. Sometimes the worst boy in the neighborhood would sing a popular song, to the great delight of his audience. It did him good, too. He could not be quite so rude after that. A ten-minutes' Gospel talk was always given at some time during the meeting, and frequently a friend would come and sing or recite. Soon there were twice as many children in this service as in the Sunday School, and they were children who did not ordinarily attend the school.

A fine concert course can be arranged, weekly, with singers from the quartette choirs of the city, or from some conservatory of music, where there are always good voices looking for practice. An offer to send a carriage to their homes and to see them safely back is usually all that is needed to secure their services—excepting some tact in telling them what one is trying to do in a musical way for the neighborhood, in order to win their sympathetic interest. Sometimes one may secure an orchestra in the same way. Recently the pastor in a Western city secured the best orchestra in town and gave a concert with a ten-cent admission. They were charging 75 cents for the same programme every Sunday afternoon, in a downtown theatre, and were playing to an audience of 2,000 persons. The musicians' union, at his request, permitted the men to play at a reduced rate. It may be well, sometimes, to alternate weekly between the concert and the lecture.

A Boys' Club, with a membership of over 500, was conducted at an expense of only $30 for each year. This paid for some cheap pine tables and some printed matter, some games and a closet in which to keep them. The rooms were open every night except Sunday, and there was an average attendance of 150 per evening, although at a weekly entertainment given by outside friends there was sometimes an attendance of 400 newsboys and bootblacks.

The editor of the newspaper sold by the boys came down to tell how a newspaper is made. A college professor talked on "Habits." A surgeon told, simply, of the progress of his art. The possibilities along this line are almost limitless, and there is comparatively no expense. Friends contributed magazines and papers, and were glad to do so.

One may have small groups of boys, led by some interested men and women who have talent—it matters little what, so long as it may be made helpful. A knowledge of geology, astronomy, wood-carving, printing, music—instrumental or vocal—almost any thing that will interest boys. And if one has a passion for one's talent, it is a comparatively easy matter to interest others. A city history club will be found instructive. Study the beginning of the city's life, its early landmarks, its development, its industries, the various departments of municipal government, the administration of public utilities, etc. Anything that has to do with the life of the city may be investigated by such a club. The most approved plan is the mass club for boys, with the subdivisions suggested above. A penny a week from the boys will usually meet incidental expenses.

What has been suggested for the boys may be done for the girls, only, of course, there should be other employments, which will readily suggest themselves.

A Penny Savings Bank is always a helpful enterprise. A bankbook is given to each child or grown person, stamps of various denominations indicating the amounts deposited. A complete outfit may be secured from the Penny Provident Fund of New York City, without any charge excepting postage. A few dollars originally invested will keep the bank going indefinitely. Almost every church or mission in the poorest districts of our cities conducts a sewing-school. Its expense is comparatively small, and it may be made a very valuable feature of church work.

Fifteen dollars, invested at a wholesale drug store, will establish a drug department for a free dispensary. There are physicians in every city who will gladly give their services to such an institution, going weekly, or oftener, to the dispensary at the church. The physician will write out a list of the drugs required. A charge of ten cents for the medicine dispensed by the attending physician will keep the drug department always well supplied.

A drum corps may be maintained by the boys themselves. They can manage, in most instances, to pay an instructor a small amount, and until they can afford to purchase drums, a pair of sticks and a piece of rubber will do service. Indeed, for various reasons, it is best that they begin in this modest way.

It is a mistaken policy to continually offer privileges to any class without requiring some service or self-help. This, of itself, is an educative feature that is most valuable. I once had a Young Men's Club which was limited to ten members. They were all employed in factories near the church. The boys wanted a gymnasium. I told them that I would provide them with a room, if they would manufacture some of the material necessary for fitting up the gymnasium, and that I would help them in the matter of purchasing other material which they could not afford to buy. They soon had a simple outfit, and I had contributed only about $10. The boys appreciated it far more than if it had been given to them outright, and it was a pleasure to see how affectionately they regarded every part of that crude gymnasium. It was their own—purchased at a real sacrifice. The moral and mental discipline, acquired through this effort, was of more value than any physical training that they might have received in a more elaborate gymnasium.

One may organize many kinds of clubs for all ages and for both sexes. Whether they are self-supporting or not, they should, in most instances, be self-governing. A club spirit among the people will give the work a strong *esprit de corps* which is very desirable in any kind of enterprise. A literary society for the young people will prove an inspiration.

A flower mission may be conducted at practically no expense to the church. In this very beautiful ministry one can easily secure the interest of suburban dwellers who have gardens. The express companies usually carry, free of charge, the flowers which are sent weekly to the church for distribution. Little girls—perhaps the members of the Girls' Club—will serve as messengers in sending the refreshing bouquets to the sick and the poor.

A lack of money need not keep one from having a mothers' meeting. Music plays a most prominent part in the work of an institutional church. Why not invite the banjo club, that now meets back of the saloon, to make itself at home in the church? No doubt some of your own young men belong to it. Most churches have a chorus choir. Why not form it into a musical club for the purpose of securing a musical education? It would pay the Church to assume all the expenses of such an organization, if for no other reason than that it would give the Church a fine company of volunteer singers. But the class may be made nearly self-supporting by charging a small amount for dues.

This matter of making an enterprise self-supporting may be overdone. Making a downtown work self-supporting is not the most important thing in connection with such work. But these suggestions are offered to prove that quite a strong institutional church may be conducted under great limitations, so far as finances are concerned.

Many more things can be done than are here outlined. It may not be wise to adopt every suggestion offered, and it may be well to adapt those that are adopted. Everything suggested may be done with the amount indicated, besides what the people themselves will contribute for special privileges. Hard work? Yes. But did anybody ever do anything that was worth while without hard work?

Speaking from a purely human standpoint—there is no patent way for doing these things, besides hard work and genuine enthusiasm for it. Perspiration is just as important as inspiration, and sometimes it accomplishes more.

After all, success in this work is a question of flesh and blood, rather than a financial problem. Sometimes you can buy it, and those who have the money are putting most of it into men and women. Right here is the opportunity of the Church in its great social work. If we can secure the men and the women who will serve in the spirit of brotherhood—not "going down" but "coming over"—many of the social problems of the day will be got at, and men will be won to Christ.

REWARDING SOCIAL EFFORT

It is with a sense of satisfaction that Christian workers have noticed that the time usually comes in the experiences of these for whom we are pleading, when they have learned to live in their homes the lessons which have been taught them in the institutional church. This answers the criticism of those who oppose the institutional church, that after this work has been engaged in for a number of years, it seems to have lost its power of attraction—but really, that institutional church may have finished its work in this respect. If one were to go into the homes of the community in which the church operated, it would be discovered that these homes had been so radically changed because of the influences and teachings of the institutional church that there is no longer the need which was found at the beginning. Therefore, this apparent failure is really the sign of the greatest success.

It has been complained that rarely do those who have been the beneficiaries of the institutional church unite with the church, and that because this has been so the institutional church is a failure. A little insight into human nature will explain this seeming unresponsiveness, where this has been the case. Usually, when the ordinary man or woman has become the object of charity, they are eager to get away from the scenes and the persons who were the witnesses of their misfortune, but they generally go away with a new conception of the spirit of the Church, and ordinarily they are grateful to the particular church which assisted them in the hour of their great need, whether that assistance came through a free dispensary, the employment bureau, or some other agency of the Church. In many cases, they will unite with the Church in the neighborhood to which they have moved. Thus the Kingdom of Jesus Christ has been enlarged, and for this every follower of Him "Who went about doing good," should be grateful.

As a matter of fact, however, the institutional churches of this country are receiving more people proportionately than are being received by the churches working exclusively on the old lines. And yet, such a comparison is hardly fair to the institutional churches, because, as a rule, they are located in the hardest fields, where the old line churches have utterly failed, and because no account is taken of the great good that has been accomplished in other directions, in which respect the old line churches have almost altogether missed out.

The Protestant Episcopal Church in New York is using institutional methods far more commonly than any other Church and it is growing more rapidly than any other denomination. In this denomination, in New York City, the churches which are growing most rapidly are institutional.

The Markham Memorial Presbyterian Church in St. Louis for several years has been receiving more members on confession of faith than any other church in the same Presbytery, and it is the only Presbyterian church in the city which is recognized as institutional. During a recent year it stood eighth in this respect among the 8,000 Presbyterian churches in the United States.

The average Congregational institutional church has six times as many additions on confession of faith as the average church of that denomination.

INDEX

Activities, church. *See* Church, activities of
Adams, Henry, 227
Adaptations, xiii, xxi, xxii, xxvii, xxx, 127–301
  See also Adventism, Church of Christ (Scientist), Jehovah's Witnesses, Neighborhood churches, Pentecostalism, Revivals
Adventism, xiii, xvii, xxviii–xxix, xxx, 182, 227–262
  See also Jehovah's Witnesses
Alcuin, 8
American Protective Association, 40
Architecture. *See* Church, architecture
Armenians, 343
Attendance, church. *See* Church, attendance at
Australia, 262

Baker, Ray S., 55, 69–95
Baptist Temple (Philadelphia), xxxvii
Baptists, xix, xxv, xxxvi–xxxvii, 36, 122
Barratt, T. B., 263
Barry, Colman, 115
Bates, H. Roswell, 89
Beecher, Henry W., xxii–xxiv, xxxiii, xl, 106, 127–153, 154–201
Beecher, Lyman, xi, xxii, 137
"Black Jews," xli
Boys clubs. *See* Church, activities of
Brick Church (New York), xvi

Brooklyn. *See* Plymouth Congregational Church (Brooklyn)
Brooks, Phillips, xvi, 309
Broome Street Tabernacle (New York), 35
Duckle, H. T., 12
Businessmen. *See* Economic life of church

"Cahenslyite," xx *n.*
Calvary, 103
Calvin, John, 62
Calvinists, xix
Carlyle, Thomas, 129
Cass, Lewis, 152
Cathedral, xv
Catholic World, 227
Catholics, xx, xxiv, xxxiv–xxxv, xxxix *n.*, xl, xlii, xliii, xliv, 3, 4, 21, 30, 35, 40, 41, 46–47, 51, 56, 88, 114, 115, 116, 117, 119, 120–121, 122, 123, 227, 309
Cato, 6
Chapels. *See* Mission churches
Chicago, 16, 39, 41, 262
Children, 6–7, 10, 16, 18, 21–22, 23–24, 27, 136, 143, 317, 322, 346
Chinese, 343
Choate, Joseph H., 91
"Christian Conference" (1888), 29, 33
Christian Science. *See* Church of Christ (Scientist)
Christian Science Journal, 290
Christian Workers, xviii
Chrysostom. *See* John Chrysostom, Saint

Church
  activities of, 58, 89, 311, 342,
    343–350
    boys clubs, 315, 347
    clubs, xxxvi, xxxviii, 89, 315,
      342, 343, 344, 347
    confraternities, xxxiv
    cooking classes, 84, 342, 344
    industrial schools, 58, 84, 344
    kindergartens, 89, 344
    sodalities, xxxiv
  architecture, xvi, xl, 57, 128, 136,
    306
  attendance at, xv–xviii, xxxvi,
    xxxvii, 37–38, 83–84, 130,
    131, 135, 305–306
  culture and, xxiii, xxviii, 133, 182,
    184, 213, 219, 222
  evolution and, xxiii, 182, 184
  income, xvi, xxvii, xxxvii–xxxviii
    pew rents, xvi
    property-holdings, xv, xvi,
      69–95
  membership, xxxi, xxxiii, 29–32,
    57–58, 85–86, 352
  politics and, xxiii, 169–176, 213,
    228, 260
  poverty and, 244, 315–323
  reunion, 45–51, 59–68
  science and, xxiii, xxviii, 182, 184
  social problems and, xxxvii
  unity (*see* Church, reunion)
  See also Downtown churches,
    Economic life of church,
    Ethnic churches, Govern-
    ment and church, Holiness
    churches, Institutional
    churches, Minister, Mission
    churches, Neighborhood
    churches, Revivals, Ritual,
    Sunday schools, Village
    churches
Church of Christ (Scientist),
  xiii–xiv, xxxii–xxxiii, xl,
  267–301
Church of England, 64
Church of God, xx
  of Anderson, Indiana, xl

Church of the Most Precious Blood
  (New York), 88
Church of the Nazarene, xix–xx
Churchman, The, xvii, 93
Cicero, 6
Classes, church. *See* Church,
  activities of
Classes, social. *See* Social classes
Clubs, church. *See* Church,
  activities of
Columba, Saint, 10
Common School System, 21
Confraternities. *See* Church,
  activities of
Congregationalists, xxii, xxxvi
Connecticut River, xxii
Conversion. *See* Salvation
Conwell, Russell, xxxvii–xxxviii
Cooking classes, 84, 342, 344
Country churches. *See* Village
  churches
Country folks, xiv, xviii–xx, xxv, xli,
  99
Countryside. *See* Villages
Croker, Richard, 307
Culture. *See* Church, culture and

"Daddy Grace," xli
Darwin, Charles, xxvii
Darwinism. *See* Evolution
*Die Moralstatistik in ihrer Bedeu-
  tung für eine Christliche So-
  cialethik* (von Oettingen),
  14n.
Disease. *See* Health
Dix, Morgan, xvi, 55–68, 91
Doctors. *See* Health
Döllinger, Johann, 65–66
Douglas, Mr., 152
Douglass, H. Paul, xii, xxxi
Downtown churches, xiii, xiv–xviii,
  xx, xxx, xxxvi, 55–95,
  127–134, 305–330, 350
Drunkenness. *See* Intemperance
Duncan, Captain, 147–148
Dunn, Lewis R., 99–113
Dusen, Henry van, xli

East Harlem Protestant Parish,
xxxix
Economic life of church, xv, xxiii,
xxxvii–xxxviii, 129, 166–169,
213
See also Church, income
Economic reform. *See* Economic
life of church
Eddy, Asa G., 292
Eddy, Mary B., xxxii–xxxiii,
267–301
Edwards, Jonathan, 151, 176
Emerson, Ralph W., 11
Emmanuel Church (Boston), xxxii
Episcopalians, xvi, xvii, xxxii, xxxvi,
xxxvii, 35, 36, 70, 73, 75,
84, 305–330
See also Trinity Church
Ermenfried, 9 10
Ethnic churches, xiii, xv, xx–xxi,
114–124
Ethnic group, xxii, xxxi
Europe, 65, 223–224
Evangelical Alliance, xviii
Evangelism, xxix
Evolution, xxiii, 182, 184

Family, 5, 20–21, 22, 342
"Father Divine," xli
Federation of Churches, xviii
Fiacre, Saint, 9
Fine Arts' League, 91
Finney, Charles G., xix, xxv
Fish, Henry Clay, xxv
Foreigners. *See* Immigration
Freedom, religious, v
French, 16, 122, 123
Frontier, xi

Gastonia, North Carolina, xviii, xix
Germans, 16, 26, 116–117, 118,
119–120, 121, 122, 343
Gethsemane, 103, 104
Gilder, Richard W., 81, 92
Gladden, Washington, 40–51
Glossolalia. *See* Pentecostalism
Gnosticism. *See* New Thought
Gottheil, Gustav, xvi

Government and church, 164–166
Grace Church
of New York, 35, 37, 73
of Philadelphia, xxxvi–xxxvii
Graham, Billy, xxv *n.*, xli
Grayson, David. *See* Baker, Ray S.
Great Britain, 15, 16, 27, 34, 64,
262, 322
Greece, 4, 8
Greer, David H., 91, 92
Guizot, François, 4

Havergal, Frances R., 109
Healing. *See* Health
Health, 203–208
Christian Science and, xiii–xiv,
xxxii–xxxiii, 267–301
disease and, xlii, 263
healing and, xxx, xxxii, 264–265,
267–301
mental, xl
Henke, Frederick G., 262–266
Heresies, vi, xiii, xxii
History of Civilization in England
(Buckle), 12 n.
*History of European Morals from
Augustus to Charlemagne*
(Lecky), 14–15
History of the Spirit of Rationalism
(Lecky), 139
Holiness churches, xix–xx, xxv, xxx,
xl, 99
Holyoke, Massachusetts, xviii
Home Evangelization program,
xviii
Houses. *See* Tenement houses
Hughes, Charles E., 76, 83
Huntington, William, 92–93

I Am movement, xl
Immigration, v, xiii, xiv, xv, xvii,
xx–xxi, xxiv, xxxi, xxxiv,
xxxvi, xli, 30, 34, 40, 90,
114–124, 333, 334
Immigrants. *See* Immigration
Income, church. *See* Church,
income
India, 262

Individualism, 64, 308, 338
Industrial schools. *See* Church, activities of
Industrialism, vi, 153
Institutional churches, xiv, xviii, xxxvi–xxxix, 308, 331–352
Intemperance, 26–27, 30–31, 223–224, 293–294, 316, 319, 320
Ireland, John, 41
Irish, 117–118, 119, 120–121, 122
Italians, 123
Ivo of Chartres, Saint, 8

Jay, William, 75
Jehovah's Witnesses, xiii, xxviii, xxix–xxx, xxxiii, xli, 227–228
See also Russell, Charles T.
John Chrysostom, Saint, 7
Judaism, xvi, xx, xxiv, xxxv, xl, xli, xliii, xliv, 4, 5, 30, 35, 37, 44, 155–156, 333

Korea, 262
Kindergartens. *See* Church, activities of
King, James M., 29–32, 40

Labor Temple, 332
Laborers. *See* Workingmen
Last Supper, 103
Lecky, William E., 14–15, 139
Literature. *See* Church, culture and
Liturgy. *See* Ritual
London. *See* Great Britain
Low, Seth, 91, 329
Luther, Martin, 62
Lutherans, xx, xxiv, 121

McClellan, George B., 91
McComb, Samuel, xxxii
Mahan, Alfred, xxxvii
Manhattan. *See* New York City
Manning, William, 86
Markham Memorial Presbyterian Church (St. Louis), 352
Massachusetts, xviii, xxii

Massachusetts Metaphysical College, 271, 294, 295
Membership, church. *See* Church, membership
Methodists, xix, 29, 35, 36, 99, 122, 262
Michelet, Jules, 13
Middle class. *See* Social classes
Migrants. *See* Country folks
Millennialism. *See* Adventism
Miller, William, xxviii
Milton, John, 198, 284
Minister
    background of, xvi, 339–340
    leadership of, xxx–xxxi, xxxvii
    role of, xxi–xxiv, xxvi, xxxv, xxxvii–xxxviii, 131–133, 137–153, 154–181, 220, 315–330
    status of, xxii–xxiii
Mission churches, xvii, xviii, xxx, 58, 63, 86, 87, 88, 89, 90, 321, 332, 333, 334, 336, 340
Montalembert, Charles F., 8–9
Moody, Dwight L., xxvi–xxviii, xxix, 182, 227, 305, 202–226
Moody Bible Institute, xxviii
Morgan, J. P., xxxvi, xxxvii, 314–315, 323–330
Movements, unification, xxiv
Municipal Art Commission, 91

National Holiness Association, xix
National parishes. *See* Ethnic churches
Negroes, xv, xxxi, xli
Neighborhood churches, xiii, xxii–xxv, xxvii, xxxix, xl, 127–201
Neighborhoods, v, xiii, xiv, xxxix
Neo-orthodox revolt, xxxix
New England, xviii, xxii, 137, 139, 142
New Thought, xiv, xl, 267, 268
New York Art Commission, 91
New York City, xv, xiv, xxviii, xxxvi, 16, 29–39, 132, 133, 134, 135, 138, 151, 202

New York City (Cont.)
See also by particular church
New York Sunday School Union,
xvii
Newark Conference, 99
Norway, 262
No. 36 Bowery (New York), 35

Oettingen, Alexander von, 14
Old-time religion, xviii, xxvi–xxvii
Open and Institutional Church
League, xxxvii, xxxviii, 341

Paine, Thomas, 151
Parishes, national. See Ethnic
churches
Parton, James, 127–153, 154
Pastor. See Minister
Peckham, Rufus, 81
Pentecostalism, xiii, xxx–xxxii,
xli–xlii, 182, 262–266
See also Jehovah's Witnesses
Perfectionism, xix
Pew rents. See Church, income
Philadelphia, 16
Plymouth Congregational Church
(Brooklyn), xxii, xxiv, xxx,
xl, 127, 134–136, 137–138,
141–147, 148–149, 151,
154, 182n.
Political order. See Church, politics
and
Politics and church. See Church,
politics and
Potter, Horatio P., 91
Poverty, 244, 315–323
See also Workingmen
Pre-millennialism. See Adventism
Presbyterian Church (New York),
xvi
Presbyterians, xxxviii, 33, 35, 36,
88, 122, 331
Property-holdings. See Church,
income
Prophet. See Minister
Protestant Episcopal Church (New
York), 352

Protestants, xviii, xxviii, xxxiii,
xxxiv-xxxv, xl, xliii, xliv, xlv,
4, 29, 35, 36, 40, 41, 46, 47,
51, 56, 65–66, 88, 119, 121,
127, 154, 182, 262, 308
See also by particular group
Prussia. See Germany
Psychiana, xl
Puerto Ricans, xli–xlii
Puritans, 137, 139, 154

Quimby, Phineas, 267

Rainsford, William S., xxxvi, xxxvii,
xxxviii, 305–330
Reformed Presbyterians, 35
Regeneration. See Salvation
Reintegrations, xiv, xviii, 305–352
Religion, freedom of, v
Retrospection and Introspection
(Eddy), 269
Reunion. See Church, reunion
Revivalism. See Revivals
Revivalist churches. See Revivals
Revivals, xiii, xix, xxv–xxviii, xxix,
xxx, xli, 94, 202–226, 227,
263
Riis, Jacob, 317
Ritual, xvi, xxix, 49, 57
services, xv, xix, xxi, xxxii, xl, xlii,
61, 69, 95, 130–133,
137–138, 263, 309–310,
312–313, 343
Roman Catholic Church. See
Catholics
Rome, 4, 8, 155–156
Roosevelt, Theodore, 91
Root, Elihu, 91
Rural churches. See Village
churches
Ruskin, John, 8
Russell, Charles E., 69
Russell, Charles T., xiii, xxviii–xxix,
xxx, 227–261
Rutherford, Joseph F., xxx

St. Agnes Chapel (New York), 76,
86, 91

St. Agnes Church (New York), 75
St. Augustine's Chapel (New York), 75
St. Augustine's Church (Cincinnati), 115
St. Augustine's League, 93
St. Bartholomew's Protestant Episcopal Church (New York), 342
St. George's Episcopal Church (New York), xxxvi, xxxvii, 73, 305–330
St. John's Chapel (New York), xvii, 74, 86, 88, 89–94
St. Joseph's School (Cincinnati), 117
St. Louis, xxxi
St. Luke's Chapel (New York), 76, 88, 90, 94
St. Matthew's Church (New York), 35, 37
St. Paul's Chapel (New York), 74, 84
Saloons. *See* Intemperance
Salvation, 138, 182–226, 265
Salvation Army, xxxv, xxxvi, 331
Samaritan Hospital, xxxvii
Sanctification. *See* Perfectionism
Schauffler, Adolphus F., 33–39
Schools. *See* Church, activities of, Sunday schools
Science. *See* Church, science and
Science and Health (Eddy), 267, 270, 272, 297
Seaman's Chapel (New York), 35
"Second blessing," xix
Second Coming. *See* Adventism
Secularism, vi
Sermons. *See* Ritual
Services. *See* Ritual
Settlement houses, xxxviii, 89
Small town. *See* Villages
Social classes, xvii, xxii, xxiii–xxiv, xxix, xxxi, xxxii, xxxiii, xxxiv, xxxviii, 48, 61
  See also Workingmen
Social gospel, xxxv, xxxviii, xxxix

Society and Solitude (Emerson), 11n.
Sodalities. *See* Church, activities of
Sophia, Saint, 65
Spalding, John L., 3–28
Spring Street Presbyterian Church (New York), 88–89
Springfield, Massachusetts, xxii
Staël, Germaine de, 101
Stelzle, Charles, xvii, xxxviii, 4
Street, A. E., 265–266
Strong, Josiah, 342
Suburban churches. *See* Neighborhood churches
Suburbs, xxxix–xl
Sunday schools, xvii, xxvii, 33, 36, 39, 58, 83, 84, 87, 90, 309, 328, 339, 343, 346
Swedish Chapel, 343
Synagogues, xx

Temple College, xxxvii
Temple Emanu-El (New York), xvi
Tenement houses, xiv, xv, 31–32, 36, 79–83, 90, 95, 318, 336–338, 342
Theodulph, 9
Theological discussion, xxv, xxix, xl, 154, 162, 202
Tocqueville, Alexis de, 163
"Tongues." *See* Pentecostalism
Town, small. *See* Villages
Tracy, Charles, 314, 315
Transcendentalism, xxxii
Transformations, xiii, xviii, xxx
  See also Downtown churches
Transplantations, xiii, xviii–xxi, 99–124
  See also Ethnic churches, Village churches
Tremont Temple (Boston), xxv–xxvi
Trinity Chapels (New York), 76, 87, 88
  See also by particular chapel
Trinity Church, xiv
  of Boston, xvi

Trinity Church (*Cont.*)
  of New York, xv, xvi, xvii, 34, 35, 55, 56–60, 69–95, 131

Unification movements, xxiv
Union Theological Seminary, xli
Unity, xl
University Place Church (New York), 37
Upjohn, Richard, 57
Urban demoralization. *See* Urbanism
Urbanism, vi, xiii, xli, xlii, xliv, 13–28, 31

Village churches, xiii, xviii–xx, xxi, xl, 4, 99–124
Villages, v, vi, xiii, xix–xx, xli, 3, 4–15, 18, 24, 40, 331
Voltaire, 151

Walburg, Anton H., 114–124
Wales, 262
Wanamaker family, xxxvii
Watts, Isaac, 313
Webster, Daniel, 152
Wesley, John, 139
Whitefield, George, 151
Worcester, Elwood, xxxii
Working classes. *See* Workingmen
Workingmen, xvii, xxiv, xxvii–xxviii, xxix, xxxi, xxxii, xxxviii, 17, 18–28, 41, 47, 88, 128, 233, 245–250, 328, 331, 332, 341, 345

Y. M. C. A., xxxv, xxxvi, 35, 331
Youth. *See* Children

Zion's Watch Tower Society, xxix